ESCAPE AT DAWN

This book is dedicated to the soldiers of the Eleventh Airborne Division who rushed in by air, land, and water to rescue more than two thousand of us from the Los Banos Internment Camp miles behind Japanese lines during World War II.

In memoriam, Lt. Col. Thomas Mesereau is pictured here as a worthy example of all those brave and noble men to whom I owe my life. Awarded the Silver Star and Purple Heart, he was the officer in command of General MacArthur's Honor Guard in Japan and selected to carry the signed peace treaty to Washington, D.C.

The nobility of his thoughts expressed at some of our reunions inspired me while I was writing this book. When I stood with a cross of white flowers by his flag-draped casket in the Riverside National Cemetery at March Air Force Base, it became a sacred moment.

CAROL TERRY TALBOT

ESCAPE at DAWN

CAROL TERRY TALBOT
and VIRGINIA J. MUIR

Tyndale House Publishers, Inc.
WHEATON, ILLINOIS

First printing, November 1988

Library of Congress Catalog Card Number 88-51061
ISBN 0-8423-0736-2, cloth
ISBN 0-8423-0705-2, paper

CONTENTS

General Douglas MacArthur

TAKE THE NECESSARY ACTION TO LIBERATE
LOS BANOS INTERNMENT CAMP SOONEST
S C A P
(Supreme Command Allied Powers)
February 12, 1945

"I was deeply concerned about the thousands of prisoners who had been interned at the various camps on Luzon . . . the latest information was most alarming. With every step that our soldiers took toward Santo Tomas University, Bilibid, Cabanatuan, and Los Banos, where these prisoners were held, the Japanese soldiers guarding them had become more and more sadistic. I knew that many of these half-starved and ill-treated people would die unless we rescued them promptly. The thought of their destruction with deliverance so near was deeply repellent to me."

PREFACE
An Invitation to the Reader

The reader is invited to live with more than two thousand of us in the Los Banos Internment Camp as we try to survive behind barbed wire and threatening Japanese guns during World War II.

Enjoy unquenchable American humor, witness nobility of spirit under heartbreaking circumstances, and know the faith in God and in America that gives strength to endure.

Experience being smothered by gigantic waves of enemy oppression while the strong undertow of hunger, disease, torture, and executions drag you under until you gasp for freedom as those who are drowning struggle for air.

Then let your heart thrill with ours to the Red, White, and Blue, the magnificent greatness of America, and the overwhelming passion to keep our country forever free, with its heart and soul as great as the land we love.

To increase the enjoyment of the reader, Virginia J. Muir, assistant editor-in-chief of Tyndale House Publishers, has added a more professional touch to my impulsive midnight writing based on the hidden diary I secretly kept in the prison camp.

Carol Terry Talbot

CHAPTER 1
Castaways
December 8, 1941

MIDNIGHT IN MANILA.

A red sky flamed with fire and thundered with explosions.

I sat on an old duffel bag at the bottom of a ship's laundry chute, stunned first by the bombing of Pearl Harbor, and now of the Philippines, with our planes destroyed on Clark Field.

Most of the passengers had fled ashore, while those who chose to stay aboard were told to gather in the ship's laundry room for safety. Almost numb from shock, I listened to the conversations around me.

"The worst possible place to be in a bombing raid is aboard this ship tied to the dock. We're a sitting duck for a bomb," commented a middle-aged man.

But a young man, strong and athletic in appearance, replied, "I'd rather be in my cabin on deck than down here, even though they say steel bulkheads make this safer. If we were up on deck, we could at least jump overboard and swim for it."

"It's a long way to jump from the deck down to the water," answered Mrs. Davis, a rather frail elderly woman.

A crusty man who exuded an air of authority spoke up, "It

doesn't matter where we are on this ship. A bomb would blow us all to pieces in a moment, down here or up there."

We all hoped he was wrong.

I remembered my father's warning, "You'll get right in the middle of the Pacific and war will be declared."

This morbid conversation was interrupted by the chef's bringing cold fried-egg sandwiches at midnight, not appetizing, but still a welcome break.

Not having heard the news that morning, Marion Childress and I had gone shopping. She wanted to get away from the gossip about her aboard ship.

Forty Burma Road technicians were traveling with us on the SS *President Grant*. Shortly after we had arrived in port, one of these men invited Marion to attend a jai alai game with him, not to gamble but for an interesting evening of fun.

Word spread around that a couple of missionaries prayed for Marion because they felt it was not the thing for her to attend.

A mock kangaroo court was held aboard ship, and a judge read the verdict: "This man is guilty of contributing to the delinquency of a missionary by taking her to a jai alai game. For this crime he is hereby sentenced to be thrown fully clothed into the ship's swimming pool."

Much to the amusement of the Burma Road men and most of the passengers, the sentence was carried out in good-natured fun. Being a large man, he made quite a splash.

But a few missionaries did raise their eyebrows. Although Marion laughed about it, I think she wanted to get away from all the talk, kidding, and criticism.

After visiting the famous Manila Hotel, Marion and I went to cash some traveler's checks, only to be told by the bank clerk, "We just stopped cashing them."

Great numbers of planes were roaring overhead, their sound almost deafening. Armed Filipino soldiers and policemen were running along the streets, closing Japanese stores. It was pandemonium.

"We'd better get back to the ship, Marion. They're more aware of the imminence of war here than we are at home."

We tried hailing a taxi, but none would stop. When one slowed up near us in the traffic, Marion hailed him. The driver shook his head and called, "The government has taken over all the taxis." Not to be put off, plump Marion ran out in front of the taxi and would not move until the driver promised to take us to the dock. On arrival we saw the Pagets at the ship's railing, watching for us. Peter bellowed out, "Don't you kids know war has been declared?"

WAR! We were stunned. Thus began our night at the bottom of that laundry chute in the ship's lower regions.

The next morning an announcement came over the ship's loudspeaker that all passengers still aboard were to meet in the main lounge. The manager of the President Line office spoke to us: "After last night I know I need not tell you the danger you are in aboard this ship. Your luggage from the baggage room has been put ashore. You will please be off this ship by five o'clock this evening. The hotels are full. Taxis are not now available. I do not know where you can go, but you must be off the ship by five o'clock. I am sorry. That is all."

"When will we continue our trip to India?" I asked.

"I cannot say. On the back of your ship's ticket it is stated, 'In case of war or act of God our contract with you is finished.' "

"Have you no suggestions as to what we can do?"

"I have none. I am sorry. Good day."

Our India-bound group sat there stunned, and in our hearts we prayed.

Knowing that the Salvation Army is always ready to help out in emergencies, we paid a Filipino boy to take a note to them, and someone also phoned. We sat on our luggage on the docks, hoping and praying the Salvation Army would find a place for our group. Before long we received the welcome news that they had secured rooms for us at the Oriente Hotel, located in an old part of Manila called the "Walled City." Later

the Walled City became crowded with Japanese soldiers and
was destroyed in the fighting.

Marion made our entrance into the lobby of the hotel very
dramatic by having one of her hurriedly packed suitcases
burst open, scattering stockings, dresses, and unmentionables
all over the floor. A broken bottle of ink completed the picture.
I wondered why she had been carrying a bottle of ink in her
suitcase anyway.

Since she and I were the last to arrive and all the rooms on
the ground floor were taken, we were assigned a room at the
rear of the second floor. Every time the air-raid siren blew at
night, we had to go down a long, dark corridor, descend two
flights of winding stairs, and cross the open patio to reach the
safest place in the hotel. No real air-raid shelter was available.

We slept in a double bed covered with a mosquito net that
was tucked in all around the mattress. In the dark, when that
air-raid siren wailed, we would start to scramble out of bed,
forgetting about the mosquito net, and our arms and legs
would become hopelessly entangled in it. Since we could not
have a light, we struggled blindly, becoming even more entangled. By the time we had freed ourselves, the air raid would be
over.

After several nights of this, we gave up and crowded in with
our friends from the ship—Geraldine Chappelle, Anna Nixon,
and Dr. Evelyn Witthoff—on the main floor.

One woman, expecting her baby to be born soon, sat calmly
in a chair throughout each of those fearful bombing raids,
while her husband dived under the only table in the room and
nervously crouched there. Perhaps it is universal that God
gives incredible calm to expectant mothers while prospective
fathers become frenzied.

Another man took advantage of every bombing-raid huddle
to berate me because his son had received a poor grade in
arithmetic from a California school. He seemed to hold me
personally responsible because I was a Californian.

The night before Pearl Harbor was bombed, we had spent

the evening in fellowship with young men in our navy at the home of Mr. and Mrs. Cyril Brooks, directors of the Navigators Club in Manila. The Salvation Army told Mr. Brooks we were at the Oriente Hotel.

Mr. Brooks came down to see us. "My wife and I would like to invite you to stay at our home, away from this bombing."

It was a gracious invitation, and we all gave it considerable thought. After he left, we discussed the problems.

Our India-bound group had not started the journey as a unit but had met on the ship and become friends. Now we had to make a life and death decision.

"I feel we should stay in Manila where we're close to the docks in case the ship sails and we can get aboard," I commented. "The Brookses live clear out in San Juan."

"Here, we could all be killed by the bombs," Elda Amstutz replied. She was the senior member of our party, and it was under her supervision that I was traveling to India.

It was Elda who finally took the lead and made a firm decision to accept the Brookses' invitation. "It seems wise to get away from the military targets," she stated. "The ship could be bombed or sunk by a submarine. I'm responsible for getting you safely to India, Carol."

I had no choice but to go.

Also accepting the Brookses' invitation were Blanche Palmer and Mr. and Mrs. Paget with their daughter, Joy.

As some of us lived there, crowded into the Brookses' home, we found Cyril Brooks to be one of the finest Christian men one could meet. Days and nights passed, and the air-raid siren wailed continually. It seemed as though we were always on our faces on the basement floor. After several days of this, some of us became braver and stepped outside to watch a dogfight in the sky. After a few moments the whistle of a shell became alarmingly loud. It landed in our neighbor's yard.

During those days we refused to believe it was a losing fight. Somehow America would send help.

CHAPTER 2
The Pearl of the Orient Is Lost

MARGE PIERCE LOOKED UP at the American flag that had flown so proudly for many years at the High Commissioner's office in Manila. Now it must come down. The Japanese were approaching to take over.

In order to save it from destruction, this city the world had known as the "Pearl of the Orient" had been declared an open city and would not be defended. Radios went off the air and transmitters were destroyed.

America's High Commissioner, Francis B. Sayre, had moved to Corregidor, taking papers and items of significant importance. From there he departed for America in the submarine *Swordfish.*

Those left at the High Commissioner's office stood looking at the Stars and Stripes flying high over the building. It must not fall into the hands of the Japanese.

After slowly lowering it, George Gray and the three secretaries reverently spread Old Glory on the ground in the garden and placed all the smaller flags on top of it. Each one standing at a corner of the flag recited the Pledge of Allegiance. The four corners of the Stars and Stripes were lit at the same time. Those in charge put the ashes in a tin can and buried it there with this note:

We the undersigned, being American citizens, do on this second day of January, 1942, solemnly and with reverence take it into our hands to burn the flag of the United States of America to prevent it from falling into the hands of the Japanese army, and to bury the ashes together with this record on the grounds of the High Commissioner's office.

> *[Signed] George Gray*
> *Margaret Pierce*
> *Virginia Hewlett*
> *Elsie Flahavan*

When General MacArthur proclaimed, "We shall return," he did not know the Japanese would destroy this beautiful city and give it back to him later in the form of millions of crushed pieces and shattered lives.

Knowing that the incoming enemy would confiscate all their supplies, Chinese grocers and other storekeepers invited their customers to help themselves; warehouses were opened for people to take what they wished.

Many started looting at will. Filipinos ran down the streets, carrying all kinds of merchandise, including furniture, yardage, clothing, and food. The baggage that we had left on the docks in bond was all looted.

Some men found a large unopened box in the street and with considerable labor carried it to a convenient place. Opening it with great anticipation, they found it contained a body that had been shipped to Manila for burial.

Neither law nor order prevailed in the city. Before the ship could be taken over by the Japanese, the SS *President Grant* abandoned plans to go to India and slipped quietly and se-

cretly away to Australia, leaving all its passengers and part of
its crew stranded in Manila, and taking my big trunk and
couch to the land of the kangaroo.

On January 1, 1942, a few Japanese officials were sighted
in the city. On the next day, units of the Japanese army entered
without fanfare and by January 3 their flags could be seen flying from Malacanan Palace, Fort Santiago, and from the mast
at the High Commissioner's residence, where George Gray
and the girls had taken down our flag. It hurt to see the Japanese flag flying in Old Glory's place.

On this day when they flew their flag, the Japanese started
rounding up Americans. One of the first places they went was
to the hotels. Anna Nixon describes what happened when she
came face to face with a Japanese soldier:

"I was sitting on the floor typing a copy of a magazine arti-
cle I liked when I heard the heavy tread of military boots as
someone approached and banged upon my door. My fingers
froze on the typewriter keys. There stood a real live Japanese
soldier in full uniform with his bayoneted gun pointed directly
at me.

"I started to stand but he made a downward motion with his
hand and in Japanese ordered me to do something. Of course,
I did not understand. So I sat down on the floor again. But he
stood there as if he were expecting me to follow him down the
hall, so I once more attempted to stand. Again he made that
downward motion and gave his command, so I sat down.

"After this happened three times, the Chinese hotel proprie-
tor went down the hall in front of my room calling out very
loudly, 'Let all the guests go downstairs.'

"I quickly obeyed him, and the Japanese soldier moved on
to the next room. When I reached the hotel lobby, I found it
empty apart from two Japanese soldiers standing at the entrance. Both of them began to give commands and to make
that downward motion with their hands.

"I interpreted it to mean 'sit down,' according to my culture, and again did just that.

"They didn't seem very happy about it and began shouting at me. Only then did I see that the others were all out on the street, so I quickly rose and went out the door. It took me two more days to learn that in the Orient the downward motion of the hand always means 'come,' and not 'sit down.' "

These girls from our ship were taken to Villamor Hall, the Conservatory of Music building of the University of the Philippines. Nearly a thousand men, women, and children were jammed in there for three sleepless, hungry days, with grossly inadequate toilet facilities. The Japanese gave them nothing to eat, and they had to sleep on the floor, chairs, or benches.

Elisabeth Earle from our ship had a little juice, which she shared. The Elks Club brought in food for their members; but on seeing the situation, they divided it up for all. The next day the Chinese owner of the Oriente Hotel brought food for the girls from our ship. They in turn shared with others.

The Japanese then moved this large crowd of people to the campus of Santo Tomas University, where thousands were interned.

While all this was going on, our heroic soldiers in Bataan continued fighting against overwhelming, impossible odds. General Wainwright and the troops with him continued to hold the fort of Corregidor.

An American of Japanese ancestry risked his life to help them.

CHAPTER 3
America's "Tokyo Rose"

BORN AND BROUGHT UP IN HAWAII, Richard Sakakida had no idea of the exciting future in store for him when he graduated from high school. When our American army began looking for Japanese linguists, Richard served as a cadet officer in the ROTC. Selected to take a battery of tests, this nisei became the primary candidate.

After being sworn in as a member of our army, Richard was trained and then very secretly sent to Manila as an undercover agent to infiltrate the Japanese community. Even his family did not know where he had gone and why.

Using the cover of being a salesman for Sears Roebuck, he mixed with the Japanese people, identifying those collecting intelligence for Japan and military men posing as civilians, a big job for a friendly young man known to the Japanese as Dick.

Much later my path was to cross his, when both of us became involved in the life of a covert radio expert.

Soon after the bombing of Pearl Harbor and declaration of war, Sakakida voluntarily turned himself in at the Japanese internment center in Manila to further his intelligence gathering.

"Let me have a pass so I can get milk for our Japanese children and other necessary food," he said one day to the American commandant.

The officer gave the seemingly big-hearted young man a pass to go out and obtain all the needed food. In this way Dick won the confidence of important Japanese internees and also his own freedom to go and come. Not only did he get the food, but he continued to carry out his mission for America.

Throughout much of the war a young woman in Japan, nicknamed "Tokyo Rose," would be broadcasting Japanese propaganda in English to our soldiers and sailors, using American humor and idioms that only a person who had lived in America would know.

During the fighting in Bataan, Sakakida became America's counterpart to Japan's Tokyo Rose. Broadcasting to the Japanese soldiers in their own language, he urged them to surrender, explaining how it would be to their benefit.

On February 11, 1942, Richard had copies of the following message placed in half-inch metal pipe pieces which were then catapulted behind the Japanese lines:

IT IS CHERRY BLOSSOM TIME BACK IN YOUR HOMELAND, AND THE MILITARY HAS SENT YOU HERE TO THE JUNGLES OF BATAAN. YOU OUGHT TO BE AT HOME WITH YOUR FAMILIES AND LOVED ONES, ENJOYING THE CHERRY BLOSSOMS. SO WHY CONTINUE THIS FUTILE BATTLE? COME AND SURRENDER WITH THIS LEAFLET AND YOUR SHIPMENT BACK HOME WILL BE GUARANTEED.

A Japanese soldier within shouting distance called out, "What the —— are you firing now, American? Are you out of ammunition?"

Then, moving to another location, Sakakida set up his microphone and loudspeaker to broadcast another message. Soon the Japanese were firing on his new position.

The American soldiers were not too happy about having Sakakida in their location because of the enemy fire he drew in response to his messages!

Transferred to Corregidor, Dick's assignment was to decipher Japanese codes and monitor voice communications, until he was ordered to Australia to be a translator.

Although Richard had been hoping for a transfer to Australia, a problem came into his mind that he considered a major matter.

Sakakida requested his superior, Col. Stuart Wood, to send another civilian nisei to Australia in his place to protect the man's personal security. An established lawyer in the Philippines, he had handled matters for the Japanese Embassy in Manila. His wife, a Japanese national, and his family had been sent back to Japan with dependents of other Embassy officials prior to the outbreak of the war.

That man had been brought out to Bataan from the civilian internment center in Manila at Sakakida's request to assist him in the translation of captured Japanese military combat orders and other documents. Dick felt personally responsible for his welfare.

Richard had several reasons for making this very unusual request. He felt the Japanese might be harsher on that nisei because of his having been associated with their diplomatic service.

Sakakida also felt that as a uniformed member of the U.S. military he was better prepared to face life-threatening situations than a civilian who might be forced to compromise because his family was in Japan and subject to reprisals.

By sacrificing his place on that airplane bound for Australia, Dick exemplified patriotism and nobility of spirit at their highest. He knew it would mean his own capture by the Japanese, torture almost beyond human endurance, and possibly even his life.

CHAPTER 4
Surrender or Be Shot

REALIZING THAT THEY HAD NOT yet found all the "enemy aliens," the Japanese fanned out in trucks to different outlying areas.

When they came to San Juan, we peeked through a curtain as they stopped at the home of the Walkers nearby. They were an elderly couple and not very well. Going inside their home, the soldiers discovered a gun. Taking it outdoors and setting up a tin can, two Japanese took turns firing at it. Since neither one could hit the can, they evidently decided the gun was faulty, and, against their own rules, gave it back to Mr. Walker.

Since the Walkers were old and ill, the Japanese did not put them in the truck but left them at home. After they were gone, Mr. Walker took the gun and hit the can with one shot. Many of the Japanese seemed to have poor eyesight.

What those Japanese did not discover was the radio hidden in the Walkers' bookcase, from which we were receiving our daily news. It would probably mean a death penalty if we were caught listening to radio news from overseas.

After the Japanese left the Walkers' residence, their truck stopped in front of the Brookses' home. Our time had come!

"Keep low and out of sight," Mr. Brooks advised us. "Stay very quiet."

There were now thirteen living in his home, others having also been invited to join the group.

Peeking through the side of a curtain, Mr. Brooks watched the Japanese soldier climbing the steps to the front door. The soldier stood there for awhile and looked around. He seemed to be in no hurry.

Down on the floor we were all silently praying.

What was going through the man's mind, we do not know, but the soldier never knocked or called. After a time he turned around, descended the stairs, walked back to his truck, and spoke to the driver. They drove off and left us there.

Incredible! We felt it was something of a miracle. No one could explain that Japanese soldier's actions.

Realizing they had not found all the Americans and their allies, the Japanese issued a proclamation:

ALL ENEMY ALIENS MUST SURRENDER THEMSELVES BY JANUARY 15, 1942, OR THEY WILL BE SHOT.

Now Mr. Brooks asked each of us to pray about the matter and then tell him how we felt about it. What a decision to make!

After a time, Mr. Brooks asked each person individually, "What did you decide?"

A verse from the Bible that had come to our minds was Romans 13:1: "Let every soul be subject unto the higher powers."

The decision was unanimous. We would surrender.

We waited until the very last day, January 15. Since all automobiles had been confiscated by the Japanese, we ordered horse and buggies called *carratelas*, and at 10:00 A.M. we were standing in line at the big iron gates of Santo Tomas Internment Camp.

Standing behind Mr. Ed Nolting was Peter Paget. When the Japanese official checked their data, he looked up, smiled at the two men and said in perfect English, "I see both of you men were on your way to India. Do you know each other?"

"Yes," Peter replied. "We were on the same boat."

With an apparent attempt to be friendly, the Japanese officer replied with a bit of a twinkle in his eyes, "Well, you're both in the same boat now."

In spite of the tension, we could not help laughing at his American sense of humor and knowledge of our idioms.

When my turn came, for some inexplicable reason the officer handed me his card. An ordained minister, he had graduated from a seminary in the eastern part of the United States.

After we were all crowded into a courtyard, a Japanese officer gave us a lecture and then told us to salute him.

We stood there motionless.

"Salute!" the officer shouted.

A few raised their hands about shoulder high.

"No! Like this."

And the Japanese saluted. I could hardly hide my smile. Instead of our saluting him, he was saluting us.

Now we saluted him again, each with his own variation. No one wanted to salute him properly.

Finally the officer gave up, exasperated with our stupidity. Whether he realized it was purposeful or not, no one knows. Maybe we were embarrassing him, and he felt it was time to call a halt to the farce.

We were then given a lecture on how the Imperial Japanese Army wanted to cooperate with the churches in making their "Greater East Asia Co-Prosperity Sphere" a help to the Filipinos. To this end, religious liberty would be granted and ministers and missionaries allowed to continue their work. On the surface, these smooth-sounding words appeared fine, but we were soon to realize that they contained hidden meanings and implications not suspected by us, with our straightforward American manner of speaking.

I was not sure who this Japanese officer was, but it may have been Lieutenant Colonel Naruzawa, chief of the religious section of the Propaganda Corps, a Buddhist.

When he finished, I turned to Miss Amstutz. "I'll stay here in Santo Tomas. I don't want to be in a position where I might be asked or forced to cooperate with the Japanese."

But she had a different point of view, perhaps larger than mine. In her own quiet way, Elda put pressure on me to return with her to the home of Mr. and Mrs. Brooks. A dedicated woman, she wanted to help him in his work. "Carol, it's more important to encourage the Filipinos in their faith in God and in America than to be locked up in this camp where you can do nothing."

While I was taking a bit of time to think that through, Elda continued, "The Lord is opening the door for us to help the Filipinos in their resistance to possible Japanese pressure in the churches. They need our spiritual support."

Turning to Mr. Brooks, who was standing nearby, I asked, "What do you think I should do?"

"I'd appreciate your help with the young people," he replied, but put no pressure on me.

"I'm responsible for you, Carol," Elda added, "and you should stay with me." Usually mild, Elda could be very firm.

Reluctantly I said another good-bye to some of the girls from our ship.

Back at the Brookses' home in San Juan, we were placed under house arrest and forced to wear red arm bands designating us as enemies. Although we could attend church and minister there, we were ordered to report all our activities every week to the Japanese Imperial Army. The very thought nauseated me.

Some people on a neighboring island did not surrender themselves as ordered, and they were shot.

At Mr. Brooks's suggestion, I taught a Bible class of Filipino young adults who understood English. I also helped the two teenaged Brooks boys, Leonard and Kenneth, with their studies, because they could not go to school.

The Japanese did not stop with the red arm bands and weekly reports. After a short time they tried to force all Christian leaders in the Manila area to sign a pledge of cooperation with the Japanese Imperial Army. Of course, very few signed.

Considerable controversy erupted when Christian pastors and leaders refused to sign. Before the matter of signing the pledge was over, I think the Japanese were sorry they ever started it. The Japanese do not like to "lose face."

Because of being a transient with no church affiliation or work in Manila, I was not asked to sign, and I felt glad to be of no importance whatever to the Japanese Imperial Army. Had I been asked to do so, I would have refused to sign.

CHAPTER 5
Conflict of Church and State
January 27, 1942

THE JAPANESE PROPAGANDA MACHINE was now moving full speed ahead. Lieutenant Colonel Naruzawa called for a conference at the Manila Hotel with Protestant leaders "representing all the major denominations in Manila."

The list included twelve Americans, one British clergyman, and twenty-six Filipinos. Newspaper reporters were invited to attend, with the Rev. Dr. T. Aiura serving as master of ceremonies.

Since we were a mixed group and had fine fellowship with the Baptists who were doing excellent work in Manila with their church and school, we affiliated ourselves with Rev. Edward Bomm. He headed up the Baptist work and was highly esteemed by his peers and all who knew him. He was a man of great faith, deep American loyalty, and true Christian ethics.

Lieutenant Colonel Naruzawa invited press members of the Propaganda Corps and photographers to be present. He gave a long speech in which he dropped his gracious veneer completely and asked the heads of the main denominations in Manila to sign a pledge. The newspaper men left after Naruzawa's speech, assuming all would sign, and published it as a fact, an error that resulted in great misunderstanding. Instead, the pledge was questioned, doubted, and critically analyzed.

Rev. Dr. E. E. Tuck said, "I would not allow even my own bishop to interpret for me the will of God."

Rev. W. H. Fonger of the Bible Society asked, "What is meant by 'positive cooperation' with the Japanese Army?" And he did not sign.

When Rev. Edward Bomm, who represented us, was asked to go forward and sign the pledge, he remained in his seat, refusing to sign.

Rev. H. Bowsman and Rev. Dr. F. W. Brush also remained in their seats.

Seven Americans and the Baptist Filipino pastor, Rev. Dr. Santiago Cruspero, continued to hold out.

Dr. Holter, head of the Union Theological Seminary, who refused to sign, told a Japanese minister that for years he had taught classes in the history of Christianity and had frequently emphasized the dangers of the forced union of church and state. How could he now acquiesce? He asked the Japanese minister, "What would you do in my place?"

The Japanese replied, "I don't know but what I would take the same position you are taking. I hope that we may be able to discuss this question together after this war is over."

There was some apprehension that the men who would not sign the pledge might be taken to the torture chambers of Fort Santiago. However, due to the publicity that surrounded the event, and the intense desire of the Japanese to give the impression that everyone had signed, they just quietly picked up the following men in automobiles on Sunday morning and took them to Santo Tomas: Dr. Brush, Dr. Holter, Dr. Fonger, and Rev. Bomm, our representative. They were treated politely. On arrival at the camp, when it was realized they had no bedding or personal belongings with them, they were driven home to secure the needed articles and taken back to the camp.

However, Rev. Edward Bomm's lovely wife, Marian, was

picked up later by the Japanese on a false charge and taken to one of the horrible cells of Fort Santiago. After some time, she was released and taken to Santo Tomas Internment Camp, an ill woman.

Bishop N. S. Binsted, of the Episcopal church, was interned in a private home with Dr. Claude A. Buss, executive assistant to the High Commissioner, and did not attend the meeting at the Manila Hotel. The Bishop was asked to sign the pledge of church cooperation, but refused.

When Lieutenant Colonel Naruzawa asked the Catholic archbishop to have his parish priests distribute propaganda leaflets to the people, the archbishop replied, "I am afraid that the nature of our work, which is purely spiritual and has nothing to do with political matters, makes it impossible for me to accede to your request."

THE PLEDGE I DID NOT SIGN

"We, the Protestant missionaries and those who are connected with Christian works, will gladly cooperate with the Japanese Army as it proclaims the military administration in the Philippines, and do hereby pledge ourselves to take the duties of the restoration and maintenance of peace by observing the following items:

(1) Although we are granted the freedom of faith, we will gladly offer our buildings and their equipment whenever they are needed and are requested through proper channel for military strategy;

(2) We would never hold meetings primarily for the people of the hostile nations (worship services included) except services in the Santo Tomas Internment camp [the Los Banos Internment Camp did not exist then];

(3) We would not hold, for the time being, any meetings other than religious services;

(4) We would lead and instruct our members of the church, trusting in the Japanese army, understanding that the great ideal of the Great East Asia Co-Prosperity Sphere is on the road to its realization, and believing that the very fulfillment of that great ideal is to obtain world peace;

(5) We would positively cooperate with the Japanese Army and would not fail its generous considerations toward us."

No one in our group signed.

CHAPTER 6
"With Broken Heart"

WITH BROKEN HEART AND HEAD BOWED in sadness but not in shame, I report. . . that today I must arrange terms for the surrender of the fortified islands of Manila Bay. . . Please say to the nation that my troops and I have accomplished all that is humanly possible and that we have upheld the best traditions of the United States and its Army. . . With profound regret and with continued pride in my gallant troops, I go to meet the Japanese commander.

[Signed] Gen. Jonathan Wainwright
Corregidor
May 6, 1942

CHAPTER 7
Unflinching Loyalty

AFTER GENERAL WAINWRIGHT BROADCAST his deeply moving message of surrender on Corregidor, General Beebe made a lengthy broadcast in English to the Japanese, giving details of the surrender, which Richard Sakakida translated.

Keeping Richard on Corregidor, the Japanese Military Police, known as the Kempetai, tortured him. They strung him up for hours with his back arched over a beam and his feet dangling.

Then taking him down, they gave Sakakida the water treatment, filling his stomach with water and then beating on it. Tying his arms behind him, they strung him up again, pulling a rope over a rafter until his shoulders were dislocated.

As a prisoner for almost two and a half years, Dick did not know from one day to the next whether he would live or be executed, and neither did the Japanese.

Our intelligence officers had told Sakakida that if he were caught, he should tell the Japanese that the Americans forced him to work for them and to wear their uniform. No amount of torture could break his story:

"I am simply a civilian working as a representative of Sears, Roebuck & Co. Due to my American citizenship, the United States Army invoked the national emergency act and utilized my Japanese language ability."

The Japanese could not disprove it.

Finally, Lieutenant General Wachi decided Sakakida's fate. As Chief of Staff of the Japanese 14th Army, he said, "There's no problem in eliminating anyone. We can do that anytime. My suggestion is to utilize his service on our side as much as we can; if there's any question or doubt, then we can execute him."

Unknowingly, this important Japanese general had just saved the life of America's "planted agent," enabling Richard to continue his work. They placed him at Headquarters of the 14th Army, Office of the Judge Advocate, as orderly to the Duty Officer and interpreter at criminal trials—their interpretation of *criminal* being acts against Japanese. He translated at a trial of a radio expert with whom I was involved.

Although they watched Richard carefully, the Japanese were unable to find any flaw in his story or actions and began letting up on their scrutiny of him. When they asked him to go by submarine to America as their spy, he replied, "And get tortured again?" The Japanese smiled wryly and dropped the idea. They may have been secretly testing him.

Months later when they were not in the office, Dick smuggled out copies of their shipping schedules from Japan and gave them to ROTC guerrillas. They had the information transmitted to MacArthur's headquarters in Australia, and from there it was secretly sent to American submarines searching for just such targets.

One night Sakakida stole a plan for movement of large numbers of Japanese troops going south. He had this plan radioed on to MacArthur through the guerrilla network and their associates. Other American spies may also have reported this to MacArthur's headquarters. When eight Japanese troop transports, accompanied by destroyers, sailed from Rabaul for New Guinea, our American military was ready for them.

Continuing these undercover activities, Richard risked his life for America with unflinching loyalty. In the future he would exchange positions with his captors and become a colonel in the United States Armed Forces.

But now I would face a Japanese soldier who frightened me.

CHAPTER 8
Stormy Weather

WIND AND RAIN LASHED OUR HOUSE as a typhoon raged through the area, whipping the tree branches. We settled down in the comfort of our safe haven.

Suddenly we heard *Clump! Clump! Clump!* on our verandah and a pounding on the door.

Five Japanese soldiers stomped into the house, dripping water all over the floor. They were on one of their searching expeditions for Filipino guerrillas and guns.

I quietly slipped into my bedroom and hid the American flag fastened to one of the poles holding up a mosquito net over the bed. Before obtaining that net, I had battled persistent mosquitoes dive-bombing my face every night. Unfortunately for me, they carried malaria and dengue fever.

Having experienced Japanese search parties before, I had placed the head of a clay skeleton in a cupboard they always searched for guns. One of the soldiers now put his hand into the darkness of the cupboard. His two fingers went into the eyes of the skeleton; and when he withdrew his hand, the skull was dangling from it.

Some excited "ughs" followed and a hasty departure. We

later heard a rumor that the search had been the result of Filipino guerrillas having killed a prominent Japanese in our area.

I sat down to write the incident in my diary when again we
heard that *Clump! Clump!* While the Pagets explained we had
just been searched, I hid my diary. These five soldiers decided they would not search, but demanded food. Our empty
cupboards finally convinced them we had no food.

In order to relieve the crowded conditions at the Brookses'
home, and to keep the Japanese from occupying Earl Hornbostel's house nearby, it had been recommended that the Pagets, Elda, and I quietly move there, but still have our meals
with the Brookses. We later did our own meager cooking under house arrest, but at this time there was no food in our
house.

Dropping their rain-soaked coats on the floor, the men ordered Mrs. Paget to warm up the rice they had with them. One
soldier approached me and, leering at me until his face nearly
touched mine, he said, *"Beer!"*

Shrinking back, I answered, "No beer."

"BEER!" he shouted again, leaning toward me until his foul
breath on my cheek made me feel sick.

I tried to step away from him, but he followed, surveying me
form head to foot.

"Whose wife?" he asked.

"No one's wife," Mr. Paget had to reply.

"Whose sister?"

"No one's sister. Friend."

"Ugh!" he grunted as he moved even nearer.

Mrs. Paget chose this auspicious moment to serve the heated
rice. The soldiers shoved the silverware aside and lapped up
the rice like dogs.

While they were thus engaged, Mr. Paget steered me into my
room and closed the door. While I had not known of any
American woman who had been raped by a Japanese soldier,

one who was captured in the northern mountains of Luzon was imprisoned in a guardhouse and raped repeatedly by the guards.*

Kneeling beside my bed, I prayed, "Lord, now is the time for You to prove Your promises. Not tomorrow, but now!"

Just then the door started to open slowly. I looked at the window to see whether I could jump, but it was barred. There was no escape.

Watching that door, I held my Bible in a viselike grip, as though it were literally my shield. My eyes were glued to that quietly opening door.

A curly-haired little girl with frightened blue eyes entered, and the door was softly closed. Mr. Paget had slipped Joy into my room. The Japanese had been fondling her blonde curls.

I put my arms around the little girl and held her to me. Then we knelt by the bed and prayed, "Lord, let something happen that will make the Japanese leave in a hurry, so they won't have time to remember about us. And lay it on the hearts of folks at home to pray, right now."

A few minutes later we heard some grunting and shuffling—and then quiet. The Japanese officer in charge had suddenly decided they had been there long enough and must get on with their searching. He hustled them out.

The golden-haired child and I offered a prayer of thanksgiving.

*Grace Nash, *That We Might Live* (Scottsdale, Ariz.: Shano Pubs., 1985).

CHAPTER 9
A Dress for a Turkey?

ONE AFTERNOON LITTLE JOY AND I were alone at the Hornbostel home when a Filipino arrived with a big live turkey. We could hardly believe our eyes. Homegrown or stolen, we did not know, but the young man wanted to sell it. We were always hungry, and the very sight of that turkey made our saliva flow.

"But I don't have any money," I lamented.

"If Mummie were home, she'd get that turkey," said Joy.

After that remark, I knew that somehow the turkey had to be ours. "Will you take anything else besides money?" I asked.

After a moment or two, the Filipino replied, "Clothes."

Going to my room, I looked over my scant wardrobe. My clothes were in bad shape, but one dress stood out from the others.

It was new in the sense that I had not worn it because of its long sleeves and high neck, which made it too warm for the tropics. It was maroon and sported a rather large rhinestone pin that sparkled on the left shoulder.

After I had purchased it in California, my father strenuously objected. "Is that the way you're going to dress now? With long sleeves and a high neck because you're going to work in an orphanage in India?"

"No, Dad," I laughingly replied. "I like the dress." Now I wished Dad could see me trade it for a turkey!

When I took the dress out and showed it to the Filipino, his eyes shone as brightly as the rhinestones. He could sell it for a high price. Clothes were more valuable than money to people who had plenty of cash, but there were no clothes to buy.

The Filipino put the turkey in the kitchen for me. Had we placed it outside, the turkey soon would have been stolen. Joy and I could hardly wait until her parents came home. We were no longer eating at the Brookses' house but were on our own under the watchful eyes and guns of the Japanese.

We kept the turkey in the kitchen for a few days, and then Peter prepared it for roasting. No turkey on earth was ever more enjoyed.

Another day Peter came in with some raw, red meat, supposedly beef. But when we tried to cook and eat it, three things were wrong—the smell, the taste, and its toughness.

"It's horse meat!" exclaimed Cae Paget. "They don't slaughter them until they're old and worn out and almost dead."

Then I came up with a brilliant thought. "My father was a sea captain in the old sailing-schooner days, and I've often heard him say that they put in a supply of 'salt horse' when they started out on a long sea voyage."

On the basis of that story, we finished eating the meat.

When I told this incident to my father several years later, he laughed. "Carol, that was not horse meat. It was corned beef. We just called it 'salt horse.'"

One day Elda said to me, "Blanche is going to live in a Filipino-type home and will be all alone. She wants me to move in with her. I asked the Lord what I should do, since I am responsible for you, and He said to my heart, 'You look after Blanche and I'll look after Carol.'"

Maybe the Lord felt I was too big a problem for Elda to handle and it was time for Him to take me in hand.

CHAPTER 10
Risking My Life

THROUGH UNDERGROUND COMMUNICATIONS, Earl Hornbostel sent a secret message to me by a Filipino. Earl asked that I come into Santo Tomas Internment Camp on a certain day, bringing with me electronic parts stowed away in the basement of his home, where I was under house arrest. He indicated the spot inside the internment camp where we would meet.

Earl was setting up a public address system inside Santo Tomas for making announcements and playing music. The electronic parts were needed for this project, and some could be used in secret radio sets. He was an expert in this kind of work.

Should a Japanese guard with technical knowledge see the parts and recognize the possibility of their being used in a radio, it could mean that I would be taken to Fort Santiago and so would anyone I visited in Santo Tomas that day. The horrors, tortures, and deaths in Fort Santiago belonged to the dark ages. Earl had given me a risky assignment.

Knowing absolutely nothing about the insides of a radio, I wondered whether I could recognize the needed parts. After finally locating them, disguising them presented another problem.

Wrapping the parts up in some of my fancy underwear that I thought the Japanese might not examine, I placed them in a rather large, black patent leather purse. It had been a bon-voyage gift from Miss Prosser, a former dean of women at Biola. I had some misgivings about the whole project and a feeling my mother would not approve.

Saying good-bye to the Pagets, I left in a two-wheeled horse-drawn buggy called a *carratela.*

At the entrance of Santo Tomas, I bowed properly from the waist to the Japanese guard at the big iron gates. It was not my custom to make the required bow quite that respectfully, but with those suspicious parts in my purse I did not want to risk the sentry's wrath.

I was directed to the office of the Japanese Commandant in the main building. Seated at a long table were eight armed Japanese soldiers. At one end sat an officer with an interpreter at his side. On each side of the table were three armed guards. An empty chair at the other end of the table was indicated for me.

Was that officer the Japanese Commandant? I wondered.

This frightened me a little. Why were eight armed soldiers necessary to interview me? Some of those electronic parts in my purse suddenly seemed to be like sticks of dynamite that could blow me to pieces at any moment.

Questioned extensively through an interpreter, I answered quietly, briefly, with as few words as possible. I made my answers simple and endeavored to seem calm and unperturbed, but my heart was racing. I smiled and tried to appear coopera-tive.

From their questions I could not figure out why they were suspicious of me. They seemed to be zeroing in on my family background and the reason for my being in Manila. I did not know then that the Japanese make a great deal of family history.

I avoided telling them that Dad had been an officer in the navy during World War I and that my brother Jack now served as a naval officer in this war against them.

Generations of the Terry family had lived on Long Island in New York State. Jeremiah had served as an officer in George Washington's army, and Thomas had become a colonel in the colonial wars. Strongly patriotic blood ran right through our family history. My parents were living on Long Island when their first son was born on the birthday of Teddy Roosevelt, a person my father greatly admired as a man of brave and bold action, and whose home was located on the island at Oyster Bay. Dad named his son "George Roosevelt Terry."

A family tale handed down through the years is that one day Dad had a bicycle collision with Alice Roosevelt there on Long Island, and she did a good job of telling him off.

Now Franklin Roosevelt served as president of the United States. I was relieved when the Japanese made no association of that name with my brother's name. After a grueling period of questioning, I was given a pass and dismissed. Making sure I was not being followed, I met Earl at the appointed place and gave him the electronics parts he had requested, glad to be rid of them. I then sought out my former cabin mate from the SS *President Grant*, Anne Nixon, and enjoyed a short visit with her.

Walking through those big iron gates to the road outside, I breathed a sigh of relief when no one from the dreaded Kempetai (Military Police) picked me up.

If the Japanese had discovered in my purse the electronic parts that were usable in radios, I could have been taken to Fort Santiago and possibly executed. Now Earl faced that danger.

A horse-drawn *carratela* took me back to the Hornbostels' home in San Juan, but Japanese military soon ordered us put out of the house.

CHAPTER 11
From House Arrest to Imprisonment

THE JAPANESE SOLDIERS who had tromped through our house in the storm did not forget us. They came back with a written order instructing us to leave, which in effect said:

> *This our house now*
> *Get out*
> *And please bow.*

They had first placed us under house arrest and now ordered us out of the house!

The Brookses had been very kind, but we did not feel like imposing on them again. As we prayed about what to do, the Pagets were invited to live with a couple of women stranded on their way from China to America.

Then Ruth Woodworth offered to share her room with me at the Baptists' home in Manila, the group represented by Rev. Ed Bomm, who had refused to sign the pledge and with whom I had affiliated myself in that matter. He was in Santo Tomas Internment Camp, and his group was put under house arrest.

A few days after moving in with Ruth, I became very ill. My temperature climbed up and up. Chills shook my body. No doctor was available, and we had no medicine except aspirin.

Ruth nursed me night and day. Knowing I was an added burden to her, I kept asking Ruth to send me away somewhere. She just smiled and kept putting cool packs on my forehead and feeding me aspirin. Either dengue fever or malaria was wracking my body.

When my fever started coming down, Ruth asked me, "Carol, who is going to win the war?"

"America, of course. Why do you ask?"

Laughing a bit, she explained, "Some people say that if you think the Japanese will win, then you have dengue fever, as it can cause depression. But if you feel the Americans are going to win, then you have malaria."

I did not have malaria, but no amount of dengue fever could cause me to predict a Japanese victory.

Thanks to Ruth's fine nursing, I recovered; but soon after that two Japanese soldiers appeared at our door and then marched into the house.

"Line up!" was the curt command through an interpreter.

The officer clicked his heels together, drew himself up to the fullest height of his small stature, expanded his chest, and with a flourish whisked out a paper.

"Are you all here?"

"All here," we promptly replied, trying to hide our smiles at his pompousness.

"I have a proclamation to read."

After we listened to a long series of the strange sounds of Nippongo, the interpreter read to us in English the fact that we were to be taken to the Santo Tomas Internment Camp at nine o'clock the next morning.

"How much luggage can we take?"

"Two suitcases and a folding cot. A truck will call for you. You are responsible for one another to see that no one tries to run away."

"Can we take some food with us?"

"No! The Imperial Japanese Army will feed you," the officer stated emphatically. We should have had him put that in writing and sign his name to it!

We began to make almost frantic preparations for our internment. Grabbing my purse, I ran to a nearby store to buy what little I could—soap, toothpaste, medicines.

Being a bunch of women, we all thought of shampoos. We showered and washed our hair, knowing it would be the last time we would have warm water. We went to bed at 2:00 A.M. and were up again at four.

The news spread rapidly, and by morning the house was crowded with strangers wanting to send messages to loved ones interned in Santo Tomas. Filipino friends arrived, expressing sympathy, bringing gifts such as a few cakes of soap, rice cakes, a can of fish—giving out of their little. It was obvious they loved these Americans.

Ruth Woodworth later described the scene: "After praying, the Filipinos said, 'Now we will put all your boxes, suitcases, cots, and rice on the curb. When the truck comes, we will load it all for you and there will be no problems with the Japanese.'

"No sooner had they placed everything on the curb when the Japanese truck drove up. The soldiers surrounded our house with fixed bayonets. The officer got out and started toward our gate. Being the senior, I went out first. I saw that the officer was very angry. Immediately the Lord brought to my mind words from one who had lived many years in China; 'Never show fear in the presence of the Japanese.' As the officer waved his hand over all our boxes and luggage, he shouted, 'You cannot take all this.'

"As he stood with his back to the curb, I looked him squarely in the eye and said quietly, 'Now see here, you promised us that we could each take two pieces of luggage and there are seven of us going from here.' I spoke very slowly so he could understand me. Then I explained, 'Seven times two is fourteen, and there are exactly fourteen suitcases here. We will count them.'

"Meanwhile, the Filipino men were throwing all our things into the truck as fast as they could. Two boys had climbed into the truck to catch them. Greg Tingson, supervising it all, had things flying. The officer turned around to stop them, but I got his attention again on the number of cots we were taking. He asked what was in the sacks. When I said rice, he was really angry and ordered two soldiers to take the rice.

"The officer shouted for us to get into the truck, but it was impossible for us women to climb into the back. Our friends had to lift us up into the truck. All the time the Filipino boys continued to throw in the boxes until the very last one was loaded. The officer took his seat beside the driver, and the soldiers climbed in with us. As the truck started up with a terrific jerk, we were all thrown together in one big huddle—boxes, soldiers, and all of us. It struck us so funny that we burst out laughing, to the amazement of the Japanese soldiers. They must have been thinking, *What queer people these Americans are—laughing their way to prison.*

"Our stuff was placed in front of Santo Tomas along with that of others who were being reinterned. How about our boxes stenciled with the words, 'U.S. Navy'? That was enough to send us to Fort Santiago. We closed our eyes for a brief moment to cover those boxes with prayer.

"As we opened our eyes, we saw a Japanese officer with a very kind face and gentle manner coming toward us, and then in perfect English he asked us if our things were ready. When I pointed them out, without having me open one, he marked them all with Japanese characters and disappeared."

Ruth felt he was an angel sent by God for that situation, as she thought of a verse from Psalm 50: "Call upon me in the day of trouble: I will deliver thee."

However, if he was an angel, he did not come near me. A Japanese soldier was pawing through all my things in the suitcase he made me open. In it was my Viking camera.

Without looking up, he asked, "Camera?"

Just as I was about to answer, another Japanese began examining someone else's suitcase and asked her a question, to which she replied, "No."

The soldier bending over my suitcase thought I had said that "No" and accepted it.

My mind struggled with my conscience. Should I let the Japanese continue thinking I had denied having a camera? Would that be an unspoken lie? And what if I let him think that I said "No" and he found the camera? In those few moments, thoughts whirled in my mind and struggled with my ethics. It was my camera, not his.

My conscience finally won, and I admitted having a camera, which the soldier promptly confiscated with the greatest of joy. It became obvious he intended to keep it for himself, and that made losing my camera hurt even more. I couldn't fight him, but I fought back some tears, keenly aware that the iron gates of Santo Tomas had closed behind me a third time.

Two freckle-faced American boys about fifteen years of age grabbed my handbags and escorted me down a long walk to the gymnasium. "You know you're goin' to Los Banos, dontcha?" one of them asked.

"No, I didn't." They passed on some other tidbits of news en route to the gym. Later I heard they were reprimanded by the Japanese for talking and walking with me.

We sat on the floor of the gym for endless hours, hundreds of us with not a cushion or chair.

Each group was asked to appoint a typist, and ours gave the job to me. An alphabetical list had to be typed in this order: Name, nationality, sex, age, address.

Many errors made purposely or otherwise by the typists exasperated the Japanese. Some of the internees enjoyed their frustration at our seeming inefficiency. My turn came last, and by then their patience was exhausted. I decided to do mine accurately. Never did I type so carefully, lining things up correctly in evenly spaced columns, making sure it was alphabetically correct.

I finished without making any mistakes and proudly presented my original copy with its four carbon copies.

The Japanese officer was standing on the stage, and I was standing below looking up at him. As he took the papers out of my hand, I gasped. The carbons had printed on the back sides of the sheets. I had evidently placed them in backwards! I almost panicked, wondering whether he would be angry enough to strike me. Should I tell him or let him find out for himself?

With bated breath, I timidly spoke, "Would you mind letting me do that over again? I'm afraid I put the carbons in backwards."

The Japanese did not quite understand, so I pointed at the back of the sheets.

He looked at them and sort of grunted, saying something like "Carbon print both sides."

Puzzled, I went over and looked at the carbon paper. I had never seen any like it, made so that it printed on both the sheet in front and the one behind it.

I breathed a sigh of relief, only to find myself permanently assigned to the office as a typist a few days later in the Los Banos Internment Camp.

Some rice and stew were served to us for lunch and dinner as we continued to sit on the floor in that gymnasium and nurse our aching bones.

The whole evening was taken up by roll call. At first we were told to answer by giving our ages. The first name called happened to be Dr. Tuck, seated way at the back of the gym.

"Fifty-five," he shouted out. Such a roar of laughter went up that for a few moments the Japanese seemed daunted by the unquenchable spirit and humor of Americans even under the dire circumstances of being prisoners under armed guards.

Each time they called the roll, it came out wrong, not tallying with their records, until they seemed exasperated with us. Eventually we stretched out on the floor and tried to sleep, not knowing that a nightmare of a trip awaited us.

At 2:00 A.M. we were roused, fed a little something, lined up, and marched out quietly, almost stealthily, so as not to awaken the prisoners in Santo Tomas. The rain poured down on us in the darkness of a moonless night.

Herded into trucks completely covered with canvas and totally dark inside, we did not know whether we were to be executed or taken to the Los Banos Internment Camp.

When the trucks stopped and Japanese soldiers ordered us out, we found ourselves at a railroad station. Armed guards ordered us to board the waiting train.

Machine guns were mounted on the train, and six guards with guns were placed between all the coaches to keep us from escaping and to prevent Filipino guerrillas from rescuing us.

Still not knowing whether we were to be executed or taken to Los Banos, we were encouraged by those familiar with the area who felt we were on our way to that internment camp. We had hardly slept at all for two nights. Crowded into third-class compartments, we were tired to the point of exhaustion but too uncomfortable to relax, even though some of us women did find places to sit on the board seats.

Upon arrival at the Los Banos station, we were lined up in the tropic sun to wait for trucks. Eventually my turn came to be jammed in with others, and we arrived at the internment camp. Roll call was again taken while we sat around on the ground.

Heavy clouds appeared overhead. All our luggage was in one big jumble on the ground, and we were ordered to find our own. I located mine, but my bed was missing. It was never found. Maybe someone else had taken it. Later Mr. Smallwood, known as "Chips," found a metal cot for me.

As rain threatened to drench us, we quickly headed for our assigned barracks. Made of woven *sawali* matting and thatched roofs, they looked rather fragile.

We now became part of the 2,146 prisoners in the Los Banos Internment Camp.

The American sense of humor is a marvelous thing.

At first the Japanese officers were very strict in making us bow to them. Since bowing is not a part of our way of life, we tried a slight nod of the head. They discovered that getting Americans to bow properly to them was as difficult as teaching us how to salute. We were purposely poor learners.

Virginia Chapman has described what happened when she first arrived at Los Banos:

"They said, 'Every American must bow to a Japanese soldier when he goes by, or if they pass the sentry post.'

"We had a meeting on that. Then we decided, 'Well, all right, we'll do it, but we'll also bow to each other.'

"So we went around the camp and we bowed. Every time we met, we bowed; and we bowed also to the Japanese. We would bow to a pole or anything.

"After a week the Japanese asked, 'What's all this bowing going on?'

" 'We were told to do it,' was our reply.

"They suddenly realized we were making fools of them."

We heard that in another camp bowing was enforced and the Japanese returned the bows. One day sixteen women lined up behind a building, in front of which stood a Japanese soldier. One after another, with some space between them, the women walked by him and bowed properly, each bow being duly returned by the soldier.

Each woman had bowed only once, but the Japanese soldier had bowed sixteen times, bobbing up and down like a cork in the waves of the sea. After a short time the women walked by him, bowing again, until he had bowed to them a total of thirty-two times!

CHAPTER 12
Color Me Purple

"HAVE YOU ANY IDEA what these bites are?" I asked Ruth Woodworth, pointing to my arms and legs.

"Could be mosquitoes," she suggested.

"But I also have them on my body in places covered by my clothes."

"What about fleas?"

"I haven't seen any."

"You borrowed that bed, Carol. Those bites could come from bedbugs, which are prolific here in the tropics."

Ruth had some boiling water poured on my bed, but the next day there were more bites. They were spreading all over my body.

Examining them closely, Ruth made another diagnosis. "They're beginning to look like blisters, and a few of them are oozing. Maybe they're not bites."

Looking at her in horror, I asked, "Not smallpox?"

"I just don't know what it is."

Then Mona Kemery gave me great news. "Carol, I've heard that a clinic is being set up nearby for those needing only minor medical help."

Our men were making a lean-to shelter at the end of a barracks for an examining room. As soon as they could find more nails, they were going to make it sturdier. For the present, the men were just leaning some boards at an angle against a very sparse framework extending from the *sawali* wall to the center aisle of the barracks. The next day I made my way to this temporary clinic, fearful of the possible diagnosis.

A nurse administered aid to us, while serious cases were sent to Dr. Nance at the camp's "hospital." Nurse Ruth Meinhardt examined me in the little lean-to. She was an attractive, capable, blonde young woman any soldier would enjoy having for his nurse. I stood before her speechless, afraid to ask the verdict.

At last it came. "Carol, this is impetigo."

Not realizing the rough road still ahead of me, I breathed a sigh of relief, grateful that it wasn't anything worse. "How did I get it?"

"I don't know," Ruth replied. "Maybe on the crowded trucks or train that brought us down here. I've heard that impetigo is common among the Japanese soldiers."

Since the sores ranged from my face to my toes, I had to take off all clothing.

Using a pair of forceps, Ruth Meinhardt removed the crust from each of the couple of hundred sores, and then applied gentian violet, a brilliant purple medicine.

While she continued to paint me purple, someone inadvertently leaned against those unnailed boards. With a resounding crash, they all fell down like dominoes.

There I stood, covered only with the garment Mother Nature provides—and purple medicine.

A middle-aged man sitting about six feet away was keeping the clinic records. He looked up in stunned alarm, his eyes surveying every inch of me. I blushed with embarrassment.

About twenty patients were waiting in line for treatment, most of whom were young men studying to be priests. They all stared, so startled they forgot to be gentlemen. When they came out of shock, the men hastened to put the boards back up again.

I crouched down, and the nurse threw my clothes over me.

That afternoon an internee heard one of the student priests saying to another, "Were you in the clinic this morning when the boards fell down?"

When the other priest replied that he was not there, the first priest said with a twinkle in his eyes, "Well, brother, the vision that was beheld cannot be told."

The story quickly spread through the camp, and people started walking by the cubicle I shared with others. They were looking for the woman "clothed in purple." They kept a safe distance away but wanted to know all the details.

Because everyone else thought it was humorous, I went along with their humor, quoting a rhyme I had once heard:

I've never seen a purple cow,
I never hope to see one;
But I can tell you anyhow
I'd rather see than be one.

They had a good laugh, which brightened their otherwise dreary day. But that night when I was alone in bed with all my sores, tears of humiliation quietly slid down my cheeks. Still young and sensitive, I was mortified with embarrassment and offered a little prayer, "Lord, help me keep smiling."

CHAPTER 13
The Camp Leper

"DON'T TOUCH THE CAMP water buckets, faucets, or anything anyone else has to touch, and keep your hands out of water," ordered Nurse Meinhardt when she came to see me the next day.

"Because impetigo is so contagious," she continued, "I'm moving you to the empty cubicle across the aisle from where you are now. You'll be in isolation until you are past the contagious stage."

"Do I continue going to the clinic for treatment?" I asked, feeling very subdued and not wanting to risk having those boards fall down again.

With an understanding smile, she replied, "No, I'll come here every day and take care of you."

I thanked her, and in my heart awarded her the medal of honor for doing extra, unpleasant work when she was starving like all the rest of us.

Before leaving, she said there was a place reserved for me in our crude bathroom that served two barracks.

Since we had no dishes, I used half of an empty coconut shell, holding it out like a begging bowl for Ruth to pour water into it when I was thirsty or put in food when there were weeds, mush, or slugs to eat.

As I continued to get worse, people shrank away from me, and I did not blame them. If my impetigo spread through the two thousand people in camp, it would be horrendous.

I became the "camp leper," repulsive, foul, unsightly, and odious.

In my isolation, I ate alone, walked back and forth in my cubicle, or sat alone on my box. We had no chairs.

One woman walking by said, "We'd love to have you come into our cubicle and visit, but of course you can't."

And another commented, "I'd like to do something for you, but I can't touch anything you've touched."

Some of them really wanted to help, but they didn't know how because everyone was afraid of getting my disease.

Nurse Meinhardt tied a string across one end of my cubicle and hung a sheet on it to provide privacy when she treated my sores. But one day in the midst of the treatment, the string broke and down went the sheet. There I stood again in all my purple splendor.

I was in a women's barracks, but Mr. Smallwood was standing in the aisle a few feet away, talking to Evelyn Congleton. I grabbed the sheet and threw it around myself as he turned to see what all the commotion was about.

Since his name was "Smallwood," everyone called him "Chips." Later, when he married and had a baby son, people nicknamed the little boy "Splinter."

"Chips, you get out of here!" I ordered firmly, but with just a trace of a friendly smile, as I knew him well.

Sizing up the situation quickly, he had an impish look in his eyes as he replied, "No, Carol, I plan to spend the afternoon here!" But after a few more facetious remarks, he left.

One missionary stood in the aisle by my cubicle every evening and read to me from the book of Job in the Bible, and soon I started feeling like Job.

A number of Job's "comforters" walked down the aisle of our barracks from time to time, pausing by my cubicle, asking questions and suggesting reasons why, of all people in camp, I should have impetigo.

One woman, meaning to be kind, said, "Do you think you made a mistake starting out for India and God has stopped you on the way? You are quite young for such a commitment."

The woman's remark raised a question in my mind. Had I made a mistake in starting out for India to work in the orphanage there?

I recalled the words of one of our professors at the Bible Institute of Los Angeles (now Biola University), Dr. John Hubbard, who said three things must coordinate when you make an important decision:

1. It must be in ethical accordance with the moral principles set forth in the Bible.
2. There must be an affirmation in your own heart.
3. The circumstances must make it possible.

The first two requirements were met, but what about the third?

Am I just an accidental victim of war? Or are the present circumstances a meaningful detour to deepen my values in preparation for better service in India? Or is my becoming a prisoner a roadblock, stopping me from making a serious mistake with lifelong implications?

These questions pierced my innermost being. I did not want to make a disaster of my life, but it seemed as though I was doing an excellent job of exactly that.

Sitting in solitude on my box in that prison barracks, my mind traced the events that had led me into this wretched condition:

As a teen-aged student at Woodbury College in Los Angeles, I felt money would buy everything I wanted in life, including happiness. The college promised to secure good positions in the business world for its graduates, and I studied hard to make my dreams come true.

But my cousin, Dorothea Cox, suggested to some of her

friends that they invite me to the Lyceum Club and Church of the Open Door in Los Angeles. The special speaker one Sunday evening at church was Mel Trotter. As he spoke on the love of God, I realized for the first time something of the wonder, magnificence, and redemptive power of that love.

Although I had attended a Presbyterian Sunday school and church now and then while growing up, I had failed to grasp the challenge of sharing that love with others.

As I felt moved to give my life in the service of helping people in need, there came to mind the marvelous things I was going to buy with money earned in the business world, and I felt they were too valuable to sacrifice, so I answered, "No."

But as Mel Trotter continued his message, those material things began fading. Overwhelmed by the majestic greatness of God's love, I dedicated my life that night to His service wherever in the world He could use me.

Feeling God would have me start among my classmates, I decided to establish a Bible club at Woodbury College, even though I had never owned a Bible. I felt that somehow He would take care of all the details.

The next morning at college my best friend said to me, "Carol, did you become engaged to be married last night?"

"No, why?"

"You look so radiantly happy."

Before the week was over, about twenty students, both men and women, asked me why I seemed so very happy. It was the beginning of our Bible club.

But one evening my parents called me into the living room for a "conference."

Mother started it off, "Your father and I feel that you will get yourself in trouble with the authorities at Woodbury College if you continue organizing this Bible club, and the school authorities will not get you a good position when you graduate. Therefore, we want you to stop the club tomorrow or we'll take you out of school."

Wow! I offered up a little prayer for help.

The next morning at college I was surprised to find a letter for me from the owner, who was also the president of the school, R. H. Whitten. The students called him "Pop."

Dear Carol:

How about that religious club you were planning on organizing?

Mildred brought it to my attention some time ago with a little hesitance. I guess she thought I would not favor it, but I surprised her by stating that I liked the idea immensely.

Right after that I took a vacation and have just returned. I have hardly had time to get my balance, but I have thought of the matter many times, and have hoped that you would go through with it. We need proper balance of organizations, and with so many inclined toward social activities, we certainly want to have one along religious lines. . . .

I am really proud of you, Carol, for conceiving this idea. . . . You are just the kind of a girl we like.

Sincerely yours,
Pop

When I showed that letter to my parents, they withdrew their ultimatum, and I said, "Thank You" to the Lord.

We named our group the "Philologus Club." A translation from the Greek is "Lover of the Word."

My next idea was to give a banquet for all new incoming students and present to them the ideals of our club. I had no money to pay for the banquet or the stamps on the invitations, but I offered another little prayer for help.

I went to the office manager, Mrs. Dora Kirby, and made a request: "I would like the names and addresses of all new incoming students for the next semester."

Looking astounded, Mrs. Kirby replied, "Why, Carol, we never give that information to anyone."

"But I was just going to invite them to a banquet so we could tell them about our Philologus Club. Here's the letter I was going to send them."

Glancing over it, Mrs. Kirby replied, "This will have to go to Pop Whitten for approval."

The next day a smiling Mrs. Kirby said, "Carol, Pop liked your letter and the idea so much that he's going to have us type the letters here in the office. We'll sign your name, stamp them, and Pop's going to pay for the banquet."

I glanced heavenward and said another "Thank You."

Pop arranged for me to have a student body assembly hour in which to present the purpose of the club. When someone in the office told him I might not return to the school for financial reasons, he sent me a message: "If there is any reason why you can't be back with us, I'll work with you to plan some way to overcome every obstacle."

Pop cleared away every mountain that arose in my pathway. It almost seemed as though the Lord had appointed him to clear my way, but apart from greeting him when we happened to pass each other in the college hallways, I never had a conversation with "Pop" Whitten.

At the awards ceremony when I graduated, Pop presented me with the Leo V. Youngworth Award for outstanding contributions to the college.

The Philologus Club became part of the University Bible Clubs, in which Dr. S. H. Sutherland was a leader. As the club flourished, lives of many students were graced with higher quality and deeper meaning. There is nothing quite like college life, and what fun we had!

As I looked at my deplorable situation there in that internment camp, I couldn't help wishing that "Pop" Whitten were somewhere around to remove all my problems.

After I graduated, Woodbury's placement manager, Mrs. Louise Ware, secured for me the position of private secretary to Dr. Jules Stein. He founded the Music Corporation of America, which purchased Universal Studios. He later also founded the famous Jules Stein Eye Institute. In our office we handled contracts and publicity for famous bands, film stars, writers, and musical artists, to whose performances I sometimes received complimentary tickets.

In contrast to all that night life, my heart became burdened for the orphaned baby girls of India. Turning from the business world, I gave up my high salary and entered Biola for further training. Dr. Louis Talbot was president of the school. I never dreamed that many years later this wonderful man would ask me to marry him. Truly God's hand was still leading me.

I worked my way through the school as secretary to a faculty member, Dr. Samuel H. Sutherland, with whom I had become acquainted in the University Bible Clubs. He later succeeded Dr. Talbot as president of Biola College. Both of these men were to have a great impact on my life.

We had very little humor in the prison camp, but working for Dr. Sutherland had often been hilarious. As I sat there on my box, isolated from everyone else in the camp, I thought of former days and started chuckling. Some people walking down the aisle near my cubicle paused to find out what could possibly be humorous in my deplorable situation. I told them this story:

Our office was on the sixth floor of Biola's thirteen-story building. I attended classes in the morning and worked for Dr. Sutherland in the afternoon. When I went to my desk on Valentine's day, there lay a penny valentine with a lollipop attached and a note: "Go to the women's lounge on the 13th floor for your valentine."

In the lounge on the 13th floor was another valentine with a lollipop and a note: "Go to the sub-basement for your valentine."

There I found another one with a lollipop and a note: "Go to the library on the 9th floor for your valentine."

Following a series of such notes, I went up and down stairs and in the elevator until both my hands were filled with valentines and lollipops.

Then I found the final note: "Go to your office and look in the Dictaphone shaver for your valentine."

Back in my office, I opened the little door of the Dictaphone shaver and there found a big, juicy lemon.

His office door was closed. Opening it, I did not take time to notice that an important out-of-state official was in conference with Dr. Sutherland. The man's back was toward me.

I threw that lemon right at Dr. Sutherland. It narrowly missed both men, landing against the wall. As that lemon whizzed past the ear of the visiting dignitary, he looked startled, but Dr. Sutherland calmly explained, "It's all right. That's just my secretary reporting for work."

Laughing at the incredulous look on his guest's face, Dr. Sutherland explained what he had done. I'm sure the man must have wondered what kind of a school he was visiting.

"Did you ever get back at him?" asked one of the women standing in the aisle of our barracks.

"I tried a couple of times, but it's pretty hard to get the best of Dr. Sutherland. Somehow he's always out there ahead of you."

"Tell us how you tried."

It was the first time since I had developed impetigo that my barracks neighbors had encouraged me to talk to them, so I continued the story:

When Dr. Sutherland was recuperating from the measles, his lovely wife, Eleanor, phoned to ask if I could come out to their home and take some dictation from her husband. Although still in bed, he felt much better.

A student named James Vaus happened to be in my office at the time. "I'll drive you out there, Carol."

When it was time to leave, Jim appeared at my desk with a box of Mrs. Sees chocolates as a gift for Dr. Sutherland.

"I'm not sure he will feel like eating chocolates, Jim. He's sick," I commented.

"I'm going to make these very special so he will really enjoy them," answered Jim as he opened a pocketknife and started slicing the bottoms off of the creams.

"Why are you doing that?"

Without answering, Jim pulled some rubber bands out of his pocket, stuffed them into the chocolates, and then stuck the bottoms back on again.

Watching wide-eyed and remembering the lemon incident, I didn't object.

Mrs. Sutherland welcomed us to their home and we went into the bedroom, where Dr. Sutherland was propped up with pillows and looking quite capable of coping with almost any situation.

Dr. Sutherland started dictating as I took it down in Gregg shorthand. There were no tape recorders in those years.

After about half an hour the doorbell rang, and in came Dr. Kenneth Monroe, highly esteemed as one of our professors and as dean of Biola. He sat down near a table where Jim had placed the chocolates. Not wanting to interrupt the dictation, Dr. Monroe remained quiet, while Jim kept urging him to have one of the luscious candies.

Finally giving into Jim's urging, our distinguished guest reached over and selected a cream, and then kept chewing and chewing and chewing.

Now Dr. Monroe was a scholar of great acumen, high intelligence, and wonderful teaching ability. With it all, he was a man of quiet dignity and greatly respected by the students. No one ever played a joke on him. He was every inch a dean and later became president of Westmont College.

After working on that chocolate for some time, he excused himself and went to the bathroom.

When he returned, the dean sat quietly waiting for an explanation while Dr. Sutherland went on dictating. After a few minutes, Monroe selected another candy, which also contained some of the rubber bands. Chewing on that one for a time, he then went to the kitchen.

Coming back to the room once again, Dr. Monroe studied the faces of all present, while Jim and I struggled to keep our expressions "deadpan."

During a pause in the dictation, our discerning dean said, "Sam, have you had one of these chocolates?"

When Dr. Sutherland innocently responded in the negative, Professor Monroe extolled their qualities in such scholarly fashion that Jim and I could no longer control our laughter.

Explanations had to be made to the dumbfounded Dr. Sam Sutherland, who escaped the trap set for him.

We had no idea Dr. Monroe could be such a good sport. He topped it all by saying, when leaving, "May I have one of those doctored-up chocolates to give my secretary?"

The women's laughter drew others to the nearby aisle. They all wanted to hear more stories about Dr. Sutherland.

"Did you ever get the best of Dr. Sutherland?" one of them asked.

"Well, maybe just once."

"Oh, tell us about that!"

Happy to have some companionship at last, I agreed to share one more story:

Among Dr. Sutherland's many responsibilities at Biola was teaching a class on the last book in the Bible, Revelation, which is one of the most difficult to understand. When final examination time came along, the students were restless. Since Dr. Sutherland's examinations were sometimes unpredictable, none of us knew how to study for the exam.

The night before the exam, the irrepressible Jim Vaus came up with a plan. Borrowing another car, he invited the student president of our class, Bill Heath, along with Eleanor Hill and me, to go out to the Sutherlands' home early in the morning. We were all in Dr. Sutherland's class. Jim had prepared picket signs for us to carry, stating in humorous ways that Dr. Sutherland's exams were unfair to his poor students.

When Dr. Sutherland saw us picketing and read the signs, he came to the door and asked, "What are your demands?"

Actually, we had none, so Jim called out, "Bacon and eggs for breakfast."

Always gracious, Mrs. Sutherland invited us in and more than met our demands with a delicious breakfast.

All of this, however, made Dr. Sutherland late for class. He had to call the school and ask that someone tell the students to wait for him. He did not know that everyone in our class knew about the picketing. No one could have dragged a single student out of the classroom before Dr. Sutherland arrived.

When he walked into the room with the four of us traipsing behind him, the class erupted in a roar of applause, which was not for us who delayed him, but for a good-natured Dr. Sutherland whom all the students loved and respected, though he could be mighty tough when necessary. His lateness to class did make it necessary for him to cancel one question on the exam, but he chose the easiest!

As my storytelling closed, the women walked down the barracks aisle to their cubicles, and I heard one of them remark, "That must have been an interesting school to attend!"

As graduation from Biola neared, I applied to the Ramabai Mukti Mission, a large orphanage, school, and rescue home in India. I was told to be in New York City the week after graduation to meet the official board representing the mission in this country.

The Great Depression was at its height. By the time my school and graduation expenses were paid, I had no money left for a ticket to New York, but I mentioned it to no one. When I had felt led to start that Bible club at Woodbury College, all the difficulties had been overcome. I was convinced that if the Lord wanted me to serve Him in India, He would do it again, keeping me in the hollow of His hand all the way.

Sitting there on my box in the prison camp, I recalled how the money for the ticket to New York was supplied and was grateful for the way it happened.

I had been doing volunteer work as the superintendent of a Sunday school in a little Russian church located on the east side of Los Angeles. Since I would be leaving for New York, I informed the pastor he would have to get a replacement for me but said nothing about my not having any money at all for my ticket—$78 by Greyhound bus.

The Sunday before I was to leave, the pastor presented me with $50 from the Russians. At that time they were a poor people. It was hard for them to get work because they spoke broken English and had Russian names, but they had sought refuge in our country. I was overwhelmed by their gift of love.

I then needed $28 more to buy my ticket. Returning to my room, I found a note to phone Mrs. Edwin B. Young. She was an elderly lady who had very little means of her own but spent most of her time giving out monetary gifts that were donated to her for distribution where greatly needed. She could not cope with all the letter writing, so I had done voluntary typing for her.

When I reached her by phone, she said, "Carol, someone has sent me a check for $28 to be used where needed most. As I was praying about it, your name came to my mind. Do you need $28?" Did I ever!

Although I now had the exact amount needed for my ticket, I did not have money for food on the long journey, but that did not bother me. What did thrill me was the fact that the money for my ticket had come from needy people I had been helping on a volunteer basis. It reminded me of the proverb: "He who is kind to the poor lends to the LORD, and he will reward him for what he has done" (Proverbs 19:17, NIV).

It confirmed my call then and reconfirmed it now as I sat on my box in isolation, imprisoned, diseased, and starving. It was the answer to that woman's question. My leaving for India was not a mistake, no matter what happened on the way.

My family had hoped to the end I would not be able to go either to New York or India. As I was packing, my brother Jack stopped by to see me. After chatting a bit, he rose to go and dropped a ten dollar bill in my lap. With a brotherly grin he said, "Get drunk on this for me while you're in New York." He did not know he was providing food for me on the bus trip.

Dad and Mother took me to the bus station in Long Beach, California. As I settled into my seat, and just before the driver closed the big door, my father sighed and said, "Well, I guess you're really going," and tossed into my lap a check for $50. I knew how he felt about my plans, so his gift brought tears to my eyes.

I was glad Mother and Dad could not see me now.

My physical condition continued to worsen as the sores multiplied and ate deep into my flesh. I was reinfecting myself every day from my own clothes and sheets, which were saturated with oozing matter from the sores. I could not wash my sheets and clothing, and anyone attempting to do so would risk getting the disease.

I thought of John Bunyan's *Pilgrim's Progress* and felt like Christian when he tumbled into the Slough of Despond and struggled in vain to get out but could not because of the burden on his back. Finally a man named Help gave him his hand and drew him out.

But Christian did not have an odious disease, highly communicable to anyone offering help. My nurse was losing the battle as the disease spread over my body. People felt sorry for me, but they were afraid to touch anything near me.

I truly was in the Slough of Despond with no way out. How would it end?

CHAPTER 14
Warfare in My Cubicle

WE WERE LOSING THE BATTLE on two fronts—Nurse Meinhardt's and mine.

She was now spending most of her time skillfully attacking my sores morning and evening with forceps and medicine, as I continued to be isolated in my cubicle.

My flesh decided to fight back. Each time that monster, Forceps, crept up under the guise of kindness to attack a sore's protective crust, the victim, Flesh, around the sore started an involuntary, rebellious twitching I could not control.

Forceps changed tactics. It tried dive bombing the sore, tunneling under it, or slyly approaching it from the side. But Flesh had its secret radar working in every direction, and the twitching warded off each attack, no matter from which direction it came.

Our only weapon, one pair of forceps, fought valiantly, but every day the flesh was bombarded by new reinforcements in the form of fresh germs from my clothes and sheets.

The forceps had to retreat in defeat, and the germs danced in victory all over my body, capturing the nurse and me as their prisoners of war. We were both discouraged and exhausted. Retreating to her cubicle, the nurse searched for some new strategy, while I sat alone in my slough of despond.

One day an elderly lady walking down the aisle in our barracks paused to chat with me, keeping a safe distance.

"I suppose someday I'll see God's purpose in this and thank Him for it," I said to her, with a self-pitying sigh.

And she responded, "My dear girl, how much better it would be if you thanked Him now by faith."

That remark started my thought processes working. *Among more than two thousand prisoners, why me? Why am I the one to get this terrible case of impetigo?* After thinking about it for some time, I offered this little prayer: "If there is a purpose in my having this disease, give me listening ears and a heart to understand, because I'm ready to learn and learn quickly!"

Resembling a famous statue, "The Thinker," I sat on my box in that cubicle, with chin supported by the back of my hand, elbow resting on one knee, thinking.

How long I sat there meditating, I do not know, but after a time I envisioned the diseased children and adults in the villages of India. That fascinating land has beautiful, educated, wealthy, cultured, wonderful people, but it also has the poor, the needy and sick, the diseased, living in the villages, sometimes with no medical help or any other kind of assistance available, and many without hope.

As my tears started flowing, I saw in my mind's eye a sick, orphaned child holding out her hands to me for help, her body covered with sores just like mine.

Peace came to my heart, for I had found my answer. Bowing my head, I thanked God for giving me ears to hear and a heart to understand why I had become the "camp leper." It was part of my training, and I had graduated from another course in God's university.

The next day Nurse Meinhardt changed the treatment of my sores. Leaving the forceps behind, she soaked the crusts off with hot-water foments, and then applied some ointment she secured from the camp hospital. Friends and strangers now started asking how they could help me.

"What can we do for you?" asked Cae Paget one day as she looked with horror at my condition.

My eyes met hers in silence. I could not ask anyone to get involved. But she understood what her eyes saw. "Give me your clothes and sheets. We'll wash them for you."

"You may get impetigo!" I exclaimed.

"Never mind. Just give them to me."

Peter and Cae hauled water and washed clothing and sheets. Giving them back to me, Cae said, "Bring your bit of mush to our cubicle and eat with us."

As I took my coconut shell with its wormy mush to the Pagets' cubicle, their fellowship and friendship meant more than words could ever express.

"What's that on Joy's face?" I asked some days later when I noticed some suspicious sores. Their daughter was a dainty little girl with flowing blonde hair framing sky-blue eyes in a tiny, thin, starving face. Now about six years old, she had caught my impetigo! However, we cleared it up before the sores spread and deepened.

Ruth Woodworth came across the aisle every day to give me my portion of mush. "Carol, your cubicle looks like a chicken pen."

"I know, but I can't touch the camp broom."

Ruth secured a broom, which was just long strands of grass tied together, and swept my bamboo floor. The dirt and litter fell through the cracks to the ground six inches below. Now I had clean clothes and sheets and a clean cubicle.

One day Sister Robert Marie of the Maryknoll sisters sought me out. "Do they treat you the way they do me?"

"What do you mean?" I asked, surprised at this question from a nun.

"Aren't you from California?"

"That's right."

"So am I." With a twinkle in her eyes, she continued, "Some people accuse me of being a walking Chamber of Commerce for my home state."

After we chatted a bit, she invited me to go for a walk with her.

"You don't mind my disease?" I asked.

"Not at all. I've brought a book on Richard Halliburton's travels. Maybe we could sit under a tree and I could read to you."

Surprised at her thoughtfulness for a stranger, I gladly accepted. We never finished the book but walked and talked together in friendship and fellowship that still continue. Some of the Protestants in camp feared she might try to make a nun out of me, while some of the Catholics may have thought I would turn her toward Protestantism, but such was not the case. We shared the same love for the Lord and desire to help others, though sometimes we did resemble two politicians discussing the issues.

The nurse's new treatment and the clean sheets and clothes worked like magic. No more sores developed and the old ones began healing.

I came through the ordeal of being the camp leper, thankful for those who cared for me when I was in need, and with a prayer that my service to people in India would be greater and deeper and my heart more sensitive to their needs.

Free from isolation, I could carry my load of work in the camp again and was glad for the privilege.

CHAPTER 15
The Indelicacy of No Privacy

FOR THOSE OF US who were comparatively young, unsophisticated, and shy, the lack of privacy was embarrassing. Night and day our cubicles in the women's barracks were completely open on the center aisle.

Between each two barracks were toilet and shower facilities with no curtains allowed. I have no idea who was responsible for such a rule, but the usually meek and submissive nuns rebelled and insisted on having one shower curtained off for them, explaining that exposure would break the rules of their Order. We graciously let them have their curtain and did not report it to the Japanese, all the time wishing we also could have curtains.

We were a sight to see. Because of starvation, some women lost more than fifty pounds. Their skin was loose and their breasts sagged like deflated bags.

Not only did the ninety-six women in our barracks use the three showers, but they were also shared with the married women in the next barracks. Many times there was no water in the showers and none for the buckets.

The toilet facilities were an even greater embarrassment. Flat wooden seats with holes in them were placed over a trough. Suspended in the air, a bucket dangled that was sometimes filled with water. You pulled a rope, which tipped the bucket, sloshing water through the trough. They reserved a special hole for me when I had impetigo. Privacy did not exist.

And getting toilet paper became a problem. Those on the sanitation detail had a tough assignment.

One blessing in disguise for most of us women came when menstruation stopped because of malnutrition. We had no supplies for personal sanitary needs.

When we were interned, the Japanese who inspected our suitcases told us we could take only one of each item. Marion Childress had a box of twelve Kotex sanitary pads. The Japanese inspector on seeing them said in his limited English, "No! Only one."

Marion was a registered nurse, plump and merry, and with no inhibitions. Picking up one of those sanitary pads and waving it in the face of the Japanese, she said, "Do you know what it is?"

Startled, the inspector nodded that he did.

Then Marion shouted at him, "One no good! One no good!"

Almost hypnotized by her frankness, the guard nodded in agreement, repeating "One no good! One no good!" and let Marion keep her box of Kotex.

Among the internees lived a prostitute who had been in a mental hospital. I nicknamed her "Diamond Lil" because of her contrast to that famous prostitute. She lived on the side of camp called "Hell's Half Acre."

The small cubicles there were meant for two people or a small family, with partitions of matting just high enough so no one could easily see over the top. Each cubicle had an open entrance off the center aisle. If you wanted a door, you had to provide it yourself. Diamond Lil's had no door.

None of this inhibited Lil from cavorting with her "customers" in full view through the open doorway of her cubicle with accompanying sound effects. This offended all those who had to walk down that aisle. It was not a sight for children to see.

A request to have a door placed there was denied, since doors were not supplied for anyone. In self-defense, the internees themselves put up a makeshift door at her cubicle.

A missionary nicknamed "Hallelujah Mary" determined to convert Diamond Lil. Though there were other prostitutes in camp, Mary concentrated on Lil. When Mary sang hymns and evangelistic choruses, Diamond Lil would good-naturedly call out, "Swing it, Mary!"

They seemed equally matched. When little Mary Hunter quoted the Bible to her, Lil would come back with "Let him that is without sin cast the first stone."

Diamond Lil's mental capacity was not high, but with wile and guile, she humored Mary in order to wheedle treats of food from her.

Their confrontations varied from serious to humorous and good-natured, but neither one budged an inch. Listening to their sparring bouts often provided a source of entertainment for those within hearing distance. Some bet on Hallelujah Mary to win, while with others, Lil was the odds-on favorite.

One day an official of our camp committee, George Gray, told Lil she would have to share her cubicle with Hababah Rodda, who had no place to stay. Hababah was from India, middle-aged and illiterate, accustomed to a simple life. When she moved into Diamond Lil's cubicle, Hababah brought some bags bulging with her possessions. Diamond Lil threw her out, bags and all.

An incredible scene developed when George Gray came to settle the dispute. Lil tackled him with fury, hitting and biting him, shouting at this stalwart man of dignity and political stature, a gentleman who had been one of the official representatives of our American government in the High Commissioner's office in Manila. He struggled with the scantily clothed prostitute until she agreed to stop fighting with Hababah.

But that did not end the feud. Both women headed for the Japanese commandant, Tannaka, who settled it. The two women had to live in that cubicle together. There was no other place and no higher court of appeal.

Finding Hababah's name a bit difficult, Diamond Lil called her "Bombay Duck." Bouts of feuding were interspersed with an occasional truce, but neither woman wanted to put up with the other. When it became evident there would be no peace for them or for the whole barracks, someone found another place for Hababah.

In spite of lack of privacy, several romances developed in camp and a few marriages took place. This may have saved some from cracking up and going out of their minds. It gave them something else to think about besides food. Caring for another under difficult circumstances involves sacrifice and is ennobling, often deepening love. It makes the struggle to live meaningful, preventing one from giving up, strengthening the desire to live, and providing hope for a happier future.

Although we were often embarrassed by our lack of privacy in the camp, the indelicacies were not life threatening. We learned to live with these indignities, sometimes even to joke about them. The human spirit, with its marvelous sense of humor, and the hope that "springs eternal in the human breast" rescued us from the throes of this demeaning humiliation.

The demands of our bodies for food became more important than our privacy as people scrounged for weeds and slugs, some sacrificing ethics and morality, or almost anything, for a bit of nourishment. We talked about food by day and dreamed of it by night. No price seemed too high to pay for a little something to eat.

CHAPTER 16
Keep Off the Weeds—We Eat Them

"IF WE EAT THE WORMS, will they give us protein?" asked diet-conscious Elda, as we were eating our tiny ration of mush containing rice, a bit of corn, and a multitude of weevils and worms.

"Will the worms continue eating the rice after we swallow them?" I asked.

Intellectual Ruth entered the conversation. "Those worms are cooked. They can't harm you. It's the eggs on weeds we eat that will develop into living worms inside of us."

"Raw or cooked, I don't relish eating worms," I lamented. Spooning through my mush, I started pulling the big worms out, counting up to six. Then I went after the shorter ones, but they were hard to pick out because they blended in with the grains of rice.

"At least the worms don't have a strong flavor," I continued. "The hardest things for me to swallow are the slugs. My whole digestive system seems to rebel against them."

"The most difficult part of the slugs for me," Evelyn commented, "is trying to fry them. They start inching toward the edge of the pan, and I have to keep shoving them back until they're cooked."

Our stomachs were shrinking as the daily ration of mush became smaller and wormier. Everyone was so very hungry, haunted by the specter of starvation, while noble ones sacrificed part of their own meager rations for the weak and the children.

We tried to grow a leafy plant called talinum and gathered pigweed wherever we could find it. One of my room jobs was cutting thorns off the pigweed so they would not tear our intestines. Someone put up a sign, "Keep off the weeds. We eat them."

When we were able to get a banana, we fried the skin and ate it as well. Nonbearing banana and papaya trees were cut down and their edible parts consumed.

Any dogs or cats unfortunate enough to be in our camp were soon put into the cooking pot.

The men started a piggery. Sometimes instead of mush, we had stew made of one little pig and various weeds for over two thousand of us. On rare occasions there would be a few *camotes* in it, a vegetable resembling the sweet potato.

Some Japanese soldiers would scrape the refuse off their plates onto those of American men, who ate it greedily. Several of our men grabbed a bone out of a dog's mouth and that night had bone soup for supper. And soon the dog also was on their menu.

One day a Japanese truck brought sacks of rice into camp, and a few scattered grains fell on the road. Our children eagerly gathered the grains and ate them raw, dirt and all. In their excitement, some of the little boys crossed a few feet over the boundary line leading to the storehouse. The Japanese announced that any such offenders, children or adults, would be shot.

On one occasion two little girls were discussing their "lick day."

"I had my lick day yesterday."

"What did you get to lick?"

"I got to lick the bowl we get our mush in."

"My lick day was today. I got to lick the family dishes." For many of us those dishes were coconut shells.

Hunger was not only destroying our bodies, our energy, and our hopes, but it was destroying character. People's sense of values was dying with their bodies. Hunger was eating away at nerves, emotions, and even conscience. Men who had never stolen before were stealing food from each other; honor was being sacrificed for a few grains of rice or a handful of beans.

When no guards were watching, some of our men stood near the barbed-wire fence at the back of the camp and waved shirts at Filipinos who were eager to trade coconuts for needed clothing.

For a time the Japanese allowed a food stand to be set up near the camp, where supplies for our kitchen were sometimes purchased by one of our men under close Japanese supervision. The operator was Carmen Rivera, a brave girl guerrilla of "Terry's Hunters," who risked her life to hide news and messages in the food.

Except for a rare banana, coconuts were our only fruit, and they were hard to get unless you had something to trade. In muggy weather, when perspiration flowed and bathing water was scarce, we smelled like coconuts. Sometimes I felt as though I were perspiring coconut milk.

It was our misfortune to have a cruel man in charge of our food rations. He was the grubby and crude Lt. Sadaaki Konishi, a heavy drinker of unsavory reputation. When he was transferred from his responsibilities at Santo Tomas Internment Camp to ours, the internees there played "The Drunkard Song" over a loudspeaker.

We appointed a committee of men to confront Lt. Konishi and request, plead for—and even demand, if necessary— more food for us.

Sitting in his chair with his boot-clad feet on his desk, Konishi glared at them, his gold tooth blazing with scorn. He had previously said he would make every American under his control eat dirt, and now his only reply was, "You'll be eating mud before this is over."

Among the Japanese who ruled over us at various times, there were a few rare officers who sometimes were concerned and thoughtful; but in every society all over the world some men are evil.

Most of the garrison holding us prisoners were veterans of former wars who had been put out to pasture as guards in our camp. Among those removed from front-line fighting, possibly because of his limp, was our nemesis, Konishi. We heard that his injury happened during war in Manchuria. In Japan he belonged to a terror squad of ill repute and had served as a prison warden. Violence had become a way of life for him, and he enjoyed it.

Deprived of actual warfare, Konishi vented all his frustration and wrath on us. This scoundrel became our camp villain. He despised all the prisoners in Santo Tomas and Los Banos Internment Camps because in his code of tradition, surrender and dishonor were synonymous.

Since internees were dying of starvation, our committee went to Konishi again, with a request they felt he could not refuse. Enjoying the sweet-potato-like *camote*, the Japanese discarded its bitter leaves, which were high in vitamins. We asked Konishi to give us the *camote* leaves they threw away.

With his feet as usual on his desk, Konishi listened and then surprised the Americans by telling them to pick up the green tops on the camp road the next afternoon. This particular road had a base containing something like tar.

The next morning Konishi had his men take the greens and spread them thinly on this road, then declared the road off limits. The tropic sun wilted the greens and softened the tar base of the road. When the greens were hopelessly stuck in the soft tar, Konishi kept his word and said we could have them. By that time they were inedible.

Our American committee did not give up their efforts to secure more food for us. On another trip to Konishi's office they demanded more rice for all internees.

After pondering their request for a time, Konishi told them to send some men to the storehouse the next day and they would be given sacks of rice. Our men were so weak from starvation, they could hardly carry those sacks. But putting them on their backs, they stumbled along until they reached our camp kitchen. Then Konishi gave orders to bring them back. "You asked for rice and I gave it to you. Now bring it back."

Reeling and falling under the weight, our men had to carry the sacks of rice back to the Japanese storehouse while Konishi sat in the office, his feet on the desk.

Dr. Dana Nance was a man of large frame who needed nourishment to sustain him as he worked long hours under primitive conditions, giving unreservedly of his medical skill and strength in caring for all of us internees.

He invited Margaret Pierce, George Gray, Fred Satterfield, and Ed Parish to have dinner with him on Thanksgiving Day. Each one brought his own ration of rice. They were served nicely sliced steak, an unheard of treat in a prison camp. As they ate and enjoyed it, the guests silently wondered whether it could be the missing dog, Poochie.

A family who was living nearby at the Los Banos Agricultural College when the war broke out had brought their pet dog with them when they were interned in our camp. When they found out what Dr. Nance had done to Poochie, they were infuriated.

Dr. Nance was a pragmatist who felt that in the circumstances under which we were living, sustaining human life was more important than sentimental feelings. The owners of the dog vehemently disagreed and took the case to our camp court. However, no action was taken because of a camp rule that pets were not allowed in camp.

Two sons in the family, who loved their dog, which was a

mixture of friendly breeds, defended Poochie's honor by assaulting Dr. Nance in a physical encounter. The big, broad-shouldered doctor could have laid them both low, but he refrained because he understood.

Feeling a bit subdued, Nance was sorry for what he had done to Poochie; but with so many starving men in camp, someone would have had the poor dog sooner or later. He did suggest to the internees that fried cat tasted like fried rabbit, and I felt sorry for any feline that might wander into our midst.

Dr. Nance helped me a number of times, and I felt kindly toward him, appreciating his medical expertise in caring for us. My first sortie over to see Nance at the camp hospital occurred soon after the temporary clinic was discontinued. I had discovered a lump near my elbow, oozing some kind of liquid.

"Have a look at this, will you?" I had asked Ruth Woodworth. "Could it be more impetigo?"

After scrutinizing it, she had replied, "No, but you better have Dr. Nance take care of *that*."

The seriousness in her tone caused my eyes to question hers, but she would say no more.

I had thought about it during a long, restless night, and the next morning was at the hospital, with Dr. Nance examining my elbow.

Without saying anything to me, he told the nurse, "Schedule surgery for removal of a cyst tomorrow morning."

"You're going to operate?" I asked in stunned surprise. "Is it necessary?"

"No," he replied in his matter-of-fact way, "not if you prefer to go around with a leaking cyst."

"Well—all right," I answered dubiously, wondering whether malnutrition would keep it from healing.

The next morning Dr. Nance performed the surgery with expertise, and I was to count among my souvenirs of Los Banos prison camp the neat white scar from his skillful knife.

I did not have so much as a spoonful of sugar with which to

pay Dr. Nance, but he expected nothing. He was giving his time, energy, and medical skill to serve all of us, accepting as his remuneration the satisfaction of providing needed help.

It was only when I became desperate that I took another little walk over to see Dr. Nance. Being a private sort of person, I stood embarrassed before his almost overwhelming presence and struggled with having to tell him why I had come.

I'm sure a smile of amusement must have flitted across Nance's face as, keeping my eyes lowered, I timidly explained what had happened:

"A fellow prisoner jokingly said something to me I didn't like. He was only teasing, but I started to give him a very unladylike kick in the shins. Trying to protect his shins from my kick, he grabbed my foot in midair. Losing my balance, I fell to the floor, injuring my sacroiliac joint. For several days I couldn't walk. When lying or sitting on that side, I still become almost paralyzed and have to lift myself up to relieve the pressure. It seems to be getting worse."

"When did this happen?" asked Dr. Nance.

"I don't remember the date. Maybe a year ago."

After completing his examination, Dr. Nance gave me some medicine that lessened the discomfort.

The gentleman who had only been trying to protect his shins felt worse about the accident than I did.

The injury became another souvenir of my prisoner-of-war years to carry home with me. My physician in America, Dr. Boyd, was to call it my "silly acrobatic joint." More than twenty years of difficulty with that sacroiliac followed before it finally decided to stop giving trouble and cooperate, nullifying a doctor's prediction in India that I would spend most of my life in a wheelchair.

But now in the internment camp that sacroiliac joint made it difficult for me to sit several hours at a time on a hard chair as I typed in the camp office. This problem was finally solved by shifting my weight now and then from one side to the other, uncomfortable but bearable.

As our stomachs continued shrinking because of lack of food, pains in that area became intense. Each night while I was lying in my upper bunk, my tummy was pinching, stabbing, growling, grabbing, wrenching, convulsing me in pain.

I softly massaged it, kneading, pressing, holding it as I tossed from side to side. And as the food became less and less, the stomach pains grew sharper.

Then real starvation set in, and after a time the pains gradually diminished and faded away. I presumed the shrinking had reached its limit.

My youthful health and vigor disappeared, and I became dull, lethargic, and weak. Along with others, I was a skeleton walking in rags.

When I first came into camp, I often typed six hours in the camp office to complete the roster in one day, but as our internment dragged on and on, the work tired me and I found it difficult to keep typing long enough to keep up the camp roster. The typewriter was not electric, but a heavy old clunker. Each time a new roster was required, I had to spread the typing over several days.

This typing was becoming even further complicated by a numbness that was developing in my hands. I now made a third and last visit to Dr. Nance. This time I showed him my numb hands.

After an examination, Nance gave his diagnosis, typically brief, "You have beriberi."

As I left him, tears stung my eyes. Beriberi was a disease causing degenerative changes of the nerves, digestive system, and heart, also partial paralysis of the extremities, due to malnutrition's causing a deficiency of thiamine. A number of our internees had already passed away, their death certificates listing cause of death as "beriberi due to starvation."

I had watched others go down Beriberi Road to its end. Now it was my turn to walk that gloomy path.

Going to our cubicle, I picked up my Bible and walked slowly and thoughtfully to the half of a barracks we used as a makeshift chapel.

As I faced this new crisis in my life, a promising future began fading. Young and just out of school, I did not feel ready to die of beriberi in that internment camp.

Sitting on a bench in the bamboo chapel, I was glad there was no one else present. I needed to be alone with my God. As I opened the Bible to Philippians 4:19, "My God shall supply all your need," tears blurred the words and beriberi blurred their reality.

After an unmeasured time, there came to mind the scene of friends on a dock in California, waving hands in farewell as my ship slowly sailed away. Now their faces and hands faded and refocused into the multitudes of India reaching out their welcoming hands to me for help, hands that were numb from beriberi and starvation just like mine.

In the quietness of the chapel, my thoughts turned to Ephesians 3:11, "According to the eternal purpose which he purposed. . ."

Suddenly the whole experience became electric with meaning. Doubt and discouragement, self-pity and despair dropped from my shoulders like a worn-out coat. God was supplying my greatest need in working out His purposes.

"My God shall supply all your need" didn't necessarily mean "You'll never be hungry or have beriberi."

I had been seeing only the present. The Lord was seeing eternity.

I saw only my numb hands. He saw the hungry hands of India's multitudes.

I had asked Him for something small. He withheld it to give something greater.

He was turning me from a pygmy into a giant to minister to people of Hindustan who needed help.

Bowing my head, I thanked Him for answering and for giving me this tender word of encouragement from Ephesians, "I desire that ye faint not at my tribulation for you, which is your glory."

Through the gnawing pangs of hunger and the numbing disease of beriberi, India and I had become one.

But what about the little children in our camp who were fading and becoming weaker because of starvation? Would it stunt them in body, mind, and soul? I breathed a prayer that there would also be an answer for these little ones whose energy even to play was fading away.

CHAPTER 17
"That's Not Thunder!"
September 21, 1944

I WAS SITTING on my upper bunk sewing, trying to make a dress out of some royal blue material for which I had traded a treasured bon voyage gift. My clothes were barely hanging together and beyond repair. Someone had given me a few small pieces of white material and tiny bits of red with which I was going to edge the neck and sleeves, making a red, white, and blue victory dress to wear when the American army returned.

Gertrude Feely came down the aisle, a radiant smile on her face. Looking up at me, she said, "That's not thunder, is it?"

For more than two and a half years we had heard such remarks, and the sounds had always been tropical thunder. But we listened intently, every nerve taut, every sense alert.

Boom! Boom! BOOM!

Jumping down from my bunk, I raced to the front of the barracks, shouting, *"That's not thunder!"* My eyes swept the skies, and there in the distance could be seen black specks moving quickly here and there.

Jumping up and down and pointing, I shouted, *"Look, they've come!"*

The pathways filled with people. From every direction the

prisoners came running, pointing, yelling, some with tears of joy running down their cheeks, all uncontrollable with rejoicing.

Puffs of antiaircraft fire could be seen just below the planes. Like swarms of bees the planes came and then disappeared, leaving their stings behind them. We gave vent to our unrestrained joy until Japanese guards sent us back into our barracks.

But in all our buildings we could still hear the bombs. No one worked; hardly anyone even sat down. We laughed, we cried, we ran up and down the aisles of the barracks. Men punched one another, women hugged each other, some danced little jigs, mothers held their little children close to them in sheer happiness.

The sounds of bombings continued through the night. Some of the men saw the light from a huge explosion. Counting the seconds until they heard the sound, and figuring the time it takes light and sound to travel, the men decided it must have been a bomb striking a Japanese superdreadnought in Manila Bay.

The next morning when we were all lined up for roll call, the air-raid alarm sounded. Looking up, we could see black specks filling the sky. Though the Japanese sent us to our barracks, our eyes still followed a formation flying away from the bombing. Suddenly one of the planes burst into flames, hung suspended in the air, and then crashed to the ground. It was too far away to see whether the pilot had been able to bail out.

Suddenly everyone in camp became quiet, while some of us silently prayed. Most of the internees turned and went to their cubicles, a hush coming over all of us. We had seen one cost of that bombing. Whose husband? Whose sweetheart, son, or brother?

The bombings continued, but the hilarious rejoicing faded somewhat, and it was as though a heavy weight hung over the camp. We did not know the planes probably came from Admiral Halsey's fleet. We were as starved for news as we were for food.

Then on Sunday morning, October 15, we were sitting in the chapel when the air-raid alarm sounded. Each one had to go immediately to his or her own barracks. It had been raining, and as we sloshed along the paths, our eyes searched the sky. We spotted some planes, and our eyes never left them as they winged their way toward our camp. Straight over our heads they flew.

We strained to read the insignia. Instead of the enemy's markings, we saw America's insignia of the stars.

We simply went wild, shouting and waving our arms wildly at the planes.

Returning our greeting, the planes dipped their wings in salute and flew on over the tops of palm trees and away into the wide blue yonder.

They left us behind, and tears of deep emotion rolled down our cheeks. Those pilots will never know what their waggling of the wings meant to us that day. It seemed as though they were saying, "Chins up! We'll be coming back for you some day."

On October 17, 1944, the sound of a missing motor overhead brought the entire camp out of the barracks. A few hundred feet above us smoke could be seen trailing from a plane. Part of the wing was gone, and the motor kept coughing and spluttering. Lower and lower it came, turning over and nose diving to the ground. A parachute opened just above the treetops. The plane fell somewhere outside our camp.

Absolutely consumed with excitement, I kept jumping up and down, shouting and pointing. It all happened so fast that I did not notice whether the plane was Japanese or American.

Rumors flew about our camp:

"Someone asked a Japanese guard and he replied, 'American, but pilot escape.'"

Ben Edwards later explained to me what had happened:

"The guerrillas told me the pilot injured one or both legs when he landed. They hoisted him into a coconut tree where the pilot remained hidden during the day while Japanese searched for him. The guerrillas had disposed of the parachute that night. Then they returned, helped the pilot out of the tree, and took him to a safe area. The U. S. forces were contacted, and a PBY plane landed on Lake Taal and picked up the pilot."

A few days later one of the women in our barracks said to me, "Carol, I was standing in front of you when we were watching that falling plane, and my back is still sore where you pounded me in your excitement."

I had been completely unaware of so much as touching anyone. Turning around, I laughingly replied, "Pound my back as I did yours, if you wish."

She good-naturedly declined.

Because of the bombings and American planes flying over our camp, the Japanese guards became jittery, edgy, and very strict, making rules we did not always keep, such as: "There must be complete blackout after the seven o'clock roll call every evening. No one may leave his barracks after that evening roll call unless accompanied by a Japanese guard. Violators will be shot." Although it seemed they were trying to make life as unbearable for us as possible, our morale had soared on seeing American planes.

We did not know that many long, hard months were still ahead of us before our *sawali* walls would come tumbling down—cruel months of the worst privation and starvation of our imprisonment.

Every morning on awakening we thought, *Maybe our army will come today.* And every night, as darkness closed in on our crude living quarters and our hunger became increasingly severe, we hoped, *Maybe they'll come tonight.*

But it was only more hunger that came.

CHAPTER 18
Wheeling and Dealing with Weasels

I WAS STARTLED TO SEE the anguish in Cae Paget's face as she almost stumbled toward the cubicle I shared with others.

"Carol, can you come with me to the chapel?" The tone of her voice indicated she was in deep distress.

Putting down the faded blue frock I was mending in an effort to hold it together, I slipped my hand into hers. The only sound as we walked along the dirt pathway was the slapping of our wooden sandals against our bare feet.

Sitting on one of the benches in the chapel, Cae put her head down and just sobbed.

As I sat there silently praying for her, she became calmer and was able to gain control. Then like an overloaded dam breaking, she poured it all out.

"Peter has decided that it is impossible for all three of us to survive. He stands over Joy and me, forcing us to eat his portion of rice while he won't take any of it. We can't swallow his food, knowing he will starve to death. We'd rather die together than have him sacrifice his life for us."

I knew Peter was right in thinking they might not all survive, because people were dying of starvation and beriberi. Many husbands were secretly taking rice from their own rations and adding it to their wives' portions.

In the serving line it was preferred that single men ladle out the rice or mush because married men were tempted to give larger servings to members of their families.

"Maybe Peter would be willing to share his rice with Joy," I suggested, "giving more strength to her but not sacrificing his whole portion."

Cae shook her head. "I begged him to do that, but he is determined. We can't choke his food down. Our throats refuse to swallow it."

After praying for Peter, we walked back to our cubicles. Before parting, Cae said, "Thank God you're single, Carol. It's one thing to be dying of starvation yourself, but unspeakably worse to watch your husband and child weakening and dying before your very eyes."

That night I couldn't sleep. The Pagets had been wonderful to me in my need. How could I help them? Finally, I thought of a possible solution.

There were a few internees in camp that some of us called "weasels." They accepted watches, fountain pens, and jewelry from the hungry internees and traded these items secretly with some of the Japanese guards for rice, coconuts, bananas, and other types of food, always keeping a larger portion for themselves as their "pay" for the transactions. I took a dim view of this trading, but it did help keep people alive. It was the excessive amounts the weasels kept for their own use that I resented.

During the long night, I searched my mind for something that could be traded. I had no jewelry, but my thoughts finally zeroed in on a little ivory and gold traveler's alarm clock that folded up, a bon voyage gift from Jettie Tadlock of Biola days. The Japanese would like it.

Most of the "weasels" were not known to me, but I had a slight acquaintance with one of them and thought perhaps he would be the kindest of the weasels, especially since he knew the Pagets.

The next morning I took the clock out of its hiding place and called at the man's room. Somehow he had managed to have a private cubicle with a door on it. He could wheel and deal almost anything.

I told him Cae's story and said, "If Peter Paget starves to death so that his wife and child can survive, it will not only break their hearts but haunt them all their lives. For the sake of that little girl, will you take this beautiful clock to a Japanese guard and get some food with it for the Pagets?"

"By now the Japanese have all the clocks and watches they want," he replied in a disinterested manner.

Then my eyes widened as I noticed several large gunny sacks of beans stacked in the corner of his cubicle. Beans are high in Vitamin B and what we needed desperately to counteract our beriberi.

"Will you give me three pounds of those beans for the Pagets in return for this clock?"

"No!"

"Then will you give me two pounds of them for the clock? You can sell it in Manila for a high price after we are free."

"I'm sorry. No!"

I became desperate. "Will you give me one pound?"

"We don't know when our army will reach this area or how much longer we'll be interned here. I may need those beans for my own survival. I'm not trading them now for anything," this weasel replied.

He never gave me a single bean.

I knew that man well enough to be familiar with his theology, which included the belief that reaching heaven depended on the good works one does in this life.

As I turned to leave his cubicle, tears stung my eyes, and these words tumbled out; "If you are depending on your good works to get you to heaven, you'll find some rungs missing in your ladder."

A few days later, a dear woman who was a member of his own organization died of beriberi due to starvation. Some of his hoarded beans would have saved her life.

What makes some men so noble that they sacrifice their lives for God and country and for their loved ones, while others live only for themselves?

That man and I were to meet again later when he had lost all his bulging sacks of beans, and he begged for my little clock.

I wondered whether I should approach another trader. My heart and will had been sickened by the first attempt. I could go to "Mr. Weasel" himself, the disliked, big-time operator who had the largest private store of food in our internment camp. The bean man paled into insignificance beside him when it came to hoarded goods and unprincipled ethics. I struggled with the question "Should I go to the king of the weasels?"

Because of all his gains in trading, Mr. Weasel was becoming rich, while his wife was growing pleasingly plump in size but not pleasing in disposition.

During the early years of the war, each person in Santo Tomas Internment Camp received one Red Cross parcel. Among other things, these parcels contained priceless tins of nourishing food. This merchant of guile and greed inveigled some of the shortsighted internees into trading those goodies, such as little cans of corned beef or powdered milk, for diamonds, rubies, and emeralds of internees who were starving.

You cannot eat diamonds.

This knave of a man also accepted from us prisoners our costume jewelry containing large, colorful, flashy stones, mostly of glass. He traded them with the Japanese guards, who could not tell the difference between diamonds and cut glass. They often preferred the garish glass to the smaller, finely cut gems, not realizing the disparity in value.

When this "wheeler-dealer" sold a jewel for a thousand pesos, he might give the internee who parted with it only a hundred pesos.

In this process of bartering with the Japanese, King Weasel
might obtain all kinds of wonderful edibles, such as canned
goods pilfered from those parcels sent overseas by the Red
Cross for the internees, or looted from stores in Manila. One
would pay almost any price for a delectable, nourishing packet
of cheese or a cup of sugar.

Whatever the trade or sale, this rascal and the other weasels
were the profiteers, while the prisoners were the losers.

Those who received money from the king of the weasels for
their jewels could buy edibles from the camp's canteen shop.
But it closed up, and secret trading and buying started at night
through the double, barbed-wire fences, as far away as possible from the guardposts.

Filipinos were eager to help, bringing news, fruit, and whatever food they could secure and exchanging it for money or
clothes. Since they were living in rags, clothes were preferred.
But the Filipinos were so small in stature that our clothes hung
on them like oversized bags. Sometimes the friendly Filipinos
would not take anything in exchange for the coconuts and bananas they brought us.

But such trading was very dangerous. The Japanese shot on
sight without asking questions.

If we wanted extra food or money, we were at the mercy of
King Weasel. If the Japanese commandant knew his guards
were trading with him, he looked the other way. Prisoners and
guards alike furtively sneaked through the darkness to the
Weasel's stable. At night, when small children were asleep,
many a mother crept from barracks to barracks, heading for
his cubicle. She would offer him her treasured diamond en-
gagement ring, or a ruby pendant, or all the money she had.
In return, he might give her only a small portion of powdered
milk, but it meant life for her child.

This king of the weasels also had a sadistic side. He enjoyed
smoking Havana cigars in the presence of men longing, crav-
ing for a smoke, letting its aroma tickle their nostrils.

The tantalizing odor of savory food drew some of our scrawny children from their lackluster play to the door of the Weasel's cubicle. The king saw them and brought the food outside, showing it to them and waving its ambrosial odors under their noses. Then, without giving them so much as a lick, he took the food back inside his cubicle.

I knew he would not respond to any appeal of mine in behalf of little Joy Paget. In all of his dealings, the quality of mercy was severely strained, as he always secured more than his "pound of flesh."

We had in camp our own court to deal with disciplinary cases, rather than turning fellow prisoners over to the Japanese.

King Weasel was brought before this court because of his trading with the enemy, but his case was dismissed for lack of evidence. People who had given him things to trade were afraid to testify for fear they also would be charged.

However, there lived in the cubicle next to this illegal trafficker a very outspoken, loud, and fearless couple. They objected to having the Japanese guards come there at night, along with everyone else who was bringing articles for trade. Their quarreling with the Weasel and his wife became shouting matches, which everyone living in the area could hear and enjoy as a source of entertainment. They could even join in the shouting if they so desired. It ended with each couple bringing the other before the court, and they were both given warnings.

Not quite sure what to do about my little ivory and gold clock, I placed it in its hiding place for the time being.

That night I couldn't sleep, thinking about the king of the weasels. My thoughts turned to Zacchaeus, the tax collector mentioned in the Bible. When he met the Lord, Zacchaeus said, "Half of my possessions I will give to the poor, and if I have defrauded anyone of anything, I will give back four times as much" (Luke 19:8).

I prayed that King Weasel might also meet our Lord. How

wonderful it would be if he would restore to the prisoners all he had stolen from them in his trading.

But he didn't; and before long he would receive his comeuppance.

As I fretted about the weasels, I couldn't sleep that night until the words of this old hymn by Katharina von Schlegel sang themselves deep into my being:

Be still, my soul: The Lord is on thy side;
Bear patiently the cross of grief or pain;
Leave to thy God to order and provide;
In every change He faithful will remain.
Be still my soul; thy best, thy Heavenly Friend
Through thorny ways leads to a joyful end.

I did not know that the way would become much thornier before that promised joyful end would come, but we did hope Christmas might bring us something special.

CHAPTER 19
Christmas in Prison

RUMORS OF COMFORT KITS ran rampant through the camp for weeks preceding Christmas.

"They are in Manila."

"They are at Los Banos Railroad station."

"They are in our *bodega*."

"There are two. One is from the American Red Cross, containing meat, dehydrated vegetables, and milk. The one from Canada contains sweets."

"There is also a kit from the local Chinese and Filipinos containing rice, beans, and peanuts."

"There is a fourth from South Africa. They are to be distributed Christmas day."

"The Swiss representative has come to deliver them personally."

Rumors, rumors, and more rumors night and day. What a Christmas dinner we planned with the kits. We would not be hungry on Christmas!

On Christmas Eve a copy of the following message from the Red Cross appeared on our bulletin board:

"To you prisoners disseminated in a world of war, the International Red Cross Committee brings an affectionate message of comfort. It does not ignore your grief and your anxieties. It also knows how increasingly painful the separation is the longer the days of your captivity drag on.

"It is with this knowledge at heart that the International Red Cross Committee and its 3,000 collaborators in Switzerland are doing everything in their power to bring you help and relief. To all of you and to all those who are dear to you they send their sincerest wishes."

Underneath this message another was posted:

"Mr. Ito of the Commandant's office reports, 'No relief supplies of any description have reached Manila.' "

As the news spread, people began gathering at the bulletin board to read the notice, staring at it almost in unbelief.

I stood nearby and watched their reactions.

A nun quietly crossed herself and walked slowly away, her head bowed, her lips moving silently in prayer.

Many men clenched their hands into fists and swore.

Referring to the women who were professional prostitutes in the camp, one man commented, "The Diamond Lils will be busy tonight."

Tears rolled down the cheeks of a mother as her lips pressed into a grim, thin line. When she turned and walked away, her shoulders drooped and her feet lagged as she drew her little son and daughter closer to her side. It was as though all strength and hope had gone out of her. I wanted to walk by her side and put my arm over her shoulder, but held back, thinking it must be a very private moment. I offered a quiet prayer instead.

As I watched the frustration, anger, and agony on people's faces, I quenched my own disappointment and blighted hopes with the realization that nothing could take from us the real meaning of Christmas—a Savior, manger born.

The resilience of the human spirit and American ingenuity soon became evident throughout the camp. Men cut down branches for Christmas trees, created shining stars out of tin cans, and made stilts as presents for the boys in camp.

Although almost everyone's fingers were numb from beri-beri, the women made decorations from balls of cotton, and from colored bits of knitting wool and old beads.

When the children were asleep, the women gathered around the few electric lights in camp and made rag dolls and stuffed toys. They cut down their old garments into new ones for the children.

Creative people made Christmas cards, some of which carried the greeting, "A Beriberi Christmas."

Popular gifts were handmade calendars for the length of time we might still be in the prison camp. Small dishes and vases were shaped out of coconut shells.

A delightful surprise for me was a "V for Victory" pin sent to me from the Santo Tomas Internment Camp. A fellow passenger from the *President Grant*, Geraldine Chappelle, had cut a "V" out of some cardboard, wrapped it with red, white, and blue thread, and placed a tiny safety pin at the back. She sent it with someone who was being transferred from Santo Tomas to our camp. I wore it every day, and it became a lifetime souvenir.

Little surprises appeared from every side, but the best gift of all was one received by the whole camp. A formation of American planes flew right over our heads. What a tremendous Christmas present from America! We went wild with joy.

I had been teaching a young people's Bible class in our camp and gave them a little Christmas party. After some games, I served refreshments—one slim, fried strip of coconut each—not much, but I had spent my last bit of money for it. And then we had a time of prayer together. I like to hear young people pray because they are so forthright, so honest and unpretentious.

The Catholic and Protestant missionaries living in the "Holy City" section of the camp presented to the executive committee some money toward the Christmas dinner as a present to all of the internees. This meant everyone had a smidgen of *camotes*, eggplant, and the flavor of carabao meat with our mush. The Japanese permitted it because of Christmas, and Peter Paget felt free to start eating again.

Costumed in bathrobes, kimonos, and scarves, the children enacted the scene in Bethlehem, singing to us Martin Luther's carol:

Away in a manger, no crib for a bed,
The little Lord Jesus laid down His sweet head;

The stars in the sky looked down where He lay,
The little Lord Jesus, asleep on the hay.

As we listened, the song seemed to hallow our crude cubicles in the prison camp. In the evening, everyone gathered for a songfest, with the Japanese holding guns while standing guard over us.

Among our internees were a number of "Scholastics," lively young priests who formed a glee club. They turned the evening into one of rollicking laughter by singing some American folk songs, humorously changing a few words, as arranged by a student priest named James Reuter.

Taking the song "She'll Be Comin' 'Round the Mountain When She Comes," Reuter changed the word *She* to *They,* meaning our American army. Even though there were mountains near us, the Japanese guards never understood the implications. Part of the fun was their lack of comprehension.

Here are a few sample lines:

They'll be comin' 'round the mountain
When they come. . .
They'll come pourin' o'er those mountains
Just like water from a fountain;
They'll come pourin' o'er those mountains
When they come.

They'll be bringin' apple pie
When they come. . .

Oh, I do not want to die
'Til I eat that apple pie;
They'll be bringin' apple pie
When they come.

They'll be bringin' Christmas candy
When they come . . .
They'll be bringin' Christmas candy
And the choc'lates will be dandy;
They'll be bringin' Christmas candy
When they come.

Unable to grasp American humor or implied meanings in our English language, the Japanese guards must have wondered how we could laugh so heartily at the close of another song.

The guards gave us no news, but our hidden radio often picked up the Manila station operated by the Nipponese. It usually reported all American ships sunk and planes downed in each battle, while the Japanese suffered no losses. We knew this was not true, and that was the basis for this next song from Reuter's pen.

The chorus of "Oh, No, John!" represents a guard's usual reply to our questions. Whatever we asked, the answer was almost always, "No!"

Oh, No, John!

In yonder box there stands a sentry
And the war news he must know;
I'll go and ask him if we're winning,
He must answer yes or no!

Oh, sentry, please, I wish you would tell me
'Cause my spirit's running low,
Have our sailors taken Davao?
Have we landed at Zambo?

Chorus: Oh, no, John; no, John; no, John, no!

Well, have we won a single battle?
Sentry, information me!
Has there been at least one bombing?
Have we one ship left at sea?

Chorus: Oh, no, John; no, John; no, John, no!

Well, since there will be no invasion,
And since you have crushed us so,
Since this war is won and over,
Sentry, will you let us go?

Chorus: Oh, no, John; no, John; no, John, NO!

Then, changing the theme, these words by Mr. Reuter were sung out into the night air:

Glorious, glorious
One tiny pig for 2,154 of us,
Thanks be to God
There aren't any more of us.

Our laughter changed to sentimental tears as those young men sang a song picked up on the radio. None of us had heard it before: "I'm Dreaming of a White Christmas."

This memorable evening closed as the "Hallelujah!" chorus was played on an old phonograph in camp. In the light of a beautiful moon our loudspeaker broadcast the majestic music from Handel's oratorio *Messiah*.

Climbing into my bed at the close of the starlit evening, I drifted off to sleep, singing in my heart a refrain from that soaring music, "The Lord God omnipotent reigneth."

Christmas had happened in a prison camp, though the specter of starvation still haunted our lives.

We would have been encouraged had we known about a significant event unfolding on the island of Leyte.

CHAPTER 20
General MacArthur's Concern for Us
December 1944

THE WIFE OF A CERTAIN FILIPINO became ill with a strange disease, and there was no medicine on the whole island of Mindanao that would help her. Only in Manila, two islands away, could the medicine be obtained. The Filipino started on the long journey, traveling by foot and on trucks, by animal-drawn carts in the countryside and on little sailing boats called *bancas*.

Avoiding the Japanese military as much as possible, he arrived halfway on his journey at the island of Leyte, where he noted the welcome presence of many American soldiers.

Passing them by, he made it to the big island of Luzon. While heading toward Manila, he met local Filipinos who told him about a large prison camp nearby holding more than two thousand prisoners, mostly Americans. In hushed tones, they discussed the camp among themselves, the fact that men, women, and little children were starving, and the difficulties of getting food to them.

Wondering whether the American soldiers on Leyte knew about this prison camp, the Filipino stored the information in his mind, including the camp's location.

After securing the medicine for his wife, this lone little man started his homeward trip. Arriving at Leyte, he went to the first military encampment he encountered and asked to see an officer. He was questioned and then taken to Lt. Col. Henry J. Muller, G.2, of the Eleventh Airborne Division. This lieutenant colonel was responsible for intelligence gathering in the Division and was to become an honored general in later years.

Muller was delighted to see anyone just out of Manila who could supply information. Pointing to a map, he asked the Filipino to retrace his steps. "What did you see here?. . . What did you see over there?. . . What are the roads like?"

When Muller finished asking many questions, the Filipino told him about a prisoner-of-war camp near the village of Los Banos, indicating its place on the map.

"I've never heard of it," replied Muller. "How many are in the camp?"

"I'm not sure," answered the Filipino, his brown eyes looking into the colonel's grey ones, "but about two thousand, most of them Americans."

After providing the friendly Filipino with rations, Muller wrote out the report and sent a copy up to General MacArthur's headquarters.

About the time MacArthur received this information, he heard what had happened on the island of Palawan. When our warships passed by Palawan, the Japanese thought our troops were going to land there and panicked. Crowding the American prisoners into a cave and dousing them with fuel, possibly gasoline, they set them afire and closed off the cave, burning the prisoners alive and machine-gunning those who attempted to escape.

This gave MacArthur grave concern about what the Japanese might do to the prisoners at both Santo Tomas and Los Banos Internment Camps, but at that time our forces were in Leyte and operating under orders only to take Tagaytay Ridge, about thirty miles south of Manila.

CHAPTER 21
Miracle of Freedom
January 5–12, 1945

WE WERE A PITIFUL LITTLE BAND of men and women that gathered for prayer on the afternoon of January 5, 1945. The situation in camp was desperate as more and more people were dying of beriberi and starvation. We felt that none of us could last much longer.

Sick, starving, and weak, we bowed before the God of heaven and earth, asking Him to hold out His mighty hand filled with manna for us in our wilderness of desperate need.

The next night, a Japanese soldier, Mr. Ono, routed George Gray out of bed and ordered him to have all shovels, both personally owned and camp owned, brought to the commandant's office by 1:00 A.M.

Every barracks, except those housing only women, was roused and shovels collected. Speculation ran riot as to why the Japanese wanted so many shovels. Were they needed for digging more trenches? Air raid shelters? For burying some of their dead soldiers, or maybe even us? Could it be that they wanted to dig holes or caves in the nearby mountains where they could hide when the American army came? Why the rush?

In our barracks, we slept peacefully on, unaware of what was happening. But I was awakened at 3:00 A.M. by a Japanese voice speaking to our barracks interpreter, Gertrude Feely. They wanted me!

In a few minutes Gertrude came down the aisle toward my bed. "Miss Terry, get up and give me the office records. They have to be in the commandant's office by 3:30 this morning."

Questions flashed through my mind. *Why do they want the camp roster at this hour? Did someone escape? Or could it be that they are leaving?* At this thought, I shouted "Hot dog!" into the quiet of the night, and at that sound the whole barracks awoke.

How glad I was that my records were in order. I smiled as I recalled an incident that had happened recently. I had been sitting in the office, struggling with the roster, when I looked up to see the friendly blue eyes of Lester Yard watching me. He had been walking by, noticed my frown, and stopped for a few moments to chat. He knew the importance of having the census correct.

Les had been struck across the face several times by a guard because he did not bow one day when entering the Japanese commandant's office, even though Tanaka was not there at the time. It seems he should have bowed to the empty desk! Our friendly guard, Misaki, was standing nearby and gave his handkerchief to Les for wiping the blood off his face.

Lester added a little more color to our sometimes dreary days. He had been a journalist, working for the *Hollywood Reporter* in the heyday of Hedda Hopper and famous stars such as Joan Crawford and John Barrymore. Les told tales that lifted the spirit of many an internee deep in prison-camp doldrums.

"Having a problem?" he had asked me one day.

"Yes! I'm one name short and I can't find out why."

Names on the roster kept changing as new prisoners were brought in and deaths occurred due to executions, starvation, and beriberi or other diseases. There were a few births. Escapes were rare because we were deep inside enemy territory and on an island. Until General MacArthur's forces landed, there would be no place to go if one did escape. To hide in Filipino homes would endanger the lives of those friendly, hospitable people.

Les and I discussed the problem of how to identify the missing name.

Then with a twinkle of conspiracy in his eyes, he said, "Carol, that's no problem. Some of the Catholic nuns in camp have two names—a church name and a family name. Select one of them and put down both names. The number will come out right; and if the Japanese discover it does not tally with the people in camp, we can always confuse them by saying one person has two names!"

We both knew that could not be done, but the very idea of putting one over on the Japanese was absolutely delectable, almost irresistible. He had left me with a cheery wave of his hand, and I tackled my job again with new zest, finally discovering that the problem was not a missing name but a mistake in numbering. As an important official document, the roster had to be accurate. Now, as I scrambled down from my upper bunk, I danced a little jig as I ran through the aisle, singing "They'll be comin' 'round the mountain when they come!"

Women began emerging from beneath their mosquito nets and flocked around Gertrude with a barrage of questions. Always composed, she replied only, "It looks as though they may be going."

Our whole barracks erupted like a volcano of excitement.

Walking in the darkness over to the camp office gave me an eerie feeling because of a warning that anyone outside our barracks after curfew would be shot. How would an uninformed guard know I had been ordered to get the records at that unearthly hour? However, I made it without incident.

Safely securing the roster, I handed the thick document containing more than two thousand names to Miss Feely.

The camp census/according to nationality/December 1944

Americans 1,589
British (other than those listed below). 329
British Australians 33
British Canadians 56
Netherlanders. 89
Polish 22
Italians 16
Norwegians 10
French 1
Nicaraguan 1
Total. 2,146

Note: These are the total numbers. Individual names that I typed in the last roster
are in the Appendix. There were 465 deaths by execution, starvation, beriberi,
and other diseases reported for Santo Tomas and Los Banos Internment Camps.

At about 3:30 A.M., while the Japanese officers were talking
to our Administration Committee, I stealthily crept over to Barracks Sixteen, where the Pagets lived. I was so brainwashed by
the rule that we would be shot if we were out of our barracks at
night that I felt almost like a criminal sneaking along in the
dark.

Waking up Cae, I shared with her the sensational events.
Then we heard someone shouting, "There's a big bonfire out
front and the Japanese are loading trucks. The Commandant's
car looks ready to take off!"

Cae and I crept out to see. It was true! We were incredulous.
Were they actually leaving? If so, why?

Still unable to overcome my guilty feeling, I hurried back,
fearful of discovery by a Japanese. Everyone there was ebul-
lient with joy.

The whole camp was going crazy and no one was in bed.
Feeling braver, I dashed back to the Pagets' cubicle two bar-
racks away just as a man ran through, shouting, "THE STARS
AND STRIPES GO UP AT FIVE O'CLOCK. THE JAPANESE ARE
LEAVING!"

Episcopal Bishop Binsted cast aside his dignity and picked

up little Joy Paget, swinging her in the air and shouting, "Double mush for breakfast!"

That would be the final, unmistakable proof that the Japanese were leaving—to have more food. It was the one evidence the most hardened cynic could not doubt.

"Let's eat our saved-over mush," said Cae Paget.

For the first time I noticed that I was still in my nightgown! Scurrying back to my cubicle, I put on the red, white, and blue victory dress I had made for just this occasion.

Digging out my well-hidden little flag and holding my small dab of cold mush in a coconut shell, I rushed back to the Pagets', wooden clogs slapping against my bare feet as I ran.

In one of the walkways I bumped into a khaki-clad man of small stature with a mustache. Thinking he was the Japanese patrol, I whisked the flag behind my back, my heart pounding, frightened I might be shot. He turned out to be an American as excited as I.

At the Pagets' cubicle, the blonde, blue-eyed Joy came in with a long face.

"What's the matter, dear?" asked her mother.

"Oh, it's all just a rumor," Joy replied.

Hundreds of times it had been so, and she could not believe it was true.

Although eating our treasured, saved-over mush was very convincing, conservative Peter remarked, "Now, don't get reckless."

Everyone's desperate obsession with food led to an event of importance going on at the same time that was known only to a very few.

Michael O'Hara and Charles McVey had watched the Japanese trucks leave and assumed that the Japanese were gone. They did not know the commandant's car was still in camp.

Going into the officers' barracks, the two men searched for food. They found everything neat and in good order, desks tidy, but no food. Suddenly the two men heard boots approaching and dived under the beds, scarcely daring to breathe.

They were not discovered, and as soon as the Japanese officer departed, the men fled, O'Hara grabbing a Philco radio as he ran. It was a table-top model, small and square.

Michael O'Hara was well known in camp as monitor of Barracks Nine. One of our internees, Mr. Lee, saw him running with the radio and watched with dismay as a tube from it fell to the ground, and O'Hara accidentally stepped on it, crushing the tube. Realizing it was inoperative, Lee asked O'Hara to give him the radio.

It was now of no use to Mike, but he did not feel like just handing over the radio. Thinking about his two hungry children and the fact that Lee had a supply of mongo beans and brown sugar in his cubicle, O'Hara bargained with him. Mr. Lee gave Mike five pounds of the mongo beans and a couple of pounds of brown sugar. O'Hara's family was happy about that deal.

But Lee did not want the Philco radio for himself. He gave it to the electrical wizard in camp, Gerald Sams, who somehow could make almost any radio work.

After the Japanese left, some internees looted other things from the Japanese barracks, including the commandant's rice bowls bearing the Imperial flag.

About five o'clock on that exciting morning of January 7, all of us gathered together in an open area. The stars of the Southern Cross were shining like diamonds set in a sky of black onyx. It seemed to be God's blessing on this momentous occasion.

The first official voice to be heard was that of the secretary of our Administration Committee:

"Ladies and gentlemen, this is George Gray....Before twelve o'clock last night I was awakened and told that a representative of the commandant's office wanted to see me.

"Mr. Ono appeared in a most disheveled state and informed

me that the commandant had ordered that all shovels in camp, both privately and camp owned, should be turned over to the commandant's office. After a bit of stirring around and waking most of the people in camp, we managed to produce a few of the shovels, and they were turned over at one o'clock.

"I took occasion to go over, and there was Konishi with a towel around his head and a bottle on the table. He was packing his personal belongings.

"It was not, however, until three o'clock this morning that the chairman of the Committee, Mr. Heichert, and Mr. Watty (who was the vice chairman, and British) were called to the commandant's office for a council.

"Mr. Heichert, Mr. Watty, Mr. Downs, and I went over and found things in a very upset state at the commandant's office, with cars and trucks standing out in front. The commandant, or should I now say, the former commandant, said only a few words. He was excited, but by the time he got through speaking, it was not he, but we who were excited.

"He said this: 'From now on, after five o'clock on the morning of January 7, 1945, all internees are released from my care. By sudden order from our superiors I release all the internees of the Civilian Internment Camp, Number Two, Los Banos, in the Philippine Islands. I release all internees to your Committee and leave in your charge the entire camp. We are willing to leave all food provisions, which will last for at least two months.'"

Then Mr. Gray commented, "I might add that this was according to the old ration! That summarizes things up to that point, and you all took part in the remainder."

A wave of laughter and happy conversation swept over the crowd but quickly quieted down when the chairman of our Committee, Mr. M. B. Heichert, spoke. Here are the main points of his message, slightly condensed:

"Ladies and gentlemen: As this camp was officially released to the Administration Committee, your Committee declares you free. Until official control of the camp is taken over by representatives of the American army, we warn you:

"1. We have no news of actual landing on Luzon. It is known that we have landed on Marinduque.

"2. While the Japanese have left the camp, we have no knowledge that they have abandoned the surrounding area.

"3. We have in operation facilities for getting in contact with our forces by radio.

"4. Maintain your same organization and sense of discipline and responsibilities. To this end, an Emergency Patrol Unit has been established and is responsible for order in the camp. This is the most difficult and dangerous period of our internment. We warn you that two Japanese sentries are still at the gate, and we are informed that they are attached to a unit that is still in this area. It will, therefore, be unwise for anyone to leave camp.

"5. Breakfast, lunch, and dinner will be served with full rations for all.

"6. The camp is hereby designated Camp Freedom.

"7. At sunrise this morning there will be a simple flag-raising ceremony in front of Barracks Fifteen. Immediately thereafter the flag will be lowered, as we do not wish to risk any form of enemy retaliation.

"Your Committee declares you free."

No words can describe our jubilation. It felt as though a smothering weight had been lifted from our shoulders, our hearts, our very lives.

When the starry Southern Cross and black velvet of the night faded into the splendor of a golden sunrise, we gathered for the flag-raising.

We came clad in nightgowns, pajamas, rags, clothes that were worn and patched; we came barefooted, or wearing slabs of wood with strips of rubber or cloth across the toes; we came on crutches and with canes; we came limping; we came sick and weak, with ankles and faces swollen with beriberi, but more than two thousand of us came—Americans, Australians, British Islanders, Canadians, Netherlanders, and a few Italians, Norwegians, and Polish, one Nicaraguan, and one Frenchman.

We were reverent and quiet when Bishop Binsted led us in prayer, thanking God for deliverance and praying for our soldiers and sailors on land and sea. Then everyone joined him in repeating the Lord's Prayer. Heads bowed and hearts became hushed in the solemnity and sacredness of that moment.

The Rangers, camouflaged name for Boy Scouts of America, stood at attention as one sounded reveille on his bugle.

With its stars and stripes waving in the breeze, Old Glory was raised to the top of a bamboo flagpole, and beside it the Union Jack. While tears streamed down our faces, shoulders that had been drooping from weakness now squared themselves and chins came up.

From an old gramophone, which I think had been given to the camp by the YMCA, crooned the voice of Bing Crosby, singing "The Star Spangled Banner." As we tried to join him in singing our national anthem, we choked up and could hardly get those glorious words out.

Strong patriotism ran through our family and I had always loved my country, but never in my lifetime had such deep love for America and our flag flowed so freely through my veins and throughout my being. I prayed our flag would fly forever "o'er the land of the free and the home of the brave."

Here's to Our Flag

Here's to the Red of it!
There's not a thread of it,
No, not a shred of it,
In all the spread of it
From foot to head,

But heroes bled for it,
Faced steel and lead for it,
Precious blood shed for it,
Bathing it Red.

Here's to the White of it!
Thrilled by the sight of it,
Who knows the right of it,
Through day and night.

Here's to the Blue of it!
Heavenly view of it,
Star-spangled hue of it,
Constant and true.

Here's to the whole of it,
Stars, stripes, and pole of it,
Here's to the Soul of it,
Red, White, and Blue!

John Daly

In honor of the many British in our camp, we also sang "God Save the King."

A man of the cloth commented, "I never cry at funerals, but my, I couldn't help crying at the flag-raising."

Two pleasant surprises still awaited me. It was reported that one of the Japanese officers, Mr. Ito, as adjutant, had returned all the money he had taken from the individual internees, a kind gesture from a fleeing soldier. While some of the other officers made us bow at roll call, Mr. Ito never did. I heard that he had embraced the Christian faith, but I never found any confirmation of this rumor.

The second discovery gave me a real thrill. After the Japanese left, I learned why they had Miss Freely rout me out of bed at three o'clock in the morning. The commandant had asked our Administration Committee to sign my roster as a kind of "receipt" showing that the Japanese were turning over to the control of the Committee all the internees listed in that roster.

I felt as though I had typed the official "surrender document" setting our camp free.

So much excitement in my weakened condition caught up with me, and I nearly fainted. Others were feeling faint also, but a double-mush breakfast renewed our strength.

On this Sunday morning of liberation, the same group who gathered on Friday to ask the Lord for food now met to thank Him for His spectacular answer. We had come to the end of our resources, only to find it was the beginning of His.

A miracle of freedom had overcome barriers of guns and our barbed-wire fences. Food began flowing into camp. I thought of the lines from an old hymn: "God moves in a mysterious way His wonders to perform."

On that bright and shining Sunday morning, Communion was served at church while heads bowed in worship of our God. He had opened His mighty hand and provided an abundance of food as "manna" in our wilderness of starvation and desperation. Evening vespers were filled with hymns of thanksgiving.

That afternoon Filipinos met with our Committee and made arrangements to supply needed food for the camp. Since we were located on the grounds of the Agricultural College, they underwrote us for unlimited credit.

The Filipinos brought chickens, vegetables, bananas, milk, and coconuts, with the chickens loudly squawking their protests. They even brought a prized carabao (water buffalo).

Our men butchered the commandant's bull, and the carabao, for our cuisine. We confiscated pigs from the Japanese piggery, but I must say the pigs did squeal about it.

The kitchen crews worked hard to provide good meals for us, and now there was no grousing at the chow time, only smiling, laughing, and enjoying.

At eight o'clock that evening, everyone gathered under a sky of black velvet displaying sparkling stars with no earthling lights to dim them. Over the loudspeaker we heard a radio broadcast from our homeland. It began: "THIS IS THE UNITED STATES OF AMERICA."

What a thrill! After the newscast came the voice of President Roosevelt in a stirring address.

Because the Japanese had given us our freedom without a shot's being fired, Mr. Cook remarked, "How silently, how silently, the wondrous gift was given!"

But as we returned to our barracks, looking forward to a wonderful night of sleep with no hunger pangs to drive it away, a new group of Japanese soldiers arrived and made us prisoners again. They would not believe we had been freed.

There was no officer with the soldiers, who were wearing fishnets, evidently their idea of camouflage. Our Administration Committee tried to convince these Japanese that we had been given our freedom. Bewildered but stubborn, those soldiers held their post.

What a day! And what a night!

By late in the afternoon of the next day, however, the fishnet-clad Japanese gave in, to the extent of letting the camp order food.

Some internees were so ravaged by hunger that they ate more than their weakened bodies could handle and landed in the hospital. Although suffering stomach pains, I did not require hospitalization. Camp officials had to ration food to protect us from the results of our own hunger.

Filipinos were eager to bring us extra food, trading it for clothing or anything we wanted to give them. What friends they were!

A radio in camp supplied news, but its exact location was known only to a few. We heard most of the reports as they were passed along one to another, not always certain whether we were hearing truth or rumor:

"MacArthur's convoy is close."

"Our planes bombed and strafed the nearby railroad."

"They're targeting the escaping Japanese."

"Our army is within forty miles."

"They will be here tomorrow. Get the Japanese barracks ready for them."

"No, do it today. They're coming this afternoon."

On January 10 we heard that General MacArthur and his huge convoy had reached Lingayan Gulf, about 150 miles north of us. Wide plains and good roads would speed his tanks to Manila.

A raging typhoon was tearing up the Lingayan area, but as MacArthur and his magnificent flotilla of ships approached, the typhoon bowed and moved off in another direction, leaving the waters calm and smooth. So great was the mystique that had grown up around MacArthur in the minds of the Filipinos that those watching from the shoreline felt that either the General himself had caused it or God's hand upon him. They would not have been surprised to see him walk ashore on top of the water.

While we were excited that MacArthur had returned in force, we were also dumbfounded. We had thought our rescue was imminent.

How long would it take his forces to land, organize the troops and motorized vehicles, fight their way through enemy territory to Manila, take the city and rescue the internees in Santo Tomas Internment Camp, and then fight their way on down to us? None of us knew that we were to face stark starvation again before that day arrived, and some of us would not live to see it.

For the moment we were free, but Japanese soldiers were in the area—about ten thousand of them only two hours of marching time away from our camp.

It was too dangerous to leave, so it seemed best for the present just to eat and sleep and recover our strength.

Called upon to type a new roster, I worked in the office January 11 and 12, typing the list and verifying its accuracy. I was now too weak to complete the roster in one day. According to the information available to me, it appeared that only two men had left camp. I heard they were both aviators.

With the roster finished, a full stomach, and a feeling of being unshackled, I went to bed that night looking forward to a contented, refreshing sleep, only to have it all shattered before the dawning of the morning.

CHAPTER 22
Our Disgruntled Captors Return
January 13

A MAN'S VOICE SHOUTING into the darkness startled me out of a sound sleep at three o'clock in the morning.

"AN IMPORTANT ANNOUNCEMENT: KONISHI AND THE COM-MANDANT HAVE RETURNED. KEEP AWAY FROM ALL SENTRY BOXES."

Could I be having a nightmare?

Soon the whole camp buzzed with many questions and no answers.

Commandant Major Iwanaka and the whole Japanese garrison who guarded us before had returned in force. They were disheveled, tired, and haggard. Half-drunk, Konishi staggered toward his bed.

Some members of our Administration Committee had moved into the barracks of the Japanese officers. Mr. Watty awakened to find Konishi's grubby, bleary-eyed face glaring down at him. Poor Watty really thought he was having a nightmare. Misfortune had placed him in Konishi's bed.

In order to save face, the Japanese officers simply explained, "We have been on a mission."

Rumors and questions among ourselves sprang up all over the camp.

"Where did they go?"

"Who ordered them to leave?"

"Why have they come back?"

"What caused them to be so disheveled and seemingly frustrated?"

"Why didn't we escape while the Japanese were gone?"

"How could two thousand men, women, and children escape through miles of Japanese-occupied territory?"

"Have all the Japanese in the area fled or just our guards?"

In our ignorance of facts, we thought our guards had run away because the American army was very near and the Japanese were fleeing for their lives.

One of our guards, Daikichi Okamoto, later wrote me, "Regarding on the 7 through 13 January, 1945, by order of our HQS Manila to assemble and retreat to Mariquino mountain near Manila, then we came back and transferred under Fujishige Division." Near "Mariquino," as he spelled it, is a large area the Japanese used for assembling purposes. Our guards were seen conferring with the Japanese officers in Santo Tomas. An early curfew was imposed on the camp that evening.

One of our former guards named Misaki had been a civilian before the war and spoke English quite fluently. Within certain necessary limits, he had tried to help us. Now he happened to meet our fleeing guards in Manila, and they told him of their departure from Los Banos. Concerned for our welfare, Misaki went to the Santo Tomas Internment Camp and asked to see Earl Carroll, a leading member of the internee committee there whose special responsibilities included finances.

Informing Mr. Carroll of our situation and need for food, Misaki asked for a letter authorizing him to purchase food for us and charge it to the account of the Philippine Red Cross. Mr. Carroll arranged for such a letter to be provided.

Then Misaki told Mr. Carroll that the internees in the Baguio camp up in the hills had been transferred to Old Bilibid Prison in Manila and some were in desperate need of medicines, which he wanted to obtain for them.

For trying to get the medicines to those in Bilibid Prison, the Japanese executed Mr. Misaki. Japanese guard though he was, Misaki had tried his best to help, at the cost of his own life.

Perhaps news of General MacArthur's approaching with his fleet of ships had caused our Japanese guards to panic and flee. MacArthur and his forces arrived at Lingayen Gulf on January 10.

Whatever our guards' reasons may have been for leaving, those of us who had met and prayed for food had an additional explanation. We had been praying desperately for more food, and now large supplies of rice the Japanese had stored away became available to the whole camp. In addition to this, Filipinos outside the camp started bringing us fruit and chickens. All this extra food now enabled some to survive who otherwise would have died in the worst period of starvation still ahead.

The raising of Old Glory and singing of the national anthem had done wonders for camp morale, and the week of nourishing food renewed our stamina.

Angry at the things we had done, the Japanese demanded return of their carabao, their chickens, and other food supplies. But it was quite impossible to give them back, we explained, because they had all been consumed. There are no words to express how the Japanese felt about that!

Hot as their wrath was over losing the food supplies they had hoarded, it was nothing compared to the tempest over the missing radio.

Frustrated and exhausted, the Japanese now refused to see anyone and took a long, recuperating sleep. We could not help but chortle a little, though, realizing we would be in deep trouble when our captors awoke from their long winter's nap. After their deep sleep, the Japanese felt better, but they were still angry at our having devoured all their food supplies. Since nothing could be done about that, they demanded we return the few things we had carried off, especially the radio.

We chuckled at their frustration and did not feel the least bit guilty. When our captors turned the camp over to our Administration Committee and then fled, they said not a word about coming back or of saving their carabao and chickens for them. In our wildest imaginations we never dreamed they would return and take us captive once again.

In order to calm things down a bit, a typewriter and a few other items were returned, but the officers were obsessed with finding the missing radio. Most of us did not know its hiding place, and the few who knew it was in the hands of our electronics expert, Gerald Sams, were keeping quiet.

On Sunday afternoon, January 14, just one week after they had fled, the officers ordered all of us out on the main road for roll call at 1:00 P.M. sun time. Even babies in arms had to be present. For a seemingly endless time we stood under that scorching, glaring sun. People were too far gone physically to endure it, and one by one the women began feeling as though they were going to faint.

Gradually it dawned on us that there was to be no roll call. The order had been a ruse to get us out of the way so the Japanese could search our barracks.

Our men became furious, and one of them called out, "Are we mice or are we men?"

The men of our group were tall and skinny, so weak and starved their ribs looked like coat hangers. Although the women tried to discourage them, they advanced, empty-handed and barefooted except for wooden clogs, to confront the husky, heavily shod, khaki-clad armed soldiers.

The Japanese could have mowed down those ragtag prisoners, but instead they let out a war cry for help and additional soldiers came running with hand grenades, but they did not throw them. The situation became dangerous. Finally, in the presence of our Administration Committee, the Japanese were allowed to search the barracks, while the men living there were permitted to watch.

Forcing a confrontation with our captors seemed a brave but

unwise move on the part of the internees, who could have been shot. They had nothing on their side except spirit and courage injected into their souls by that week of freedom, but the Japanese had guns.

By the time this fracas was over, most of us had drifted back to our barracks, only to be ordered out again on the road for roll call. When we finally all staggered out under the burning sun and were lined up, an officer simply said, "Tomorrow," and dismissed us.

Later in the day, officers came to all our barracks, taking roll call in an effort to discover how many had escaped while they were gone.

The next few days were filled with tension. Although the Japanese could not do anything about the food we had consumed, they continued to demand that the radio be returned.

Mr. Heichert and Mr. Watty of our Administration Committee asked Mike O'Hara, "Is the radio still in camp?"

"Yes, it is," he replied.

But the men did not ask, or even suggest, that Mike tell them who had it.

Needless to say, Jerry Sams kept a low profile.

Then someone wanting to calm troubled waters put a radio where Mr. Watty would see it.

Overjoyed on finding it, Watty exclaimed to O'Hara, "Thank God, we've found the radio!" Unfortunately, he did not show it to him.

And when poor Watty, a very fine British gentleman, presented to Commandant Iwanaka this radio, nicely shaped in cathedral style, the commandant became furious. His radio had been square!

This made matters much worse. Now the Japanese realized we had kept a forbidden radio of our own in camp all the time, the penalty for which was death. Try as they might, the officers could not find out who owned it. The internees were united in this matter, and those who knew would not tell.

Serious as the situation now became, most of us could not help being amused at the predicament of the commandant.

Then as suddenly as the furor started, it subsided, and we heard not another word about the radio. Mike O'Hara explains it this way: "If the Japanese Military Police, who were like the Gestapo in Germany, heard about the radio, it not only could have meant death for some of us, but Commandant Iwanaka himself would have been in deep trouble for letting a radio fall into the hands of an enemy. He evidently decided the better part of wisdom would be to let the whole matter just drop."

From this time onward, the Japanese became more contentious and ill-tempered, probably because they were losing the war. Konishi remarked, "You know and we know your army has landed. It is just a matter of time. It may be a week. It may be a month."

When two of our high school boys scampered up a tree to watch American planes flying overhead, some guards took them to headquarters. It took an hour and a half to convince the Japanese that the boys were only having a "look-see" and were not signaling our planes.

When I went to work in the office, the Japanese would not give me any typing paper. How could I type a new roster? But I did not feel unhappy about it because I heard that three more internees had escaped, making five in all. A fresh roster would reveal that.

As the Japanese now cut down our food drastically, a riot began brewing in camp. The landing of the Americans had made our adrenaline flow and our courage soar.

Some of the women marched en masse to the Japanese headquarters and demanded more food. One girl, bolder than the others, sat on Konishi's desk, and she is reported to have said to him:

"Listen, Konishi, we want more food and we're going to get it. You told us you were giving small rations because food is hard to get. We've fed ourselves for a week and proved that's not true. The guerrillas are outside ready to kill you at the first opportunity. Our army has landed. You're doomed! Now come across and give us three meals a day or your life won't be worth anything."

No one would have risked speaking to a Japanese officer in this manner before our army landed, and I don't think our men would have dared do it even at this point of time. But facing the wrath of a group of women, with MacArthur's forces now on our island, was a new experience for Konishi. After balking, objecting, and growling a bit, he agreed to give us some rice for lunch.

We were all beginning to feel very brave. A mass meeting was pending.

"The Japanese gave us our freedom."

"By what right do they give us orders now?"

"We're no longer their prisoners."

"They set us free!"

"Are we mice or are we men?"

Tension increased throughout the whole camp. Filipino guerrillas outside knew of the situation and were standing by, ready to aid us in case of a riot. One of them stumbled and fell near a guard who saw the Filipino's gun and shot him. That Japanese then fell, hit by gunshots from guerrillas hiding in the area. A truck filled with fully armed soldiers roared away in search of them.

At 7:30 P.M. the lights all over camp suddenly went off. The air became permeated with excitement. Americans guarding our kitchen supplies were afraid the Japanese would steal the rice we had in our custody for feeding the camp.

Under the cover of darkness our men silently removed practically all the sacks of rice and placed them under the beds of various prisoners. All through the night no one expected to sleep, but the hours passed and daylight broke on a seemingly peaceful camp.

In the morning we discovered that Japanese reinforcements

had arrived. One of the officers summoned Mr. Bennett, who supervised our kitchen, and informed him that he would be put before a firing squad if we did not return the rice immediately, not to our kitchen-supply place as before, but to their custody.

We could have objected but Mr. Bennett's life hung in the balance.

Then an officer called for our Administration Committee and held them under guard without any food while our men carried the sacks of rice on their backs and shoulders to the Japanese. Konishi sat back in his chair, with his feet on his desk, directing the operation.

Were we mice or were we men? We didn't know.

The fitting close to this scene was a formation of American planes flying directly overhead. Becoming scared, the Japanese started diving into ditches or fleeing into a cement building for protection, while we were standing out in the open, rejoicing and waving wildly at the pilots who dipped their wings in salute.

Now who were the mice and who the men?

Excited and thrilled that General MacArthur had now landed on our island of Luzon, we did not realize in our euphoria that some of us would die by starvation or execution before his soldiers could reach our camp.

CHAPTER 23
Love Your Enemies?
January 17–28, 1945

Two men look out through the same bars:
One sees the mud, and one the stars.

A RIFLE SHATTERED the eerie silence of early dawn. Fear seized the hearts of all who heard it.

He had been a friendly American with the unlikely name of Jan Howard Hell, but everyone called him "Pat." With courage and daring, he made secret sorties outside our fences to bring in chickens and vegetables for himself and friends, though they begged him not to take such risks. This time a Japanese guard saw him returning to camp, and suddenly Pat was dead.

For bringing in bananas, a chicken, and a coconut, Pat lost his life at thirty-eight. He had endured imprisonment for three and a half years. Now, when the Americans had landed and deliverance seemed near, Pat would not live to enjoy it.

All of us prisoners grieved for him. Captivity and hunger can drive a person beyond self-control, twist one's reasoning, and alter values, but Pat was bringing in that food for a needy friend.

Our captors had warned us: "Anyone going near the fences

or attempting to escape will be shot!" Our own committee faithfully reminded us of the danger.

Los Banos Internment Camp had been hastily constructed in the country near the hills, so there were no confining cement walls. Instead, we were held in by fences made of barbed wire and *sawali*. The presence of Japanese guns inside and outside our camp restrained us from escaping or slipping out for food. Beyond those flimsy fences, we had no refuge even if we did manage to escape. Friendly Filipinos who hid any American risked swift, brutal execution.

The nearby home of the Espinos became a secret rendezvous for guerrillas and a source of food for starving internees slipping out of camp. Romeo Espino had been a student at the Los Banos Agricultural College. Now he served as a guerrilla leader, disguised with the name of Colonel Price. His wife, Helen, handled confidential communications with guerrillas and Americans. Both of them risked their lives day and night.

On January 27, 1945, about a week and a half after Pat Hell was shot, George Louis slipped out of camp. He foraged for food and then may have rested at the Espinos' home. The next morning about dawn George started scrambling back over our fence when a Japanese guard pointed his gun at him.

Friends shouted, "Don't come over, George. Someone's watching."

His alertness dimmed by starvation, disease, and probably by lack of sleep, George Louis kept climbing over that fence into camp, so a guard shot him in the shoulder.

At that moment, a formation of American planes flew by, as though in protest. The Japanese took cover, keeping a rifle aimed at the wounded prisoner.

Dr. Nance and a church bishop tried to reach the bleeding man, as did George Gray of our Administration Committee, who had been an official in America's High Commissioner's office in Manila.

Threatening the men with his gun, a guard shouted something that sounded like *"Utsu zo!"* meaning "I'll shoot!"

The prisoner had not been escaping, but coming into camp, so there was no justification for his being shot. Our men tried to intercede with the commandant, but Major Iwanaka became inflexible and refused to see them. He had made the rules and would not break them. The fact that his rules were against international law for the treatment of civilian internees did not seem important to him.

While George Louis, this former Pan American Airlines mechanic, continued writhing in pain and bleeding for an hour and a half, Dr. Nance tried again and again to reach him, but each time the Japanese raised their guns menacingly at the physician.

Then several Japanese guards rolled the wounded prisoner onto some *sawali* matting fastened to a frame and carried him to a corner of their guardhouse. With Major Iwanaka present, Konishi handed a gun to one of the soldiers standing nearby, who shot George in the head, blowing his brains out.

Shock settled on the camp. Such inhumane, insensible, unjustifiable, raw cruelty! My heart burned with an anger I considered "righteous indignation," and I felt like Jane Eyre when she exclaimed: "My brain was in tumult, my heart in insurrection. 'Unjust, unjust!' said my reason."*

With tears stinging my eyes, I picked up my Bible and sought refuge in our crude chapel. I had to be alone with God.

While I sat in this makeshift sanctuary, struggling with my anger, our Administration Committee was writing a formal protest to Commandant Iwanaka. Here is an excerpt:

You, as Commandant of this camp, have no power to order the imposition of the death penalty upon any internee here for any offense whatever.

We call your attention to Articles 60 to 67 of the Geneva Convention of 1929, which soon after the outbreak of the present war your government agreed with the government of the United States to follow in its treatment of civilian internees.

Jane Eyre by Charlotte Bronte

Under those articles only a court may order the death penalty. The procedure is prescribed. . . The right of the prisoner to defend himself is safeguarded as well as his right to have counsel and to appeal; and these articles expressly provide that no death penalty may be executed until three months after the protecting power is notified of the imposition thereof.

You have disregarded all these provisions in ordering the execution of Mr. George Louis this morning.

From no point of view was Mr. Louis guilty of any offense involving the death penalty. At the worst he could only be considered as in the act of escaping when first shot. The facts are to the contrary. He was actually returning to the camp and hence was not an escaping prisoner.

In any case, under Articles 47, 50, 51, 52 of the Geneva Convention of 1929 an attempted escape is only an offense against discipline and the punishment thereof may not exceed 30 days' arrest.

There can be no doubt that the refusal to permit medical attention to be given to Mr. Louis after he was first shot and the order for his execution within an hour and a half thereafter without any court action whatever constitute a record unlawful, inhuman, and shocking.

While that protest was being written and delivered to Commandant Iwanaka, I struggled with my own intense feelings. In the quiet of the chapel, my fingers restlessly flipped pages of the Bible from Old Testament to New, back and forth, here and there, seeking help. Nothing seemed to apply. Then my eyes fell on this verse:

"Love your enemies. . . pray for them which despitefully use you, and persecute you" (Matthew 5:44).

Staring at those words, I cried out incredulously, "No! This *can't* be Your answer, Lord. I'm willing to *pray* for them, but I cannot *love* them. This time You're asking too much of me."

My thoughts turned to our enemy's cruel and unethical bombing of Pearl Harbor and the thousands of American

young men who lost their lives in that perfidious sneak attack.
I recalled the death march in Bataan, when the Japanese
treated our soldiers so despicably.

"And what about Frederic Stevens?" I asked the Lord. He
was head of the American Coordinating Committee in Manila.
The Japanese took him to Fort Santiago and, among other
things, sliced off some of Stevens's skin, shoved it into his
mouth, and commanded him to eat his own skin, while other
soldiers stood by laughing.

Many punishments were so severe the victims lapsed into
unconsciousness.

As I thought of those who were made to kneel on sharpened
points of bamboo, I became aware of my own uncomfortable
position on that hard bench with its rough spots.

Moving to another bench, I thought about my diary, hidden
in a tin can. I heard the Japanese were sticking sharp sticks of
bamboo up the fingernails and toenails of those keeping records or diaries. I had become afraid and destroyed my writ-
ings several times, but writing served as a form of emotional
release for me, and I risked the bamboo sticks and Fort Santiago to keep writing in my diary, burying it in a tin can between
times.

But I realized it meant a foolish risk, as faces of some of my
friends came before me. Dr. Hawthorne Darby, a woman beloved for her kindness and mercy, had helped me when I was
under house arrest and in need of medical treatment. Dr.
Darby and her associate at the Emmanuel Hospital, Helen
Wilk, had been temporarily released from internment to carry
on their work. They became involved in the guerrilla underground when Mrs. Mary Stagg, who had also been released,
sent wounded Filipino guerrillas to them for medical care.

Helen Wilk dangerously extended her activities, even to supplying guerrillas with a radio transmitter set. Everyone knew
that because the Japanese feared the guerrillas, the penalty
for such an act would be certain death.

One day the Japanese swept into Emmanuel Hospital and

carted off Dr. Darby and Helen Wilk to the torture dungeons of the infamous Fort Santiago.

At about the same time, the Japanese Military Police surrounded the church where Mrs. Stagg served as pastor.

Just at that moment, a Filipino named Ramon Magsaysay had an appointment with Mrs. Stagg. He was chief of the Zambales resistance and had commissioned Mary Boyd Stagg as a first lieutenant in the underground. As his car approached her church that day, he spotted the Japanese Military Police and drove past. Had he gone into the church, Magsaysay most certainly would have ended up at Fort Santiago under the knife of an executioner instead of becoming president of the Philippines.

The Japanese took Mrs. Stagg and her sixteen-year-old son, Sam Boyd, to Fort Santiago. They threw the boy into a cell and forgot about him for a seemingly unending time, eventually interning him in Santo Tomas.

Only the silent walls of Fort Santiago witnessed the vicious tortures inflicted on Dr. Darby, Helen Wilk, and Mary Stagg, as the Japanese tried to wring from them names and locations of guerrillas.

One torture common in such cases, and most assuredly used on them, was the "water cure." A hose is put through the nose and water poured down until a person can take no more. Then the stomach is struck a hard blow. This is repeated every few hours while attempts are made to wrest information from the victims.

Whether Miss Wilk broke under torture beyond human endurance, or whether her own principles demanded that she tell the truth, I shall never know.

In the sanctuary of the chapel, I shuddered. The gentle Dr. Darby and the more aggressive Helen Wilk and Mary Stagg had been executed by decapitation.

Mary Stagg's brother was Dr. E. Forrest Boyd, former Chief of Staff at the Hollywood Presbyterian Hospital, and an adjunct member of the faculty at Biola College. He had been my personal physician when I attended school in Los Angeles. He would be one of the first persons to see me if I lived through the war and arrived safely home. How could I tell him that the Japanese had cut off his sister's head?

Mrs. Stagg pastored the Cosmopolitan Student Church in Manila, but had been under house arrest since the arrival of the Japanese army. Her husband, who helped build the church, had left the country.

Known in the underground network as "Mother Stagg," she secretly aided loyal Filipino and Chinese guerrillas who were on the most-wanted list of the Japanese Military Police. She sent the ill and wounded to Dr. Darby and helped others escape to the hills with their families when the Japanese were in pursuit. She found hiding places for those in need of refuge.

In order to supply them with money, Mary Stagg purchased "guerrilla notes," a monetary unit of exchange that had been authorized by America and would be redeemable after the war.

Mr. Go Puan Seng was the publisher of a pro-American newspaper called *The Fookien Times*. He and his wife were devout Chinese Christians. When the Japanese were in hot pursuit of Mr. Go and his family, Mother Stagg risked her life to help them reach the sanctuary of the hills, where they survived the war by moving from place to place in heavy foliage.

Brave, loyal, and courageous, Mother Stagg became trapped because she was not perceptive of deceit. A slick, smooth-talking Filipino, serving the Japanese as an enemy agent, made up a story that he had come in by submarine and was an agent for General MacArthur. He forged false guerrilla promissory notes to entrap buyers and then turned their names over to the Japanese.

Helen Wilk believed this traitor and introduced him to many Filipino leaders of the guerrilla underground. Mrs. Stagg purchased from him many of the guerrilla promissory notes which, unknown to her, were fake. He gave the Japanese all the information he secured.

The next day after taking Mrs. Stagg to Fort Santiago, the Japanese excavated the backyard of the church and found there all the evidence they needed—incriminating papers, guns, ammunition, and lists of pro-American people who had purchased guerrilla promissory notes.

They had caught "Mother Stagg," and the torture she must have endured is beyond words.

Victims who survived Fort Santiago related excruciating stories of cruelty. Men were kicked or hit in the testicles with sticks. Filipino women were hung upside down and submitted to agonizing sexual tortures, unfit for printing in this book, as the Japanese tried to secure information regarding the location of guerrillas. Some lost consciousness under this extreme sexual brutality. However, the brave woman guerrilla, Carmen Rivera, who helped our imprisoned American soldiers and us at Los Banos Internment Camp, was never captured.

Frederic Stevens describes nighttime in Fort Santiago:

"Lying on the wooden floor, listening to the groans of tortured prisoners, with the floor acting as a sounding board for the clanging and dragging of leg irons on the prisoner in the next cell; hearing the cries and seeing the tears of those who in the nighttime let their emotions go, could not help but bring forth the cry that has echoed down through the centuries from that tortured soul on Golgotha, 'My God, my God, why hast thou forsaken me?' "

As my soul trembled at such thoughts, I looked down again at those words in the Bible, "Love your enemies."

"Are You really asking me to love people who are so brutal?" I asked the Lord. "What about Lieutenant Konishi, member of an underground terrorist group—repulsive, crude, dirty—the foul-smelling drunkard responsible for the starvation of many of our internees? He is vile, threatening to have us eat dirt."

As I sat there struggling, the Lord said to my raging storm, "Peace, be still." The words of a majestic old hymn written by Katharina von Schlegel penetrated the depths of my being:

Be still, my soul:
thy God doth undertake
To guide the future
as He has the past.
Thy hope, thy confidence
let nothing shake;
All now mysterious
shall be bright at last.
Be still, my soul:
the waves and winds still know
His voice who ruled them
while He dwelt below.

The waves in my storm grew calm. I became aware of a star trying to shine through the clouds that had darkened my mind.

I thought of the Japanese officer who asked to see Gertrude Feely one day. Having lived and worked in Japan, she spoke the language fluently, and served as an interpreter in camp.

"I'm leaving for Japan," he told her, "and will be returning here. I'll be glad to take letters from you to your friends there."

Gertrude had worked with high school students in a community center in Japan where English, cooking, flower arranging, and sewing were taught. This center had a kindergarten, and Gertrude had lived in the section where it was located. The officer had a child in that kindergarten.

"Iie, yoroshu gozaimasu," (No, thank you) Gertrude replied graciously, and then continued in Japanese, "I do not wish to send any letters."

She feared that his offer might be a trick to obtain the names of workers, who would then be questioned.

When the officer returned from his trip, he came to the camp office with a handful of letters and asked for Miss Feely. On greeting Gertrude, he handed her the letters. "I went to the community center where you worked and brought these letters for you from your friends," he explained.

Gertrude was overwhelmed. His offer had not been a trick after all, but a kind gesture of appreciation for her fine work in his homeland.

Sitting there in that rough chapel, I bargained with the Lord, "I could love *that* Japanese officer for you. Why aren't they all like him?"

I realized that outside the walls of Fort Santiago, it was not all mud. There were still a few stars shining. I thought of that famous couplet by Frederick Langbridge:

Two men look out through the same bars:
One sees the mud, and one the stars.

So I added a couplet of my own:

But through barbed wire I see them both,
And pray the stars my soul to touch.

As I sought for those stars, the memory of another rare deed of kindness lit up the darkness. My thoughts turned back to the day of arrival at the Los Banos Internment Camp. There had been no water to drink on the hot, crowded train trip, none in our section of the camp, and no way of obtaining any. Everyone was tired and thirsty. Little children were crying.

While standing guard over us, some of the Japanese soldiers had given their canteens of boiled tea to the mothers and said, "Divide it up for the children."

Then I became aware of light from another star shining faintly on the mud of our camp. One of the Japanese officers handed a missionary from Japan a letter addressed to his wife.

"After the war," he said, "if you get back to Japan and I do not make it, would you take this to my wife for me?" With his letter were several pictures. None of us ever heard what became of the soldier.

Some internees considered the star of a soldier named Mr. Ito to be fickle. He could be both kind and gruff, and his star shone on and off. In one shining moment he gave a gift to a woman in our camp who had taught him English in Korea. Now he served as an interpreter for the Japanese military! The guard Okamoto sometimes tried to help.*

One of the commandants in Santo Tomas Internment Camp, R. Tsurumi from the Japanese Consular Service, showed concern for the internees there. The glow of his star did not falter, but the Japanese military transferred Tsurumi. Commandants were often reassigned, possibly so they would not feel compassion for their prisoners.

Other commandants were antagonistic, as exemplified by Lieutenant Colonel Hayashi, a cruel, hardened military career soldier. Our Commandant Iwanaka seemed unreasonable.

Japanese officers who had civilian backgrounds were more humane than those with military careers. The heirs of the *Samuri* were indoctrinated with the theory that discipline is accomplished only by punishment.

Among the very small galaxy of Japanese stars, a music lover who used to play the cello startled Grace Nash one day while she played her violin in one of the barracks. At first she feared he might take her violin, but he only wanted to listen. Time and again he came, appreciating her skill as a concert violinist, requesting classical numbers. Sometimes he secretly provided some beans, a bit of coffee, and once a little brown sugar for her tiny son.

Among the stars that illuminated our years of "mud," Misaki's shone the brightest. He had very little respect for our

*See Appendix B.

commandant and none at all for Konishi. As I recalled how Misaki had risked his life, trying to get food for us from the Philippine Red Cross, and his execution because of his efforts to help American and British prisoners that had been transferred from the Baguio Camp to Old Bilibid Prison, his star would shine on my feelings and relations with Japanese civilians for years to come. (I have since learned from Daikichi Okamoto that a Japanese army officer killed Mr. Misaki there at Old Bilibid Prison, evidently because he was helping American and British prisoners.)

Sounds of children playing nearby filtered through the *sawali* walls of this barracks used as a chapel, and my thoughts traveled back to a little Japanese playmate of childhood years in Long Beach, California.

While my mother would be buying fresh vegetables from Mr. Tanaka's stand during the weekly market day at the park, his little daughter and I played happily together. We became close friends. But when little Miss Tanaka became a teenager, the parents took her to Japan for marriage.

Could her husband be fighting against us now or were they both interned in America? Somehow through the bombs and fires and barbed wires that now separated us, little Tanaka's face kept smiling at me like a tiny star twinkling in my black sky. I knew we could never be enemies.

I began to see more of the stars and less of the mud. "Would it be all right with You, Lord," I timidly asked, "if I just loved Tanaka, Japanese people as a whole, and the few officers, guards, and civilians who show a bit of kindness? Can I leave out the Japanese Military Police, the men who bombed Pearl Harbor, those who were in charge of the Bataan Death March and the insufferable conditions of Cabanatuan Prison and the horrors of Fort Santiago? I'll pray for Konishi and let You love him. If You can love these people through me, Lord, all right, but I can't do it of myself."

A young lad named Tom Bousman found himself going through the same struggle. His close friend, Burt Fonger, who was one of our finest boys in camp, a Cub Scout and budding musician, died of cerebral malaria. All of us grieved over losing Burt, and Tom held the Japanese indirectly responsible for his death.

Burt's father had been head of the American Bible Society in Manila and firmly resisted Japanese pressure on him to cooperate in carrying out their purposes. Both father and son were of the highest caliber. While standing by Burt's grave, Tom saw no stars, only mud. It would be some time before stars would light Tom's pathway and lead him to become a Presbyterian minister. For now we both struggled with the mud.

Fourteen-year-old David Blackledge also had to face hard realities. Not only did Dave have to cope with the death of his friend, Burt Fonger, but he later learned that his father, Captain Blackledge, had been wounded, captured, and sent to Japan on one of the "Hell Ships" carrying American military prisoners of war. David's father had been in reasonably good health when placed on that prison ship, but when it reached Japan, he was carried off on a stretcher and died three days later due to inhumane treatment aboard the ship. It would be years before his young son, David, would see stars instead of mud, but in due time he would become a tall and handsome colonel in our armed forces.

I had learned as a prisoner of war in that camp the necessity of listening to the Lord in times of deep distress, finding His answer to the problem, and letting Him work it out in the depths of my soul.

As I sat in the chapel for an unmeasured time, I became quieter, and felt the Lord was saying to me, "I don't love the evil they do, but I love them. They need to know Me and the meaning of Calvary love. Some of them in the military, like the

Roman centurion and the thief on the cross, may believe and be redeemed, and then their lives will change. Let that love flow through you."

They were the victims of their background, the products of a lifetime under Japan's military training, with its strange codes, twisted disciplines, and mind control. What would I have been like under such circumstances?

To forgive is divine, but I was only human. Feeling that their excruciating cruelty did not warrant pity, I prayed, "If You can let Your divine love flow through me to them, all right, but I cannot do it of myself."

Feeling I had settled the matter by being willing to let the love of the Lord flow through me for my enemies, I left the chapel and went back to my barracks.

Then, during the long, dark, and restless night, as I tossed from side to side in my bed, those thoughts of love and shining stars began fading into the terrors of Fort Santiago menacing me on two counts.

I recalled smuggling those radio parts into Santo Tomas Internment Camp for Earl Hornbostel. He had been caught distributing news sheets, and the Japanese imprisoned him. Would he break while suffering inhuman treament and tell the names of any who helped him? I felt almost certain he would not, but it could mean Fort Santiago for me.

And if any of our guards discovered my hidden diary, I would probably be thrown into one of those blood-stained cells in that chamber of horrors. I trembled at the thought. Inside the hoary walls of Fort Santiago, would I feel pity for my captors, with Calvary love flowing through my soul for the executioner?

Feeling weak and helpless at the very thought, I believed the answer would be no, and I began wondering whether even God could cause me to love my executioner.

A few of the stars had touched my soul,
But some of the mud remained.

Then these words from the Bible wrote themselves across my mind, "My grace is sufficient for thee, for my strength is made perfect in weakness. . . . Be still and know that I am God."

CHAPTER 24
The Hidden, Forbidden Radio

WITH ELBOW RESTING ON HIS KNEE, and chin cupped in one hand, Jerry wrestled with the difficult problem of finding some kind of electric power for his hidden, forbidden radio, with its exhausted batteries.

Gerald Sams, known to everyone as Jerry, was an electronics genius who had operated a radio in our camp almost continuously from the beginning of our internment in Los Banos. Starting from scratch, he required some time to build the original radio, which was battery operated; and it took a bit of doing to acquire or make parts for it.

One day Jerry felt a strong compulsion to change the hiding place of the radio parts. Taking the parts out of the Klim cans in which they had hidden them, Margaret and Jerry quickly threw them out the back door into the weeds.

Moments later the Japanese guards were at their door and went straight to the Klim cans in the cupboard. Throwing the parts into the weeds had saved Jerry's life. Their cupboards were never searched before or after that.

Margaret commented later, "We've always given God credit for saving Jerry that time, perhaps many times."

How the Japanese heard about the radio parts in the Klim

cans remains a mystery. I heard a rumor that the king of the weasels had "squealed" in order to receive benefits from the Japanese, but I do not know for sure how they found out.

News is a lifeline to a prisoner of war, giving wings to one's spirit. Jerry let it trickle through the camp as rumors, lifting us out of the doldrums and preventing dullness of mind and despair.

But now the radio's batteries were dead and could not be revived. Jerry continued struggling with how to create some kind of electric power.

We could hear sounds of bombings and tremendous explosions in Manila, more than forty miles away, and a glow from the towering inferno of fires lit up our evening skies.

Although the radio had created a strain almost too much to bear in their starved, weakened condition, Margaret and Jerry missed the news. All of us craved to hear news concerning the war.

Before the present impasse, Jerry had borrowed a one-quarter-inch Black and Decker drill from a man living nearby in their barracks. They had put a hand crank on the chuck and used the gears in the drill to increase the motor speed.

Electrically, it worked very well, but the sound was unbelievable and caused Margaret to tell Jerry, "All those things you are operating create a terrible noise. Every time you work I nearly have a nervous breakdown. If I were a Japanese guard, I most certainly would investigate all that racket."

But the guards seldom came near the area, and Jerry continued experimenting.

However, because of malnutrition, no one was strong enough to turn the crank by hand for more than a minute or two. As a result, they were forced to look for another compound-wound motor that could be used as a generator.

While all this kept turning around in Jerry's mind like wheels in a machine, Dr. Dana Nance came over from the hospital to see him. For the sake of our mental health, the doctor felt it more important now than before that we have some source of news that would give us hope and encouragement to keep on enduring.

Dr. Nance offered Jerry any motor they had at the hospital—refrigerator, washing machine, centrifuge.

As they discussed the problem, Jerry made some comment about "foot power."

The doctor's face lit up. He told Jerry about a man in camp who had stolen the Japanese commandant's bicycle. Because of having grown a beard throughout the three years he had been interned, the man would be easy to locate.

"That's our answer!" exclaimed Jerry.

This added to the hazards. Having another person know about the radio would increase the risk. But Jerry had faith to believe that a man who had stolen the commandant's bicycle would not further endanger his own life by letting something slip about the radio.

Dr. Nance and Jerry made up an explanation, an alibi, to give the Japanese in case they were discovered. There was just one unrealized problem. In the excitement and rush of getting the equipment together and operating it, they forgot to tell the bearded bicycle man the alibi to be used if they were caught!

The men worked on their project until they had enough power to light up a hundred-watt bulb, and then they decided to try it on the radio.

The barracks containing the carpenter shop was farthest away from everything, so they chose that place for the experiment. The men selected an afternoon hour when everyone took a siesta and the building would be vacant.

When Jerry left the cubicle that had become home to him and Margaret in the internment camp, he headed for the barracks where they were going to conduct the experiment. He carried a bag containing the radio, which they concealed in a sewing box as a disguise. The box had been cleverly fashioned by a missionary friend named James Lee, known to be handy in woodwork.

Margaret watched Jerry as he walked away barefooted, shirtless, and wearing only worn-out shorts and a straw hat. He was so thin that she could count every rib.

Everything within Margaret reached out to him at that moment, clothing Jerry in love and longing to protect him from what might happen. She could only do what army and navy wives in America were doing—wait and pray.

The men gathered in the carpenter shop barracks and set up the equipment. Since Jerry was the only one who knew how to operate the radio, that would be his special job. The other men were to take turns pedaling the bicycle, which was attached to the generator.

As Jerry looked over the scene, he thought, *What if a Japanese guard should suddenly walk in?* He decided to take the radio to the other end of the barracks and operate it in a partitioned-off tool room.

He connected up with their electric line, which they had run into the tool room, closed and locked the door, and turned on the radio.

The voice of the announcer from radio station KGEI came over the radio and then it went dead. Realizing it needed more power, Jerry was about to shout out at Dr. Nance to pump harder on the bicycle, when in God's providence, he felt compelled to be silent.

As Jerry peered through a crack in the flimsy wall of woven matting, he was filled with consternation at what he saw.

Sitting on the bicycle, Dr. Nance appeared as though he were frozen, with one foot on a pedal poised in midair. He and a Japanese guard were staring at each other in startled, unbelieving, stupefying surprise.

On hearing the noisy machinery, the guard had come to investigate. He was as dumbfounded as the men.

The man with the beard recovered first. Anyone clever and brash enough to steal the commandant's own bicycle would possess enough *savoir-faire* to handle a guard. He broke the silence by saying with a friendly smile, "Want to swapi watchi?"

It was like bursting a balloon in their midst. The Japanese suddenly became unfrozen and ran to call some more guards.

At that moment it seemed as though both God and America came to the rescue of the men because two American planes flew very low over our camp. The Japanese all dived into ditches, certain that the planes were after them.

Picking up his radio, Jerry fled, hardly aware that he had bolted right through the flimsy wall of matting.

When the planes were no longer in sight, the Japanese guards scrambled out of the ditches and hastened to the barracks where the men had been discovered, but they found only an empty room.

The guards had not seen Jerry, hidden with the radio in that partitioned-off toolroom, but it was a simple matter for them to trace down Dr. Nance and the bearded man.

The Japanese have ways of making a prisoner talk. Jerry feared that one of the men would be forced to tell of his part in the operation, especially since the bearded man did not know the alibi.

While Margaret worried until she felt almost ill, Jerry made plans to escape during the night through the barbed wire double fences surrounding the camp. They both knew that if the men were forced to tell what was going on in that room, Jerry would be executed; and if any guard saw him escaping, he would be shot on sight.

As Margaret realized she might never see Jerry alive again, the love she felt for him welled up inside her and almost overcame her ability to help plan his escape. Margaret felt she could not face life without him.

The suspense of waiting in that small cubicle, their tiny "home" in the internment camp, became so heavy it seemed almost too much to bear. Every noise, every footstep, every voice they heard sounded ominous and made them tense up and hold their breath.

To share their plight with anyone else would endanger other

lives. They had to bear it in secret, as the very air in their cubicle seemed filled with the threat of momentary discovery, one minute of fear ticking off into another. Their ears strained to hear the dreaded sound of any approaching Japanese guard, but all seemed strangely quiet.

During those excruciating hours of waiting, Jerry felt like making a run for it, but to try an escape in daylight would be committing suicide. However, waiting too long could mean being executed.

Word reached them that both the bearded man and Dr. Nance had been interrogated by the Japanese, and Jerry chided himself that he had not given the alibi to the bearded man. Margaret felt their only hope was to pray.

It seemed to take the sun longer to set, but gradually, slowly, it disappeared and then dusk faded into welcome darkness.

While Jerry kept hoping for some kind of word about what the Japanese knew before he made his escape, Dr. Nance and a friend arrived at the cubicle. In low whispers they told Jerry the events that followed their discovery.

The bearded man had been quickly picked up by the Japanese after they returned to the barracks and found it empty. Although he did not know the planned alibi, this incredible man told the Japanese that since his work in the camp was in the electrical department, they were trying to make a generator for the hospital to be used in case they had an emergency operation at night but no electricity. This satisfied the Japanese, who allowed him to return to his cubicle.

Then they sent for Dr. Nance—impressive, bold, broad-shouldered, and seemingly impervious to fear and subjugation. The Japanese could neither humble nor frighten him. He had their respect because of his medical skill, and he was by nature a man whose very presence commanded esteem. In addition, he towered over them in personality and stature like a giant among pygmies.

Possibly to show his fearlessness and allay suspicion, Dr.

Nance walked into the commandant's office in response to the summons, sat down, and put his feet up on the desk.

The Japanese commandant became infuriated at his arrogance and disrespect for authority.

Throughout the tirade, Dr. Nance sat there unperturbed, coolly waiting for the commandant to calm down. "Doc" was probably the only man in camp who could get away with such behavior because the Japanese needed his medical skill as much as we did.

When the commandant cooled down, he asked Dr. Nance if he knew the bearded man.

"Yes," replied the doctor.

"Have you talked to him recently?"

Knowing that the bearded man had already been questioned, Dr. Nance replied, "I saw him on the road the other day and chatted with him."

Staring hard at the doctor, the commandant asked, "Did you tell him anything?"

Not knowing what the bearded man had said under questioning, Doctor Nance took a risky chance, "Yes. When I saw him last week I told him that we were likely to have a night operation at any time, and I wondered if it would be possible to make some sort of a generator that would give us enough electricity to perform an operation."

The story sounded so similar to what the bearded man had told him that the commandant believed it and let Dr. Nance go.

The men were off the hook, and the Japanese never did know of Jerry's involvement or the radio.

Jerry had left a radio tube behind when he bolted through the wall of the partitioned room. It could have been their downfall, but it had been picked up by someone, either a good samaritan to cover their activities or a Japanese guard who didn't know its purpose.

The relief for the men and Margaret seemed like a cool, refreshing shower on a stifling, hot, muggy day when the air seems too heavy to breathe.

When Dr. Nance and his friend left the cubicle, Margaret and Jerry held each other for a few moments. Then they settled down to the most important issue facing them and the whole camp—eating their tiny portion of worm-filled rice to help ward off death by starvation. Death by shooting had been avoided once again.

CHAPTER 25
Heroes in a Holocaust
February 3, 1945

DISTANT EXPLOSIONS RENT THE AIR, causing great excitement in camp. We figured they were at Manila Bay and Fort McKinley.

A few American planes were circling low over the Santo Tomas Internment Camp in Manila, forty miles from us. One of the pilots tied a message to his goggles and dropped them into the camp as he flew by.

Swiftly picked up by the internees, who had been waving at the planes, the note proclaimed the message "Roll out the barrel!"

Rumors raced through the camp that it also said, "Santa Claus is coming."

The words became electric with meaning, and the news spread like lightning, striking everyone. The message was interpreted to mean that the American army would liberate them in the next day or two, and shouts of "Merry Christmas!" rang out like church bells.

Gen. Douglas MacArthur and his forces had accomplished a great landing at Lingayen Gulf, about a hundred miles north of Manila. Fearful that an attempt might be made by the Japa-

nese to harm the internees at Santo Tomas, MacArthur issued
the following order on January 30 for the 1st Calvary Brigade:

*Go to Manila. Go around the Nips, bounce off the Nips, but go
to Manila. Free the internees at Santo Tomas. Take Malacanan
Palace and the Legislative Building.*

The 1st Cavalry raced as fast as tanks can go in enemy-held
territory, crossing rivers and speeding through towns. When
the Japanese put explosives under one bridge, the cavalrymen
captured the bridge just before it would have blown up. Where
bridges had been destroyed, our tanks forded the rivers in
shallower places. When they came to a bridge where the Japanese lit dynamite fuses and then ran, these incredible men of
the 1st Cavalry seized the burning fuses and snuffed them out.

When a Japanese convoy of trucks carrying soldiers started
to turn onto the road on which the 1st Cavalry was traveling,
the American soldiers waved for them to halt. The surprised
Nipponese did just that. The cavalrymen opened fire on the
astounded Japanese and then sped by and out of sight before
the enemy fully realized what had happened.

Arriving in Manila, this armored division started right down
Rizal Avenue past Japanese soldiers who seemed paralyzed by
the sudden appearance of American tanks.

Speeding straight for the Santo Tomas Internment Camp, the
bold-spirited 8th Regiment, 1st Brigade, of the 1st Cavalry Division reached the iron-rodded gates at 9:00 P.M. on February
3, 1945. Everything was dark, with not a light or a person visible in the eerie silence.

Carl Mydans of *Life* magazine rode in on one of the tanks.
He had been interned in Santo Tomas, repatriated, and had
now returned for its liberation. Listening in the dark quiet of
the night, he is reported to have said, "I'm certainly scared of
what we may find when we go in there. I don't believe there's a
single American left alive."

Our soldiers also feared they had arrived too late.

Suddenly shots rang out of the darkness and hand grenades exploded, injuring the commanding officer, Col. H. L. Connor, and the Filipino guerrilla who had guided the tanks from the perimeters of Manila to Santo Tomas.

Some of the tanks then crashed through the gates, their powerful searchlights and glowing flares crisscrossing the camp, whose large concrete buildings lay several hundred yards in front of them, still in darkness.

Inside the buildings, excited internees had heard a loud rumbling becoming a roar. Pressing their faces against the windows, they peered into the darkness.

"Are they Japanese trucks bringing reinforcements?"

"Could they, oh, *could* they be Americans?"

And then suddenly those tremendous searchlights lit up the whole campus.

"They've come!" someone shouted.

"The Japanese don't have lights like that!"

Bedlam broke loose as internees scrambled for the doors, but in the main building the Japanese guards would not let them out.

Walking in front of the approaching tanks was Maj. J. C. Gearheart. With him was Capt. J. L. Walters, who served as a mine-detecting expert. The major called out, "Hello, folks!"

And from somewhere among the soldiers came a shout, "We're here!"

The internees thronged past their Japanese guards and went running, rushing towards the American soldiers, wild in their joy, weeping, cheering, wanting to touch or embrace these brave men who had come to rescue them.

Then, with surging emotion, they burst into song, singing "God Bless America," followed by "America" and "The Star Spangled Banner."

Four Japanese, of whom three wore swords and one carried

a pistol, walked solemnly toward our American officers. The Japanese had two American men with them, internees who had been leaders in the camp.

Although unasked, Lieutenant Abiko followed the group.

Raising their hands in the internationally recognized sign of surrender, these Japanese approached our American officers. As Lieutenant Abiko drew near, he was ordered to raise his hands, but he reached for a hidden hand grenade.

Quick as a flash, Major Gearheart snatched the gun of a soldier standing nearby and shot Lieutenant Abiko.

The Japanese stated that their terms for surrender were safe conduct out of camp and permission to take their military arms with them. This was not acceptable to Major Gearheart.

Hoping reinforcements would come, the Japanese decided not to surrender. Barricading themselves in the Education Building, they held about two hundred fifty internees as hostages on the upper floors.

A few of the American men began escaping by sliding down ropes, but in their weakened condition some could not hang onto the ropes. Those among the hostages who had military backgrounds started sending valuable information to the American officers by signals through the windows.

Our tanks moved in closer. Firing at the Japanese section of the building became so intense that several of the Japanese moved to where the hostages were on the third level. Stepping over the hostages, who were keeping low on the floor, the Japanese started firing through the windows at the American soldiers below. They knocked out the lights of a tank, killed one of our soldiers, and wounded several others.

Since some of the hostages, as well as American and Japanese soldiers, were being wounded and killed, a truce was called. Both sides hoped reinforcements would come soon.

No one had been allowed to bring in food for the hostages, who were desperately in need of nourishment. At about noontime the Japanese permitted stew to be brought into the building, helping themselves first and leaving the remainder for the hostages.

By morning, Brig. Gen. W. C. Chase of the 1st Cavalry had arrived, and the grounds were filled with more American soldiers, tanks, trucks, jeeps, and army tents, but no reinforcements for the Japanese. It was reported that General MacArthur would approve of lenient terms if no internees were harmed.

When the commandant of the camp, Lieutenant Colonel Hayashi, heard the Japanese would be allowed to take small arms with them, he met personally with our Col. C. E. Brady. They agreed that the Japanese could take their swords, pistols, and rifles with them and they would be escorted safely out of the camp by American soldiers.

That evening plenty of stew was provided for the hostages.

On Monday morning, February 5, the Japanese, carrying the small arms permitted, were escorted out of Santo Tomas by one hundred American soldiers led by Colonel Brady.

Some of these Japanese had been kind to the internees while others were often cruel, but they were all set free at a place in Manila chosen by the Japanese, a courtesy shown to them because they had not massacred their prisoners. Only America would be so gracious.

Two Japanese snipers, disguised in the white robes of priests, began firing from the roof of the seminary building. American sharpshooters soon picked them off.

As the American flag was raised to fly over the main building at Santo Tomas, tears ran down almost everyone's cheeks. Hands and arms were lifted toward the flag, and soldiers joined the rescued internees in singing "God Bless America" and "The Star Spangled Banner."

Now the internees had time to mingle with the soldiers and to look at the motorized vehicles of the 44th Tank Battalion. A source of amusement and delight were the names the men had inscribed on their tanks, such as "Georgia Peach," "Ole Miss," and "San Antone."

The first tank to enter Santo Tomas was "Battling Basic." Among the soldiers it carried rode Lt. Robert E. Lee, descendant of America's great southern general.

Truckloads of food were brought from Lingayen Gulf, providing new life and strength to thousands of men, women, and children in Santo Tomas.

Excitement continued to build in the camp because General MacArthur was coming to greet the rescued prisoners. Just as thousands of internees were gathering to welcome him, huge shells hit the camp, exploding at the gate and inside Santo Tomas, causing much destruction and fear that the shells were meant for the general himself.

But General MacArthur strode toward the former prisoners with all his magnificent bearing and confidence, saying, "I have returned." Even the shelling stopped for a time.

A great roar of welcome greeted him from the jubilant internees overflowing with thankfulness for their rescue. The crowd became almost hysterical in their desire to get near him. The surging, wildly cheering throng crowded about him. He was unable to reach a microphone that had been set up for him to speak to the rescued internees.

General MacArthur became so overwhelmed and deeply stirred that the freed prisoners saw the stately general wipe away his tears.

Later he wrote,

I cannot recall, even in a life filled with emotional scenes, a more moving spectacle than my first visit to the Santo Tomas camp. It was still under bombardment. When I arrived, the pitiful, half-starved inmates broke out in excited yells. I entered the building and was immediately pressed back against the wall by thousands of emotionally charged people. In their ragged, filthy clothes, with tears streaming down their faces, they seemed to be

*using their last strength to fight their way close enough to grasp
my hand. One man threw his arms around me, and put his
head on my chest and cried unashamedly. A once-beautiful
woman in tatters laboriously lifted her son over the heads of the
crowd and asked me to touch him. I took the boy momentarily
and was shocked by the uncomprehending look of deprivation
in his eyes. They wept and laughed hysterically, and all of them
at once tried to tell me 'Thank you.' I was grabbed by the jacket.
I was kissed. I was hugged. It was a wonderful and never-to-be-
forgotten moment—to be a lifesaver, not a life-taker.*

A thanksgiving service scheduled by the ministers in Santo
Tomas had to be canceled because of heavy shelling on the
camp. The worst tragedy of their whole internment still awaited
those in the Santo Tomas Camp.

After America's courtesy in setting free the Japanese
guards, the Japanese army turned their heavy artillery on
Santo Tomas. More than four thousand men, women, and children, who had valiantly endured three and a half years of starvation, now found themselves bombarded with murderous
shells that blasted their buildings, killing and injuring at ran-
dom. Many suffered shell shock, but there seemed to be no
hysteria, due to complete confidence in our American soldiers.

One of my shipmates from the *President Grant,* Marion
Childress, was talking with Gladys Archer in the room they
shared with others. As they finished their conversation, Marion turned and walked through the doorway. In that instant a
shell exploded, decapitating Gladys and killing several others.

The Rev. Dr. and Mrs. W. B. Foley had just gone into the
room for a few moments. The shelling killed him and blew off
the arm of his wife. Unaware of Dr. Foley's death, the camp officials were calling for him again and again over the loud
speaker because his ministerial services were needed among
the wounded and dying.

Having to leave their destroyed room, some more shipmates

of mine, Geraldine Chappell, Anna Nixon, and Dr. Evelyn Witthoff, were among those sitting against a wall in the hall of the main building. They were seeking some shelter from the murderous explosions.

Anna Nixon describes what happened:

There was a buzz over our heads, a loud crash, and then cement, glass, and dirt came tumbling down around us. We ducked our heads and huddled close together. . . . Another blast shook the building, and everything became hazy and dark. We covered our faces and braced ourselves as the building tumbled about us. . . . A nurse, the color drained from her face, ran down the hall followed by two soldiers carrying a stretcher bearing two children dripping blood.

We huddled together like hunted animals, realizing that the next moment might bring death. I was too stunned to pray, but as I waited in that haunting silence, knowing my face was as ashen as those around me, and knowing we all shared a common hope for life, the words of a grand old hymn sang themselves through my mind:

O God, our help in ages past,
Our hope for years to come,
Be Thou our guide while life shall last,
And our eternal home.

Then suddenly there was another blast, a direct hit on the corner room of the main building. Down through the crowded halls again came the casualties, blood-streaked, frightened people running with stretchers and mangled bodies. More explosions! The whole side of the building seemed to be caving in. . . . Shells that sounded like eggs frying in hot grease whizzed over our heads. *

*Delayed Manila by Anna Nixon

In the midst of these collapsing walls and exploding shells, and with death threatening every moment, my former shipmates heard a voice that sounded to Evelyn Witthoff as tender as a mother's cooing to her baby. It came from a soldier fighting for their lives.

Covered with the dust of battle, helmeted, and carrying his gun, that young man of the 1st Cavalry came over to Evelyn and those huddled with her at the foot of that threatened wall. In a soft, calming voice, he gently said, "You are in danger there. Follow me, and I'll lead you to a safer place."

In all that carnage and horror, the one thing that stands out above everything else in Evelyn's memory is the tenderness in that soldier's voice during that devastating holocaust.

Those fine young men in that 1st Cavalry Brigade were all heroes, brave and daring, well trained and battle-experienced soldiers, but with the internees they were gentlemanly, helpful, polite, and charming. They seemed like the hosts of heaven to the rescued prisoners.

American reinforcements arrived in Manila, and soon the shelling of Santo Tomas ceased and was directed toward the city, where fighting raged and fires were blazing.

Santo Tomas became the safest place for civilians, with many of the wounded stumbling and limping through its gates for medical help and to our flag for refuge.

And Old Glory continued to ripple its stars and stripes out over the camp, signaling its message of hope and freedom for the future.

But I could not flee to Santo Tomas for safety. Locked in an armed camp forty miles from Manila, more than two thousand of us were still in the hands of a fiercely fighting enemy.

Our guards were becoming increasingly brutal in their treatment of the internees in our Los Banos Internment Camp. Would there be any heroes to rescue us from this violent holocaust of war?

Unknown to us, those heroes were landing on Tagaytay Ridge.

CHAPTER 26
Paratroopers Land on Our Island
February 4, 1945

CLAD IN OLIVE-DRAB GREEN and shod with paratrooper's boots, Jim Holzem jumped from the plane. He was trusting his white parachute to billow out in the sky and carry him safely down, but something went wrong and he was jerked into unconsciousness. Below this twenty-year-old soldier glistened a lake of azure blue nestled in an ancient volcano on our island of Luzon.

These paratroopers from the Eleventh Airborne Division were headed for a landing on Tagaytay Ridge, which had a sheer drop of twenty-four hundred feet to the blue water in the crater below. This was not the time to miss the landing zone, but somehow the signal to jump had been given prematurely.

I'll let Jim tell his own story:

"As a machine-gunner, it was my task to get the equipment chute containing the machine gun and all its ammunition out the door at the proper moment. This particular bundle was heavier than usual as it also contained John Blansit's Browning Automatic Rifle, which we simply called the BAR. Scheduled to jump first was Lt. Roger Miller, while I would be last out the door along with the equipment bundle.

"We were still several miles from the drop zone and about

two thousand feet above the ground. We knew the pilot would soon be dropping the plane to seven hundred feet, slow it down to ninety-five miles per hour, and then give us the green light to go. Lieutenant Miller was to start jumping when he saw the men in the lead planes jump.

"Suddenly Miller turned to me and said, 'They're going! Let's go.'

"Following the others, I pushed the equipment bundle out the door and shoved away from it as the static line played out.

"Then came the opening shock of the parachute. Bang! I was unconscious, then awake, strangling. Still only half conscious, I couldn't understand what was choking me. Nothing like this had ever happened on a jump before.

"My kicking feet found the musette bag to stand on, relieving that pressure on my throat. The bag was hanging by the brass strap ends. My parachute harness had stretched, and the breast strap was at my neck. I lost my carbine, but thanked God for that musette bag, which I had worn just below the reserve chute.

"We had jumped several miles too soon at two thousand feet, going 140 miles per hour. Half the outfit lost their weapons and other gear.

"Regaining my senses, I loosened the breast strap from my throat and saw the equipment chute descending at a faster rate than I and about two hundred yards to the south. Steering my chute toward it, I watched it settle down in a gully about sixty feet deep.

"Then, ironically, I experienced the softest landing I have ever had. My chute settled over the top of a large clump of banana trees, and my feet just barely and gently touched the ground.

"By now I began worrying. Deep in enemy-held territory on this invasion jump, I had no weapon. If I did get to the equipment chute, there would be no way in the world for me to carry a machine gun weighing forty-two pounds, as well as eight boxes of ammunition at twenty pounds per box, plus the Browning Automatic Rifle and its ammunition.

"I had noticed just before landing that there were no chutes closer than three or four hundred yards, so I probably wasn't going to get any help. And what if some Japanese showed up before I had the equipment bundle unrolled?

"I rushed to the area where I saw the equipment chute come down, found a path going to the bottom of the gully, and located the bundle. While unrolling it, I looked up, and my heart raced.

"Coming toward me down the path were four short-statured men in strange uniforms, all with their weapons aimed at me. We had fought the Japanese in Leyte, so I knew what their clothing looked like. These men were wearing Japanese uniforms and Japanese army shoes.

"I thought of the automatic rifle but did not have time to get it.

"Then in a flash I realized that the weapons in their hands were United States M-1's. Their uniforms were not real uniforms but a conglomeration of Japanese army clothes, United States army fatigues, and civilian clothing, with the Japanese clothing predominating.

"In broken English, the leader said, 'Please don't hurt us. We're Filipino guerrillas.'

"I wondered how he thought I could hurt him. I was weaponless and he had a loaded M-1 pointed at my chest, but he actually seemed more frightened than I.

"Deciding to take the initiative, I grabbed the M-1 from his hands, noted that he had the safety off, and told him to help me unload the bundle.

"The last guerrilla was leading a burro. Providence indeed! Since there were no troopers near to assist me, the burro and guerrillas were just what I needed.

"We loaded the burro with most of the ammunition, and portioned the rest of it and the machine gun among the guerrillas. The leader wanted his M-1 back, so I obliged him and carried the BAR. Then we climbed out of the gully and headed for the proposed assembly area.

"We had jumped several miles too soon, but all the troopers headed in the direction that would have been right had we jumped at the correct place.

"Soon it wasn't just a lonely paratrooper, four Filipino guerrillas, and one overloaded burro. Trooper met trooper, and then we were all together, everyone talking at the same time, each with his own tale of what had happened on that fouled-up jump. Most of the men had lost their weapons. My showing up with the machine gun, the BAR, and ammunition brought them a happy surprise. John Blansit was especially glad to get his BAR back.

"It turned out that just our First Battalion had jumped prematurely. The Second and Third Battalions jumped in the right place and secured the immediate objectives. We finally all assembled and slept that night on Tagaytay Ridge.

"We linked up with the troops who had come ashore at Nasugbu. There were some trucks available. In the morning the Second Battalion took off towards Manila in the trucks, but the rest of us had to do it on foot.

"We covered thirty miles or more, meeting plenty of cheering Filipinos, and one town even had a band playing for us.

"Just about dark we arrived at the front line, starkly marked by the Paranaque Bridge in a suburb south of Manila. Darkness descended swiftly. The bridge was partially destroyed, with Japanese soldiers on the other side.

"The next morning those Japanese opened up on us with ninety-millimeter antiaircraft shells, which exploded above us and sent fragments downward. Quite a few were being wounded, so we were told to dig foxholes under the houses.

"Earl Hooper, my assistant gunner, and I were reluctant to start digging because we figured we wouldn't be at that location long. Then came a particularly close barrage of ack-ack. I ran over to where shelling was going on, and found some A Company boys bleeding profusely.

"Earl and I were convinced. Back we went to our machine gun and started digging under one of the houses. After digging for a few minutes, we looked up. Standing there were two Filipinos, one about fifteen years old and the other about twenty-five. We offered them a T-shirt and a pocketknife if they would dig our hole. They agreed and started digging.

"While we were watching our hired help, Earl and I decided to eat. As we were opening a can of sweetened condensed milk, the two Filipinos put down their shovels, and, with pleading in their eyes, asked if they could be paid with the can of condensed milk rather than the knife and T-shirt.

"This aroused my curiosity, so I pressed for an explanation.

"The older man was married to the younger man's sister. She had a baby but was unable to breast feed it. All these people were suffering from malnutrition. The baby was about to die, they said, and the milk would help keep it alive.

"The story was sad enough for me. Nothing to do but get the baby more milk!

"While the two Filipinos finished digging, I made the rounds of A Company and B Company (paratroopers), canvassing them for sweetened condensed milk. I must have been a pretty good salesman because I returned with two full cases. It was not usually in our rations, and we did not know its source.

"The next day we were preparing to leave the positions when up traipsed the whole family. After a little speech telling me how they knew their little baby was going to make it now with those two cases of milk, they offered me the young digger as a mascot, servant, indentured slave, you name it. They said I would need help digging foxholes, carrying ammunition, and in doing other such jobs.

"I assured them they owed me nothing, but they wouldn't buy it. I had to take 'Oscar' with me. His real name was Rosendo Castillo, but I nicknamed him Oscar after my grandfather, who complained because he couldn't enlist at the age of seventy-six.

"Oscar and I became very close. I was his big brother, adviser, father, and friend; and I became his nurse when he had attacks of malaria, which occurred about once a month. His eagerness to please and his look of adulation amply repaid me.

"Oscar helped in digging foxholes, in carrying ammunition, and in filling canteens. He translated and took his stay-awake turn at night. But what he did best was scrounging for food. My rations were always supplemented with rice, chicken, eggs, and vegetables. He would be with me when we stood off *Banzai* attacks from the Japanese, and by my side when we crossed machine-gun and mortar fire on the approach to Fort McKinley.

"When a long-range Japanese machine gun fired a burst into the area, killing our radio man, Glen Fox, the smallest man in our company, Oscar asked if he couldn't have his boots.

"I was shocked and said something like this, 'No, Oscar, Glen died with his boots on and should be buried with them on.'

"But our Platoon Sergeant wasn't as much of a romanticist as I, and he told Oscar to go ahead and take them.

"On went the paratrooper boots, and up stood a ten-foot-tall Filipino."

CHAPTER 27
General MacArthur Orders Our Rescue
February 2–12, 1945

TAKE NECESSARY ACTION TO ASSIGN ONE OF YOUR UNITS MIS-SION LIBERATING LOS BANOS INTERNMENT CAMP PLANNING SHOULD BE STARTED IMMEDIATELY SCAP [Supreme Commander Allied Powers]. This message was sent by General MacArthur to Lt. Gen. Robert Eichelberger on February 2, 1945.

Heavy Japanese firing on the afternoon of February 4 slowed the progress of a Forward Command Group. Headed by Brig. Gen. Al Pierson, and including elements of the 511th Parachute Infantry Regiment, the group's first mission was to locate a suitable site for the Forward Command Post. Captain Tuschon moved on ahead and discovered a vacant three-story house near Paranaque that faced the war-troubled waters of Manila Bay. This spacious home had known gracious living, but now a large bunker loomed in the front yard and gave indications that the Japanese had recently abandoned it.

After checking out the bunker, the group took shelter there while the ordnance team searched the house for hidden bombs. When the "all clear" was given, everyone moved in, and General Pierson radioed General Swing their location.

As daylight faded into darkness, enemy shelling increased,

and the command group had to seek shelter again in the bunker.

When Japanese firing tapered off, Major Magagieu and his traffic control section set up lighted markers down the road and in front of the house to guide General Swing, who would be arriving later in the evening.

It was now dark, and General Swing's driver, reputed to be a bit of a hot rodder, did not discern the significance of the lights indicating the new headquarters. He drove on past toward Manila and onto the Paranaque Bridge. There were Japanese on the other side, and the bridge was partially destroyed.

The driver made a skillful and swift turnabout on the bridge! Along with General Swing in that jeep were Quandt, Oliver, Lopez, and the driver, DeBacca.

"Hopping mad and grim," General Swing finally arrived back at the Forward Command Post and "chewed out" General Pierson, Colonel McGowan, and Major Magagieu for not having marked the house more clearly. However, the men responsible felt it had been done adequately.

General Swing calmed down when McGowan told him that Colonel Schimmelpfennig, Chief of Staff, graduate of West Point, and a Rhodes scholar, had been killed late that afternoon by a Japanese sniper. Col. A. N. Williams replaced him as Chief of Staff, with the following as his Assistant Chiefs:

Lt. Col. Glenn McGowan . . . . .G-1 Personnel
Lt. Col. Henry Muller .G-2 Intelligence
Lt. Col. Doug Quandt . . . . .G-3 Operations
Lt. Roy Stout . . . . .G-4 Supply

As each officer settled into his assigned space and work in this Forward Command Post, often referred to as Division Headquarters, the air was filled with questions, problems, and secret plans to rescue the more than two thousand prisoners from Los Banos Internment Camp before it became too late. Their decisions could mean life or death for us.

Lt. Col. Henry Muller, later to become a general, describes how he ferreted out significant intelligence:

"Col. Quentin Gellidon had been the administrator for large estates in Luzon and was highly respected by the guerrillas. He was like an elder statesman to them, and they would listen to him because of his prestige. Quentin stayed with me and kept me informed about the information guerrillas were bringing regarding the Los Banos Camp.

"When we were in Paranaque outside Manila, there were so many guerrillas coming in with information we had to set up a special section.

"In charge of this activity was Major Vanderpool, who had served with the guerrillas and knew them well. He was good at discerning those who were really telling the truth. Some Filipinos came in to give information they didn't truly have, just to show their friendship and helpfulness, and maybe get some rations, but most of them had information that was useful.

"We had to be very careful. Colonel Gellidon and Major Vanderpool, with the help of some of our Counter Intelligence people, interrogated the guerrillas, sorting the wheat from the chaff.

"We heard reports that the Los Banos prison camp had now become a serious matter. The prisoners were reaching the point where they were dying of starvation and would not be able to last much longer.

"Vanderpool and others began to caution me, 'This is now getting very serious.'

"They also told me, 'We are in touch with several of them. It is not hard getting in and out of the camp, and some want to come talk with you.'

"I kept saying, 'We've got to be careful. We have no units to send in there now.'

"I was absolutely convinced that if the Japanese were tipped off to our making a raid on the camp, they would execute all the prisoners, possibly turning their machine guns on them. We knew that from what they did in Palawan, and from the be-

havior of their naval troops in Manila, where they killed many
thousands of innocent Filipinos senselessly and brutally. The
massacre of the Los Banos internees was a real possibility.

"Why would they spare these Americans at Los Banos and
kill the ones in Palawan?

"Among the official records is this statement, possibly origi-
nating with Gen. Masaharu Homma, the Commander of all
Japanese forces in the Philippines, and passed on by General
Fujishige:

Kill all American soldiers brutally.
Do not kill with one stroke.
[Signed] Masatoshi Fujishige

"This man, General Fujishige, was the officer in charge of
from eight to ten thousand Japanese soldiers located two hours
of marching time from the Los Banos Internment Camp.

"We had to get the prisoners out of Los Banos to prevent
their being massacred, and we had to do it as soon as possible.

"Although we did not have the authority to accomplish it at
that time, I figured the only way we could rescue them would
be a parachute jump. We sent the reconnaissance platoon over
there to scout things out, the men creeping through the tall
grass at night and getting close enough to size things up.

"As the reports became grim, I told General Swing, 'It's getting much worse, and I don't know that we can wait. All reports
indicate that the number of deaths from starvation is increas-
ing rapidly.'

"General Swing was sympathetic, but at that time we were
involved in heavy military action, with virtually the last man
committed either on Nichols Field or at Fort McKinley.

"As soon as our forces had taken Nichols Field, General
MacArthur and General Swing met there. Among other matters, Swing is quoted as having told MacArthur, 'Things are
getting pretty grave at Los Banos. I'm getting these reports that
the situation is becoming very, very serious down there.' "

When asked later what kind of an order General MacArthur gave him about Los Banos, Swing replied, "Well, it wasn't exactly an order. I know General MacArthur pretty well, and he said: 'I wish you'd go down to Los Banos, Joe, and get those people out of there as soon as possible. . .but do it right.' "

Gen. Joe Swing was a commander of the highest order, and whatever he undertook, he did it right.

Colonel Muller commented, "It does not suggest a lack of confidence in Swing, but rather MacArthur's awareness that our Division had very little to spare and might be tempted to try the operation without adequate means. I always interpreted MacArthur's 'Do it right' remark as authority for us to divert temporarily troops employed on official operations directed by Sixth Army and XIV Corps."

The following message was sent by General MacArthur and handed to the duty officer, Col. Glenn McGowan, on February 12, 1945, at the Division's Forward Command Post:

TAKE THE NECESSARY ACTION TO LIBERATE LOS BANOS INTERNMENT CAMP SOONEST. SCAP [Supreme Commander Allied Powers]

And there, at the Forward Command Post in the house by Manila Bay, the rescue was being planned with infinite attention to details, human compassion, and the finest of military expertise.

Colonel Muller reveals some of the sources from which he gleaned vital information necessary for our rescue:

"We had photographs and a wealth of information from the Filipino guerrillas. We knew the location and movement of the Japanese troops on southern Luzon.

"The Japanese used Filipinos to dig in for them and bring supplies, and these guerrillas could tell us where their artillery pieces in southern Luzon were emplaced. When we received artillery fire in that area, we knew in advance where the gun was located. The guerrillas were a gold mine of intelligence.

"The first day of our operation in Luzon we captured the Japanese sergeant who was in charge of delivering supplies to all the artillery units in southern Luzon, and he spotted each one of them on our maps. The guerrillas verified as true everything he said.

"When Japanese soldiers were captured, they felt everything was lost, including their honor, and gave us all the information we wanted. They had been told that we would kill them. When, instead, we treated them humanely, they seemed to feel morally obligated to cooperate with us.

"But we had to be cautious. If any word of the intended rescue reached the Japanese, there was a danger that all the prisoners at Los Banos would be executed."

The Japanese in Manila were massacring over a hundred thousand innocent civilian Filipinos, burning hospitals after tying the patients in their beds, gouging eyeballs out of babies, and destroying Manila as they fought fanatically.

What would they do to the men, women, and children of the enemy that was defeating them? Those in Santo Tomas Internment Camp had been snatched from the Japanese by the First Cavalry, but the Japanese could still vent their wrath on the prisoners they held at Los Banos.

The order to rescue us had been given, but the "how" and "when" presented problems mountain high.

In the midst of war, humanitarian causes may be included but do not usually supersede vital, strategic warfare. We were located in an out-of-the-way area of no military value, some distance behind enemy lines. Troops to rescue us would have to be taken from the important and fierce fighting with Japanese at Fort McKinley.

The cost of possible delayed victory in that battle had to be weighed against the probable soon execution of about 2,146 men, women, and children at Los Banos. It would be a mission of pure compassion balanced against vital warfare.

Every passing day heightened the danger of the prisoners' being massacred, while increasingly more of them were dying of starvation and disease.

The rescue operation needed to be a quick, dangerous, in-and-out raid twenty-five miles behind Japanese lines. If that could be successfully accomplished, how could more than two thousand sick and weak prisoners be transported to safety through enemy lines?

CHAPTER 28
Led by Fireflies
Los Banos Internment Camp
February 10, 1945

WE AWAKENED ON THE MORNING of February 10 with no lights, no drinking water, and almost no food. Everything in camp seemed to be getting worse.

Night after night we were in total darkness, with nothing to light our way down the long aisle of the barracks to the makeshift bathroom.

One night while walking along that dark aisle, I heard footsteps following me. They were measured, deliberate steps. When I stopped, they stopped. When I started walking again, they followed. Fearing it might be a Japanese guard, I became frightened and yelled out, "Who's there?"

"It's just me, dear," came back a frail little woman's voice. "I'm trying to get to the bathroom and can't find my way, so I'm following you."

Our barracks held ninety-six beds, divided down the center by that long aisle. Midway, another aisle led to our bathroom that also served an adjoining barracks. Once you left your bed at night, it could be difficult enough to find the bathroom, but getting back to your own bed was like going through a maze blindfolded.

More than once a scream would rend the night air as someone started getting into the wrong bed, and the occupant would not know the identity of the intruder—a friendly internee or Japanese guard?

If you felt around a bed to make sure it was yours, you might run your hand across someone's face and scare her half to death.

Since I slept in the only upper-decker, no one climbed into mine, but I had to feel the corners of a number of beds before I found one that had posts on it reaching upward. Then I moved cautiously, so as not to step on Ruth's arm, leg, or face as I climbed up in the dark.

The whole situation did not contribute to restful nights after daytimes of stress.

One evening when we were outside studying the stars of the southern hemisphere, fireflies were flitting here and there. While watching them, someone poetically remarked, "Fireflies in the night could guide us through our barracks' aisle when all is dark."

After collecting a few small, clear bottles, we put a couple of fireflies in each one. Placed in key positions along the aisles, their little lights indicated the way for us in the darkness.

Thinking there was enough oxygen in the bottles, we did not let the fireflies go the next day, and they expired. We all felt deeply sorry about that. As a result, every evening we were like ballet dancers in the moonlight, catching fireflies. Then each morning we set them free to preserve their lives, and to say thank you.

But in the coming weeks we needed more than fireflies to light up our lives as the whole situation in camp deteriorated.

CHAPTER 29
Rescue by Guerrillas?
Los Banos Internment Camp
February 12, 1945

FREDDY ZERVOULAKOS slipped out of camp through our hidden passage during the night of February 12 on a short foraging excursion. He brought back with him the excitement of newly minted Philippine coins, fresh American cigarettes, and other items that could have been obtained only from the United States Armed Forces. But of even more importance, he carried a letter vital to our survival.

It came from an American officer, Maj. Jay Vanderpool, who served as a liaison with the Filipino guerrillas. The letter contained instructions for Colonel Ingles of a local guerrilla unit to take steps toward liberating our camp.

Using a radio and transmitter, Ingles would report enemy concentrations near Los Banos, guerrilla strength in the area, and conditions in the internment camp. The letter concluded with an order to call for reinforcements or to attack and release the camp with aid from the guerrillas.

At dawn Freddy showed the letter to Peter Miles and Benjamin Edwards. They took it to the secretary of our Administration Committee, George Gray.

Because it contained matter vital to our survival, Mr. Gray and Freddy slipped through the camp's hidden passage on the

night of February 14 and went to the nearby home of the Espinos. There they met Col. Gustavo Ingles of the ROTC guerrilla group known as "Terry's Hunters."

Ingles suggested that guns be smuggled into our camp.
George Gray told him that under International Law a civilian
internment camp could take no part in the actual hostilities,
and he explained the danger to us prisoners if an attack were
made on the guardhouses and living quarters of the Japanese.

The following information was given to Colonel Ingles ver-
bally:

1. A description of the camp
2. Condition of the internees
3. Locations of guardhouses
4. Locations of Japanese living quarters
5. Approximate strength of the Japanese garrison and their
    equipment

Mr. Gray then warned Ingles that the health of the prisoners
was very low. He asked that such a plan be carried through
only if ordered by and with the assistance of the United States
Army.

Colonel Ingles made an appointment to meet Mr. Gray
again.

A special meeting of our Administration Committee was
called and details of the negotiations with Colonel Ingles were
outlined. It was agreed that the rescue of the camp must be
left in the hands of the American forces.

Mr. Gray slipped out of camp through the hidden passage
for the planned rendezvous with the colonel, but Ingles did not
arrive. Instead, a message awaited George Gray that the guerrilla attack on the internment camp had been postponed.

After much discussion between Gray and our three brave
young men, it was decided that Benjamin Edwards, Freddy
Zervoulakos, and Prentice Miles (Pete) would escape in order
to give the guerrillas and our American army information on

the conditions of the internees, reporting that at least one a day was dying of starvation and related diseases, while many others were now past medical aid. The men were also to carry important information regarding the camp's layout, routines of the Japanese soldiers, and other details pertinent to the rescue of the camp.

CHAPTER 30
Obey or Be Shot
Los Banos Internment Camp
February 14, 1945

AN OCCASIONAL AMERICAN PLANE on surveillance now flew over our camp, sometimes quite low and dipping its wings to us, while we responded by waving and cheering. This did not please our captors and resulted in their requesting our Administration Committee to remind us that the following rules would be enforced, violators to be shot:

NOTICE TO MONITOR AND FOR POSTING
Lieutenant Kasene of the Japanese Garrison has ordered that the Camp be again reminded of the following rules and regulations:

1. No one is permitted to leave the area adjacent to his barrack after 7:00 P.M. except on Wednesday and Sunday when the period is extended to 7:30 P.M. All traffic (walking)—even crossing of roads between barracks is forbidden. *Hereafter anyone found disobeying this regulation is subject to being shot.*

2. No demonstration of any description (including congregating in groups) when firing is heard in the vicinity of the Camp or planes are seen or heard is permitted. Infractions of this rule will be severely punished by the Military in future.

3. Strict compliance with the rules governing Air Raid

Alarms is demanded. As every one knows this means aimless walking around the Camp is not permitted and that there is to be no walking on the roads at any time. Unless going to or from a Camp detail no one is to go outside his barrack area. *When going to work everyone is to pass only through barracks.* Infractions of this rule will be punished by the Military.

4. Internees not showing proper respect and courtesy to the Military will be severely dealt with in future.

5. The Philco radio formerly belonging to the garrison is still missing. The lieutenant again asks that the Camp be requested the early return of this radio.

The Committee earnestly urges every internee to comply strictly with the above rules so as to avoid further unfortunate incidents.

The Committee earnestly urges every internee to comply strictly with the above rules so as to avoid further unfortunate incidents.

ADMINISTRATION COMMITTEE

From this time on, we did not dare go outside and wave when American surveillance planes flew over our camp. When the pilots no longer saw a living person when flying over us, there was some concern, until they heard otherwise, that the Japanese might already have massacred us.

Enforcement of this "Obey or Be Shot" rule made the pending escape of Ben, Freddy, and Pete more dangerous.

CHAPTER 31
Chosen for the Challenge
Sunday, February 18, 1945

YELLOW WITH JAUNDICE and his arm in a sling, Col. Edward Lahti walked into General Swing's office at the Command Post. A battle casualty, Lahti did not appear in an ideal condition for making vital military decisions. General Swing soon determined, however, that Ed Lahti's mind and judgment were as sharp as ever.

On his part, Lahti wondered what could be so important that Colonel McGowan had called him away from his regiment now engaged in heavy battle at Fort McKinley, and why Colonel Quandt was taking him into the general's office.

When the 511th Parachute Infantry Regiment (PIR) flew in from Leyte and jumped on Tagaytay Ridge February 3, it was under the command of Col. Orin D. Haugen. After the lightning advance of thirty-two miles to southern Manila and while fighting through heavy defenses there, Haugen had been mortally wounded on February 11 and died on the airplane evacuating him.

General Swing then placed Colonel Lahti in command of that regiment of brave young paratroopers. Thirty-one years old, Lahti had been their Regimental Executive Officer since early January, commanding the Third Battalion of the 511th PIR through the Leyte campaign.

Five days after Colonel Haugen died, Lahti received an eight-inch shrapnel wound. He let the medics sew it up with twenty-six stitches, but he refused their offer to evacuate him. After a few hours he returned to his command of the regiment, which was engaged in battle.

The next day Lahti developed yellow jaundice but refused evacuation to a field hospital and continued with his responsibilities.

Now General Swing informed Lahti of crucial decisions that had to be made in rescuing over two thousand men, women, and children from Los Banos Internment Camp, about twenty-five miles behind Japanese lines.

The regiment had suffered severe losses in less than three weeks of combat in and near Manila. Many companies were now reduced to less than 50 percent of their normal number. Who should be selected for this vital mission?

Looking over the Company rosters, Lahti noted that B Company had the most men left. In addition to that, Lt. John Ringler was the commander. He had been in Lahti's Third Battalion all through training, and the colonel knew Ringler was not only an excellent officer but a real leader of men. For these reasons, Lahti made the wise decision to select B Company of the First Battalion for parachuting onto Los Banos Internment Camp.

Realizing the men of B Company should have more support, Lahti directed that a Machine Gun Platoon and a Mortar Platoon be attached to them. This increased the strength of B Company to more than 130 men.

To maintain unity of command, it then followed that while B Company was jumping onto the camp, the rest of the First Battalion would be approaching from the shores of the lake called Laguna de Bay in tractors of the 672nd Amphibious Tractor Battalion, carrying more than four hundred troops.

The whole rescue operation would be under command of the Operation Officer, Col. Robert Soule, who would be proceeding toward Los Banos with the First Battalion of the 188th Glider Infantry Regiment in trucks that could be used as a means for evacuating the rescued prisoners.

After this important meeting of the strategists, the First Battalion was detached from the 511th and put under the command of Colonel Soule.

Colonel Lahti's next responsibility was providing for the security of New Bilibid Prison, where the liberated internees were to be housed, protected, fed, and cared for medically after the rescue and until arrangements could be made for their safe departure.

When Maj. Henry Burgess reported to Division Headquarters, he had no idea of the news awaiting him.

What could be the cause for such a strange order? wondered Major Burgess and the soldiers under his command.

In the midst of their battling the Japanese near Fort McKinley, Col. Ed Lahti had just given him orders to withdraw his First Battalion of the 511th Parachute Infantry Regiment from the fighting "to rest" near Manila! Then Lahti told Burgess to report in person at Division Headquarters.

A twenty-six-year-old major and graduate of Harvard, Henry Burgess had military skill and acumen that had drawn General Swing's attention through training and combat, winning his respect.

Now at Headquarters, General Muller and Colonel Quandt explained to him that their Division would be liberating more than two thousand civilian prisoners of war in Los Banos Internment Camp, located twenty-five miles behind Japanese lines. He would be the commanding officer of the troops engaged in the actual rescue during the raid, under the overall command of Col. Robert Soule of the 188th Glider Infantry Regiment.

In rescuing the imprisoned men, women, and children, who were weak from disease and starvation, Burgess's troops would be greatly outnumbered by the Japanese soldiers.

"I was nervous and excited about the risks," commented Burgess, "and my adrenaline began flowing because of the nature of the raid and the fighting we were sure to encounter."

"Why us?" he questioned.

Burgess had proven himself to be an excellent combat commander and had confidence in his men, whom he described: "The Eleventh Airborne Division was tough both physically and mentally. Every man could march at least four miles an hour in the heat of the tropics; it could deploy its companies, battalions, and regiments very quickly and attack in much less time than the ordinary unit.

"Even under enemy fire, the Division's riflemen, machine gunners, and mortar men would stand and shoot, attack and fire. Its artillery was agile and quick to support the infantry."

Based on the First Battalion's past performance in combat, and because its numerical strength of 412 men made it the strongest in the Division, Colonel Lahti had recommended it, and General Swing approved it. Two other reasons were Maj. Henry Burgess himself and Lt. John Ringler, real leaders of men.

What kind of an officer was this General Swing upon whose shoulders rested whether we would live or die?

CHAPTER 32
Portrait of General Swing

GENERAL SWING KNEW WELL the soldiers under his command, when to be tough and when tender, for he himself had developed them from bewildered kids in their teens to the crack Eleventh Airborne Division.

"Swing ran a tight ship," would be the approving comment of my crusty father, who years ago had captained tall, three-masted sailing ships and had become an officer in our navy.

When my two brothers and I were young and sometimes naughty, we were unaware of the half-hidden twinkle in his eyes as Dad would bark out an order, "Front and center here, or I'll lay you out with a belaying pin!" (a metal bar on a sailing ship).

General Swing's orders could be equally strong but had more finesse. He put his troops through arduous drilling, allowed for no slack in training or performance, and could outmarch any of them. He expected the best from his men, and that is what they gave him.

A close personal friend and classmate of General Eisenhower at West Point, General Swing was cultured and handsome, a dedicated and brilliant leader of men, but he could shout

out orders in a way that would surpass my father's in the rugged sailing ship years. His troops admired and respected him.

Henry Burgess relates a rare instance when General Swing won the hearts of his men by revealing tender sensitivity:

"When we were on the beach in Leyte, loading onto landing craft headed for Mindoro and the jump on Luzon Island, General Swing came down. I was in charge of the Battalion, and he asked, 'Does everyone have a jungle sweater?'

" 'Yes, sir,' I replied.

"Walking up to the first man, he said, 'Let me see your jungle sweater.'

"The young men replied, 'I don't have one.'

"I was horrified and suggested that he stand up when the general spoke to him. But when the soldier stood up, it became obvious something was wrong.

"'What's the matter with you?' questioned General Swing.

" 'I was wounded, hospitalized, heard about this operation, and went AWOL (absent without leave) to take part in it, and I don't have a jungle sweater or a gun.'

"General Swing had a sweater and gun in his jeep. He went over, picked them up, and gave him his own sweater and rifle. Swing always had an automatic rifle also in his jeep.

"Don't get the idea that the Old Man wouldn't fry you, but he had a great compassion for people."

Burgess describes him: "Swing was six feet tall. And although I measured six feet and one-half inch, when he approached me, Swing looked to be about six feet two or three inches, though when we were eyeball to eyeball, I was physically a little bit taller."

Because of what he himself was, Swing developed a division of paratroopers and glider troops with a superb esprit de corps, proud, brave, and loyal. And they had discipline, a quality General Swing required of all his paratroopers.

These were the men who would be sent into battle to set us free.

Using his fine military expertise, General Swing now worked with Colonels Quandt of Operations and Muller of Intelligence on a plan for our rescue. Pressured by the need for utmost secrecy and the urgency of time running out for us at Los Banos, these top-quality officers discussed it with Major Burgess, who would become the commanding officer of the troops behind the lines during the raid.

Carefully studying the military maneuvers necessary to save us from the guns of our captors, the officers knew they did not yet have all the answers necessary to ensure a safe rescue. They needed more information about the layout of the camp, the force of the Japanese garrison guarding us, and the type, range, and placement of their guns. How could they obtain all that?

Death by starvation and rumors of possible massacre by the Japanese were now threatening the prisoners. They must be rescued without delay.

CHAPTER 33
Hidden Passage
Los Banos Internment Camp
February 18, 1945

ABOUT NINE O'CLOCK on the night of February 18, Ben, Freddy, and Pete left the barracks closest to the hospital—number eleven. Aware that they could be shot for being out of their barracks after curfew, Pete feigned illness. The other men took a lighted lantern and helped walk him to the hospital.

Arriving there safely, the men abandoned the lamp and escaped through our hidden passage, a place where the men slipped under the two barbed wire fences that passed close to a back corner of the hospital, enabling them to descend into a deep ravine running close to that same hospital corner.

Ben Edwards tells what happened on their secret journey, a continued, dangerous, hidden passage to help save our lives:

"Once under the fences, we descended into a jungle-like gully about forty to fifty feet deep, at the bottom of which I bumped a tin can. The noise seemed very loud to us. As we were well within hearing distance of the main Japanese guardhouse, we remained motionless for a few minutes that seemed to us like hours. When there was no indication that any of the guards had heard, we continued down the gully about six or eight hundred feet, where several armed guerrillas were waiting for us by arrangements previously made.

"These Filipino guerrillas had orders to take us to their colonel at Barrio Tranca. We traveled alongside railroad tracks and on paths through coconut plantations.

"Stopping at a small *nipa* hut, the guerrillas awakened a middle-aged woman, who became very frightened. While being questioned about Japanese activity in the area, she noticed the three of us and said, 'Americanos!' The relief in the tone of her voice and look in her eyes, even in the shadowy light of a coconut oil lamp, left no doubt as to where her loyalties lay.

"Arriving at Barrio Tranca about 11:00 P.M., we met Colonel Price of President Quezon's Own Guerrillas. 'Price' was an alias used by Espino, at whose home near the camp George Gray had conferred with Ingles.

"As we were talking, an American GI walked into camp. My first reaction was, 'A German!' I had not seen the new American helmets, and his reminded me of the coal-bucket type used by the Germans. He turned out to be Sgt. John Fulton of the 511th Signal Company. He had volunteered to accompany Ingles and was staying behind Japanese lines to provide communications between the American forces and the guerrillas.

"We had decided that Pete Miles would go to the 11th Airborne Headquarters just south of Manila, and that Freddy and I would proceed to a guerrilla stronghold at Barrio Nanhaya.

"Pete would send a messenger there to let us know that he had arrived at his destination. If no message was received from Pete after a reasonable time, I would then attempt to reach the 11th Airborne Headquarters. Then if no message came from me, Freddy would try to get through to the 11th Airborne.

"Leaving about one thirty in the morning on February 19, we headed for the lake called Laguna de Bay, led by a group of guerrillas. In the words of old farmers, the night seemed 'as black as the inside of a cow.'

"When we had to wade through a shallow creek, I took off my shoes to keep them dry. While I was doing this, those behind me moved on ahead and I became the last in line. After crossing the creek I could not stop to put on my shoes because I would lose sight of the man in front of me and become lost from the group. I had to continue uncomfortably barefooted for some distance. When we were approaching the rice fields adjacent to the National Highway, the leader stopped to reconnoiter the open area, and I put my shoes back on again.

"As soon as it was deemed safe, we continued towards Laguna de Bay, arriving at the lake about dawn. The guerrillas 'commandeered' two sailing *bancas*, but when the Filipino fishermen saw Americans in the group, they were not at all reluctant to let us take their boats.

"While the *bancas* were being prepared, Pete, Freddy, and I had a couple of minutes to clean up, as we were covered with mud from head to foot. When coming through the rice fields, we had trouble walking on the narrow mud dikes that separated them, and we were constantly slipping into the muddy rice paddies, much to the amusement of our guides.

"Soon Pete was in a *banca* heading for the 11th Airborne Headquarters while Freddy and I sailed toward Nanhaya.

"I fell asleep in the boat but was awakened by several shots and something hot hitting my neck. One of the guerrillas, a lad of about fourteen, had shot at a wild duck, and an ejected carbine shell casing struck me on the neck. I was relieved but a bit angry, feeling that the shots might attract unwanted attention. Fortunately, they did not.

"Arriving at Nanhaya in the afternoon of the 19th, we were taken to Col. Abdinago Ortiz of the Marking Fil-American Guerrillas. After we had related to him the events of the previous night, he assured us that if a message arrived from Pete, he would see that we received it. Colonel Ortiz was later to become head of the Palace Security for President Carlos Garcia.

"The Filipinos brought us food—fried duck eggs, fish, pork, and boiled rice that had been warmed in a skillet with coconut oil. The food was placed on banana leaves and looked and tasted delicious. A picnic on the beach had never been and probably never will be more welcome. We had not realized how hungry we were until the excitement of the escape and subsequent experiences were over.

"During the early morning hours of February 20, a Filipino boatman arrived and told us that Pete Miles had reached American territory. We correctly assumed that Pete was safely at General Swing's headquarters. It now seemed possible to relax a little, as much as feasible with only a thin line of guerrillas between us and the Japanese army."

CHAPTER 34
Pete Brings the Key
Division Headquarters
February 19, 1945

PETE'S ESCAPE from our camp and safe arrival at Division Headquarters became an answer to hundreds, maybe thousands, of prayers.

While planning just how to rescue us safely, the General Staff of the Eleventh Airborne's Forward Command Group was finding it difficult to coordinate all the action and get everything organized.

Just then Pete Miles walked in and handed them the key.

Colonel Muller commented, "Pete became the key to the whole operation. He provided us with a great deal of essential information about the camp. As an engineer, he was able to sketch it out accurately on paper. Pete gave us:

1. Location of camouflaged Japanese machine guns
2. Types of guns used and fields of fire
3. Location of guards' barracks
4. Location of men, women, and children prisoners in various barracks
5. Routine of activities in the camp
6. Daily schedule of the guards rigidly followed

"Then Pete revealed the single most important factor, which became the key to the whole rescue.

"Between 6:45 and 7:15 each morning the guards off duty took their morning calisthenics, having their guns locked in a gun rack in the guards' barracks. Pete not only indicated the location of those barracks, but even showed us at which end of the barracks the gun racks were placed.

"The information this brave young man gave us proved of inestimable value. We set the time for rescuing the prisoners at 7:00 A.M., in the middle of the guards' calisthenics."

The rigidity of the Japanese in keeping to this daily schedule of exercises became their vulnerable point. We had located their "Achilles' heel."

"When the Japanese soldier has a coordinated plan of attack, he works smoothly," commented General MacArthur. "When he is attacked—when he doesn't know what is coming —it isn't the same."

Events now moved swiftly in preparation and with utmost secrecy.

Major Burgess absorbed every scrap of information Pete could provide, along with valuable input from Lieutenant Skau of the Reconnaissance Platoon, who had been scouting out the terrain behind Japanese lines.

With Colonel Quandt of Operations and Colonel Muller of the Intelligence section, Burgess examined aerial photos taken by planes that had been flying over the Los Banos Internment Camp, studied the road network, bridges or lack of them, and location of the nearly ten thousand soldiers about eight miles from our camp.

Burgess describes the complicated and dangerous situation, extreme urgency and utmost secrecy being vitally necessary to the saving of our lives:

"An all-out, direct attack on the camp would result in the total massacre of the prisoners. There had to be a long approach march made in secret behind the Japanese lines and capture of the entire camp, which covered sixty acres. The following action would need to be taken to rescue the imprisoned people alive:

"1. *Destroy* immediately all of the Japanese guards on duty and the off-duty garrison, a total force consisting of some two hundred and fifty soldiers who were believed to be veterans with considerable fighting experience and who had been wounded and assigned to guard duty.

"2. *Neutralize* other Japanese troops in the vicinity of the camp, estimated at from two to three hundred men.

"3. *Neutralize* an additional force of from two to three hundred men in the quarry at Los Banos and at an outpost at Mayondon Point.

"4. *Delay* elements of the Japanese Eighth Division of some ten thousand men which might move on the camp from its positions eight miles from the camp.

"5. *Direct* all firing in the attack upon the camp in such a direction that the prisoners would not be shot.

"6. *Evacuate* the prisoners immediately as the ten thousand Japanese troops in the Eighth Division were within about two hours of marching time.

"The prisoners were of all ages and physically weak from inadequate nutrition. Many were nonambulatory and suffering from beriberi and various fevers. Evacuation meant transporting them. How? By truck, by water, or both? They could not walk.

"Neutralization of Japanese troops near the camp was a nightmare to contemplate. How many troops were in the area? How good were they? Did they have tanks? Artillery?

"How did one keep them at bay and out of firing range for one hour? For five hours? The situation encompassed a sector twenty-five miles long and ten miles wide.

"How alert and well trained were the prison guards?

Carol in 1940 at her graduation from Biola, a year and four months before sailing for India. Photo from Biola yearbook, *The Biolan*.

Carol in 1946. One year after being rescued from Los Banos Internment Camp, Carol still shows signs of those prison years.
Photo from Biola yearbook, *The Biolan*.

Anna Nixon, Carol, and Marion Childress, cabin mates on the ship, enjoy a stop at Honolulu.

Under "house arrest," Mrs. Paget stirs a pot of soup while I blow on the embers to keep them burning.

The oath we did not sign. English translation appears in Chapter 4, "Surrender or Be Shot."

宣誓

昭和　年　月　日

比島軍抑留所長殿

私儀如何ナル場合ニ於テモ

逃走及策動セザルコトヲ

宣誓ス

To Charming Miss Shay
With best love
[signature]

Celing waded in water almost to her hips during a storm to secure food for me.

Front page of Manila *Tribune*, a Japanese-controlled newspaper. Headlines were designed to cover up their defeats.

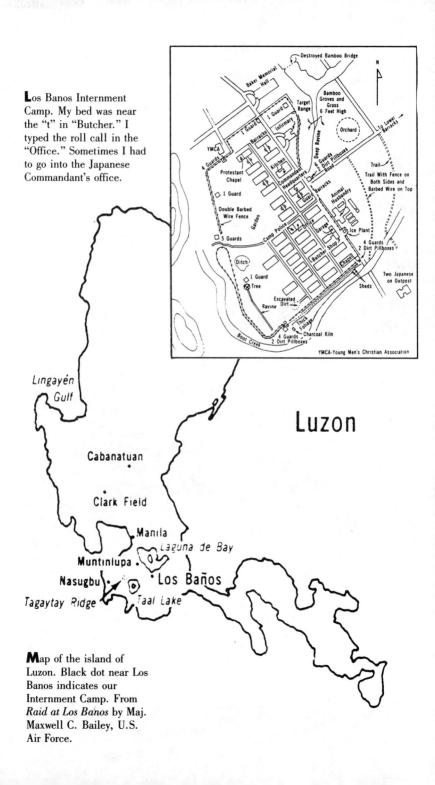

Los Banos Internment Camp. My bed was near the "t" in "Butcher." I typed the roll call in the "Office." Sometimes I had to go into the Japanese Commandant's office.

Map of the island of Luzon. Black dot near Los Banos indicates our Internment Camp. From *Raid at Los Banos* by Maj. Maxwell C. Bailey, U.S. Air Force.

Using hot-water foments, a nurse soaked the crusts off my impetigo sores while I sat on a box in isolation.

Our cubicle. Edible weeds are growing in coconut shells. The "cots," which we were told to bring with us, are for: 1. Evelyn; 2. Mona; 3. Ruth; 4. Elda; 5. Blanche; 6. Carol.

"Keep off the weeds; we eat them." I buried my diary in a talinum patch like this by our barrack.

The camp dining tables. Since it rained a great deal, we would have to eat with one hand and hold an umbrella with the other—if we had an umbrella. Later these tables were cut up to make coffins for those who died of beriberi, starvation, and related diseases or were executed by our guards.

Our twenty-eight barracks were mostly in three rows, with bathroom areas and covered walkways between the barracks, which were farther apart than they appear in this drawing. One tin can on post: Ready to be on the alert. Two tin cans: Alert. Three tin cans: Air raid. Mount Maquiling in the background.

A graduate of West Point Military Academy, Lt. Col. Henry J. Muller later became a brigadier general.

Filipino guerrilla leader Gustavo Ingles with Col. David Blackledge, who was a young boy in the Los Banos Internment Camp.

The Stars and Stripes fly over Santo Tomás Internment Camp in Manila when the 1st Cavalry liberates the internees, February 6, 1945.
U.S. Army Photo

Years after the war, when Jim Holzem returns to Manila, he is greeted by "Oscar."

Maj. Gen. (later Lt. Gen.) Joseph M. Swing,
Commanding General of the 11th Airborne Division.
The responsibility for our rescue was given to him by
General MacArthur. Swing was sometimes called
"the Patton of the Philippines."
Photo kindness of Lt. Col. Glenn McGowan

Four members of General Swing's staff who were
involved in planning our rescue from Los Banos.
From left to right: Lt. Col. Glenn McGowan G-1,
Personnel and Administration; Lt. Col. Roy Stout
G-4, Supply and Logistics; Lt. Col. Henry Muller
G-2, Intelligence; Lt. Col. Douglas Quandt G-3,
Operations.
Photo kindness of Lt. Col. Glenn McGowan

Benjamin Edwards.

Prentice (Pete) Miles.

Lt. Gen. Masatoshi Fujishige. "Kill all American soldiers brutally; do not kill with one stroke. Kill all Filipinos who oppose our Emperor."

From left to right: Gen. Joseph W. Stilwell, CG, Army Ground Forces; Lt. Gen. Oscar W. Griswald, CG, XIV Corps; and Maj. Gen. Joseph W. Swing, CG, 11th Airborne Division.

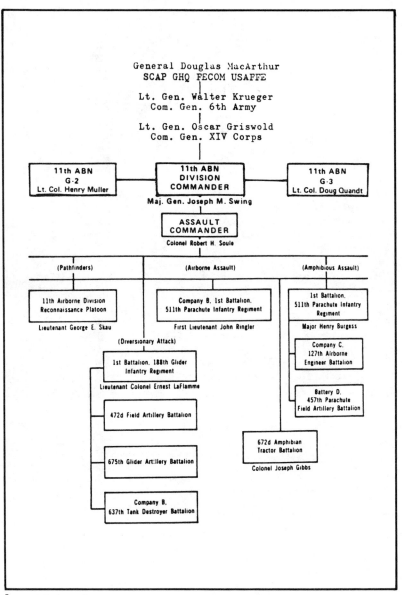

General Douglas MacArthur
SCAP GHQ FECOM USAFFE

Lt. Gen. Walter Krueger
Com. Gen. 6th Army

Lt. Gen. Oscar Griswold
Com. Gen. XIV Corps

| 11th ABN G-2 Lt. Col. Henry Muller | 11th ABN DIVISION COMMANDER | 11th ABN G-3 Lt. Col. Doug Quandt |

Maj. Gen. Joseph M. Swing

ASSAULT COMMANDER

Colonel Robert H. Soule

(Pathfinders)   (Airborne Assault)   (Amphibious Assault)

11th Airborne Division Reconnaissance Platoon

Lieutenant George E. Skau

Company B, 1st Battalion, 511th Parachute Infantry Regiment

First Lieutenant John Ringler

1st Battalion, 511th Parachute Infantry Regiment

Major Henry Burgess

(Diversionary Attack)

1st Battalion, 188th Glider Infantry Regiment

Lieutenant Colonel Ernest LaFlamme

472d Field Artillery Battalion

675th Glider Artillery Battalion

Company B, 637th Tank Destroyer Battalion

Company C. 127th Airborne Engineer Battalion

Battery D. 457th Parachute Field Artillery Battalion

672d Amphibian Tractor Battalion

Colonel Joseph Gibbs

Line of Command
Chart drawn by George Doherty

1st Lt. (later Col.) John Ringler, commanding officer of the paratroopers who jumped into our camp. He was in command of our rescue until the arrival of Maj. Henry Burgess with the amphibious tractors. (Above)

Radio operator John Fulton, on left, in typical *banca*, where he was hidden in the bottom of the boat in Laguna de Bay. (Top).

Honoring the Filipino guerrillas, Col. Frank Quesada of Terry's Hunters ROTC, Filipino guerrillas who rushed into my barracks during the rescue. (Left)

Maj. Don Anderson, commanding officer of the Air Corps Squadron of nine C-47s carrying the paratroopers to jump on our camp. Don flew the lead plane and stayed over the camp until we were safely removed.

Loren Brown, Reconnaissance Platoon. In later years he was Wing Chaplain, California Wing Civil Air Patrol.

Copy of actual "Operations Map for Release of Los Banos Internees." "Objective" indicated is the Los Banos Internment Camp.

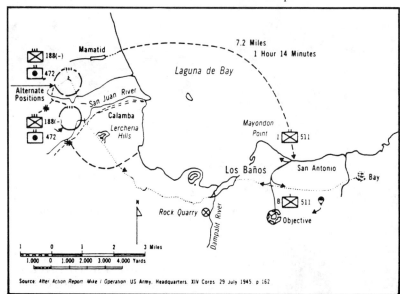

Source: After Action Report Mike I Operation US Army, Headquarters, XIV Corps 29 July 1945 p 162

"**A**ngels with wings of silk." The paratroopers who jumped into our camp were members of B Company of the 1st Battalion, 511th Parachute Infantry of the 11th Airborne Division.

Frank Smith, a newspaper correspondent from the Chicago *Sun Times*, parachuted into camp with our paratroopers. Seeing in the chapel a large pulpit Bible that would be burned in the approaching flames, Smith carried it reverently in his hands on the long walk to the lake.

Filipino guerrilla of the "Terry's Hunters" ROTC group, wearing the group's identifying rooster feather in hat, walking with paratrooper after the rescue.

Former internee Margaret Whitaker Squires returns to Los Banos years later and stands under a landmark still visible— the white, arched gateway to the Animal Husbandry that is visible in a few photographs. Some time after the rescue, Margaret married one of our rescuers—Sgt. Martin Squires, who was in the Reconnaissance Platoon.

The American soldiers set fire to our barracks to get us out of them because we were hiding from flying bullets, and they had no way of telling us we had to get out of there fast. As a barracks burns, you can see how flimsy they were.

Ready to flee with us to the lake, amphibious tractors line up in front of our barracks, waiting for the internees to climb aboard.

Escaping in the amphibious tractors, we approach the American side of the lake.

Safe on the American side, the amphibious tractors with their mounted guns.

At Mamatid, stretcher cases are placed in ambulances. Swelling of face and ankles of man in front indicates beriberi, the same disease with which I was afflicted. Note concern of soldiers caring for ambulance cases. Although not on a stretcher, I was put in an ambulance.

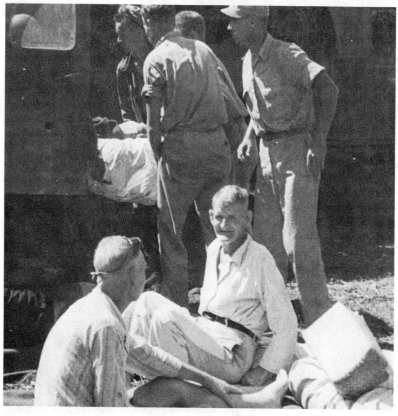

Joy Paget and I were taken in one of these ambulances to new Bilibid Prison, Muntinlupa, for refuge. The high walls, towers, and flags flying reminded me of *Beau Geste* and tales of the French Foreign Legion.

Note how thin our men were. It was felt we could not digest solid food, so while soldiers watch, we are fed our first meal— nourishing soup, ladled out to us from new tin garbage cans.

Lt. Col. (later Brig. Gen.) Henry Muller holds a Japanese saber, while Lt. Col. Glenn McGowan shows a Japanese flag, trophies captured during the rescue at Los Banos Internment Camp.
Photo kindness of Lt. Col. Glenn McGowan.

Peter, Joy, and Cae Paget before their internment by the Japanese.

At our thanksgiving service we took Communion out of gun shells beautifully fashioned into Communion cups.

Eleventh Airborne Division insignia.

Maj. (later Lt. Col.) Thomas Mesereau with Gen. Maxwell Taylor.

The American army dropped large parcels of food to us by colored parachutes at our place of refuge in New Bilibid prison, where we were protected by our army. The color of each parachute indicated a certain type of food.
Photo from National Archives.

Richard Sakakida, America's undercover agent and counterpart to Japan's "Tokyo Rose," was the translator at Earl's trial. After the war, Sakakida spent many years in Japan, continuing undercover work for America. He retired from the U.S. Army as a lieutenant colonel.

THIS IS NOT A CERTIFICATE FOR PURPOSES OF CONFIRMATION OR MARRIAGE

MILITARY ORDINARIATE
462 MADISON AVENUE
NEW YORK 22, N. Y.

BAPTISMAL RECORD

NO. 96308
(RESERVED FOR CHANCERY USE)

PERSON BAPTIZED ___Sadaaki Peter Konishi___ No. 51J104279
    (First Name)   (Middle Name)   (Last Name)   (Serial)

Rank and Unit ___W.O.___ Residence Luzon POW Camp APO 900 c/o PM, S.F., Calif.
    (Post, Station, Ship or APO, if civilian, street address)

Father's Name ___Shogoro Konishi___ Mother's Maiden Name Name Morimatsu
    (First)   (Last)   (First)   (Last)

Date of Birth ___Jan. 19, 1914___ Place of Birth ___Fukuoka-ken Yamegun Kita Kawachi Mura___
    (Month, Day, Year)   (City) #473,

Date of Baptism ___June 17, 1947___ Place of Baptism Luzon POW Camp #1, APO 900 c/o PM, S.F.Cali
    (Month, Day, Year)   (Church or Chapel; City, State)

Godfather ___Kiyoshi Nishikawa___ Godmother 2nd witness not possible

Proxy _____ Proxy _____
    (Duly Appointed by Godfather?)   (Duly Appointed by Godmother?)

If Adults

Previous Religion, if any? ___Buddaist___ Previous Baptism? _____
    (Please specify)   (If baptised: state denomination; date; name and address of church; if not baptised, please indicate.)

Profession of faith and abjuration made? _____ Absolute Baptism? _____
    ("Yes or No")   Conditional Rebaptism? _____

Absolution given in external forum? _____ Without Rebaptism? _____
    (Faculty 16)   (Please specify)

Marital Status:

Single? ☐   (Please check proper square)   If Widowed _____
    (Date of Former Spouse's Death)

Married? ☐
Widowed? ☐   Tokiko Konishi
Divorced? ☐   (Name of Spouse)   If Divorced _____
    (Place of Death—Street, City, State)

Date of Marriage ___Oct. 10, 1944___
    (Month, Day, Year)   (Date of Decree of Divorce or Annulment)

Place of Marriage ___Fukuoka-ken Yamegun, Kita Kawachi, Mura #473___
    (Church or Chapel; City, State)   (Date of Ecclesiastical Annulment)

Officiant at Marriage ___Civil Magistrate___
    (Catholic Priest; Civil Official; Non Catholic Clergyman)   (Court issuing it)

Sacrament of Confirmation _____ First Communion _____
    (Date and Place)   (Date and Place)

Remarks ___Condemned to hang as War Criminal___

        John P. Wallace, C.SS.R.
        (Signature of Officiating Priest)

    Hq. Camp Batangas, APO 1009 c/o PM
    San Francisco, Calif.
    (Residence Complete Mailing Address)

(margin, left side, vertical) (RESERVED FOR CHANCERY USE)   Acknowledged JUL 7 1947   Indexed JUL 7 1947   Approved for filing JUL 28 1947

Baptismal record of our "camp villain," Sadaaki (Peter) Konishi, who said he wanted to become a Christian before being executed and took the name of "Peter." The only surviving Japanese guard from our Los Banos Internment Camp is Daikichi Okamoto. Mr. Okamoto has identified this Konishi as the guard in our camp by means of his place of birth and graduation from the Yame Middle School. Mr. Okamoto also stated (and his own wording and spelling are preserved), Konishi "was one of the officer who is always against to my suggestion all the time. That is the reason I personally have a strong impression regard to him. He was become a Christian before hang."

Benjamin Edwards and our guard, Daikichi Okamoto, in Japan after the war.

We are brought home to America aboard the SS *Admiral Eberle*. A band on the dock welcomed us at the Port of Los Angeles.
Los Angeles Times Photo

My brother George was among those waiting near the ship to welcome me home.

The Japanese surrender and sign the peace treaty aboard the U.S.S. *Missouri*.
General MacArthur on the right in the foreground. At his far left is Lt. Gen. Sir
Arthur Percival, former commander of Singapore. Next to him is Gen. Jonathan
Wainwright, skeleton thin from years of Japanese imprisonment.

The arrow points to Maj. Thomas Mesereau, commanding officer of General
MacArthur's Honor Guard in Japan. See Chapter 51 for the full account of how
Mesereau was chosen to carry the signed peace treaty to Washington, D.C.
AP/Wide World

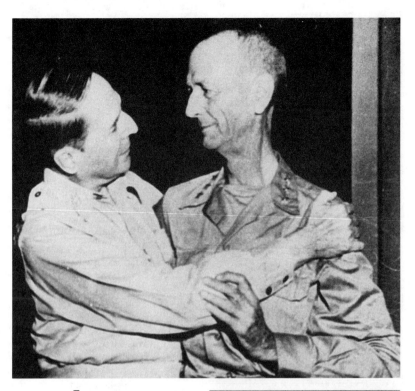

Emaciated from his years as a prisoner of war, Gen. Jonathan Wainwright is greeted by General MacArthur, who restored to Wainwright his dignity, self-esteem, and position. General Wainwright represents all of us who were held prisoners by the Japanese.

My award from General MacArthur: "Fortitude, courage, and devotion."

My original welcome to India resembled this one in 1978 when I returned to be Coordinator of an International Conference.

"Alone with God," written by Doris Kershaw when she heard me tell in a church in London, England, how the Lord used my time alone with Him to turn a resented printing press assignment in India into the reprinting of the Bible as translated into the Marathi language by Pandita Ramabai.

Alone With God

Dedicated to Carol Terry Talbot

DORIS KERSHAW
Arr. by Alice Spencer

A-lone with God, what fel-low-ship di - vine, A-lone with God, I know I feel He's mine; In si - lence kneel Be - fore the throne of grace, It's here I see The won-ders of His face.

CHORUS

A-lone with God, A - lone I am with Him. A - lone with God, I feel His peace with-in; A - lone with God, to med-i - tate and pray, A - lone with God, I kneel with Him each day.

The old treadle press on which we
printed the proofs for the Marathi Bible
in India. The women standing at the right
set the type by hand and read the proofs.
The woman on the left handed me the
paper and took the printed copies. The
woman on the right helped turn the wheel
as I stood in the middle working the
treadle. In this picture one of our girls is
learning to work the treadle.

Shaku on arrival at our home for children
in India. She was unable to sit up
without bracing herself. Her legs were so
deformed from cruel treatment that she
could not walk, and in her eyes was the
look of a frightened fawn.

After the war, a reunion in India with Peter and Cae Paget and little Joy, now grown taller.

My father with my brother Jack, both officers in the U.S. Navy—Dad in World War I and Jack in World War II.

Dr. Louis T. Talbot. Louie charmed everyone, including me.

Our wedding day.

I am awarded a Doctor of Literature degree by Biola University when I was the Commencement speaker. The degree was conferred by Dr. S. H. Sutherland, President Emeritus. At that time Dr. Richard Chase served as president.

Presentation of Colors to Dr. Carol Terry Talbot. One of life's greatest thrills and honors came my way when the formal "Presentation of Colors" with due pomp and circumstance was made to me as speaker at the reunion with paratroopers from the 11th Airborne Division. After marching in, carrying the flags, a soldier of the Color Guard saluted me and said in a strong voice, "READY TO POST THE COLORS!"

Placing my right hand over my heart, I replied, "POST THE COLORS!" When the flags were put in their appropriate places, I felt like singing out to all America:

You're a grand old flag;
You're a high-flying flag;
And forever in peace may you wave.
You're the emblem of the land I love,
The home of the free and the brave.

The Talbots, at home in Leisure World.

I am standing in the center of the photo. At my right is Maj. Gen. Philip Y. Browning of Fort Ord, who had arranged for a display of actual parachute jumps that afternoon in honor of our reunion. To my left is Mr. Cecil Fullilove of the Naturalization Service, and his wife, Mary Ann, the magnificent daughter of General Swing, the officer to whom General MacArthur gave the responsibility of our rescue from Los Banos Internment Camp.
Photo by Michael Kalamas, 11th Airborne Division.

"How many of our troops could be spared from the heavy fighting in Manila?"

These were all knotty problems with no easy answers or precedents to follow, but General Swing and Colonel Quandt were experts in military strategy.

The shadow of General Fujishige and his ten thousand troops hung over the whole operation, making what could happen a nightmare to contemplate.

Perhaps Caesar and all his hordes could have saved us from Fujishige's thousands, but Burgess was an American soldier to the core of his being and knew we had something better than Caesar and his legions.

General MacArthur has been referred to as the "American Caesar," and he said, "Get those people out of there as soon as possible." Trained to accomplish it were the indomitable troopers of the Eleventh Airborne Division with their highly skilled officers and the superb military leadership of General Swing.

But in the prison camp we were unaware of this, and the threatening shadow of a ruthless General Fujishige spread over us like a dark cloud. We prayed in desperation that God would send his angels and all the hosts of heaven to rescue us.

While General Swing, his staff, and Major Burgess were putting into action a more earthly strategy, perhaps the hosts of heaven were hovering over their shoulders.

CHAPTER 35
Strategy for Victory

CONSULTING WITH COLONELS Muller and Quandt, and with Major Burgess, General Swing approved a brave, bold, and brilliant plan for our rescue that would include a triphibious attack—by air, water, and land. Here is an outline of a report given by Burgess on that top-secret strategy for victory:

1. *An attack by air with parachutists.*

2. *An attack over water and land by amphibious tractors* that could transport the artillery and hundreds of paratroopers to increase the fighting force, and then provide a means of conveying the prisoners out of the camp.

3. *An attack by ground forces* from another direction, using trucks that could also be utilized for evacuating the prisoners. The First Battalion of the 188th Glider Infantry was selected for this assault. It would be reinforced with artillery and self-propelled guns, and have equipment to bridge rivers.

4. *An infiltration* by the Division's Reconnaissance Platoon before the attack to serve as pathfinders under the leadership of Lt. George Skau.

At 7:00 A.M. three of the Recon Platoon's men were to send

up phosphorous smoke to mark a landing zone on the beach for the amphibious tractors coming across Laguna de Bay.

Creeping into foliage near the prison camp, some of the pathfinders had the mission of sending smoke upward to mark a landing zone for the paratroopers who would be descending by parachutes. This smoke would also indicate wind direction for them so they could keep clear of the power lines and railroad tracks.

Accompanied by loyal Filipino guerrillas, more of these intrepid men had to deploy themselves in hiding around the prison camp so every Japanese sentry in the outposts and pillboxes was covered. When the planes flew in and the first parachute billowed out, these Recon men would have to eliminate the Japanese sentries, neutralize guards doing exercises, and grab their stacked guns.

All of this constituted a dangerous and Herculean mission for the thirty-one very brave men of the Reconnaissance Platoon.

5. *Evacuation* of the rescued prisoners had the safety factor of two options: in amtracs over the lake, or in trucks along the road to be cleared by the 188th Glider Infantry and the units of artillery and engineers accompanying it.

6. *In case of an emergency*, General Swing readied the Second Battalion to be called if necessary, and he would be flying over the prison camp during the raid, observing each aspect of the operation with the trained eye of an expert military strategist.

What could go wrong? Only one thing.

If any word of the rescue leaked out to the Japanese, the nearly ten thousand troops of General Fujishige just eight miles from the prison camp could commit a horrible massacre of prisoners and rescuers.

However, another means not in the plan could prevent it, and most of our soldiers and officers were to take that last precaution. In the quiet sanctuary of their own hearts, they prayed.

The rescue plan was submitted to General Griswold, the XIV Corps commander, who approved it without change.

Beginning Monday, February 19, and spreading out over the next few days and nights, an armada of amphibious tractors, trucks, ambulances, and other military vehicles began moving secretly and discreetly out of Manila by different pathways and byways.

Capt. Luis Burris, who commanded D Battery of the 457th Artillery, received very short notice and said he had to "scramble like mad" in order to secure ammunition and supplies and then get it all loaded on the amtracs.

Capt. Nat (Bud) Ewing, the executive officer, moved the Battalion out of Manila as inconspicuously as possible, shortening the distance from Los Banos Internment Camp.

Realizing that the best-laid plans do sometimes go awry, General Swing and his staff endeavored to provide for every possible contingency that could arise twenty-five miles behind enemy lines. The whole operation was fraught with danger both for the rescuers and those to be rescued.

Events now moved swiftly toward our rescue as General Swing sent for First Lieut. John Ringler, who would later become a colonel.

The reader will find in the photo section a chart showing the line of command and the units making up the Los Banos Task Force.

CHAPTER 36
"It Not Only Can Be Done, It Will Be Done!"

LT. JOHN RINGLER KNEW something big must be in the wind. His B Company had been pulled out of heavy fighting at Fort McKinley, and now Colonel Lahti was taking him to Division Headquarters by order of General Swing.

Accompanied by Ringler, Colonel Lahti walked into Headquarters with his face sallow from yellow jaundice and his arm in a sling, due to his recent severe shrapnel wound. Though wounded and ill, Lahti carried on with his responsibilities, showing great strength of character and physical endurance. He would not be part of the raiding force, but Lahti was a thorough officer and planner and had made more parachute jumps than most of the men.

General Swing had a very high regard for Lahti's combat judgment and wanted counsel from both him and Ringler regarding final details of the parachute jump on the Los Banos Internment Camp.

Later to become a colonel, Lieutenant Ringler was now twenty-six years of age, excellent as combat leader of his Company, competent, precise, intelligent, and highly respected by those he commanded in B Company of the First Battalion, 511th Parachute Infantry Regiment.

Although a very careful and masterful plan for rescue of the prisoners at Los Banos had been skillfully prepared, not only would Japanese guns be endangering the paratroopers, but also the hazards of railroad tracks and deadly high-voltage electric power lines.

General Swing wanted to inform Ringler that he would have the vital part of commanding the paratroopers jumping into the Los Banos camp.

Ringler describes what happened when he arrived with Lahti at Division Headquarters:

"Colonels Quandt and Muller told us that General Swing wanted to enlighten us about a special mission. We were taken into General Swing's office, where he explained what was involved in rescuing the internees at Los Banos.

"After he finished, we left his office, and then Colonels Muller and Quandt gave us more information, including aerial photographs showing the area of operation.

" 'Where would you like to select a drop zone?' they asked, pointing out two or three available places.

"We selected the drop zone that would get us closest to the camp and be most likely to afford maximum success.

"I briefed our platoon leaders on the operation, and they in turn informed the personnel. Then we went into detail, planning how we would execute this airborne mission. We had advanced intelligence to assist us, and we knew a diversionary force would withhold possible attack from the enemy in the outlying areas of the camp. We were also aware that Lieutenant Hettlinger's machine gun platoon would be attached to us for this operation to reinforce our fire capability.

"At Nichols Field on February 22 we would receive our parachutes and prepare for our drop. Using the ground for sand tables, we would have a briefing and orientation session as to what each person would do, each platoon, each squad, and what would happen if we were hit by the enemy on the ground at the time of our drop.

"The first phase of the mission was to eliminate any enemy resistance that was in our way, and then to organize the internees so they could be loaded on the amtracs or trucks that were to come in and pick them up for evacuation.

"We felt we had the ability to do things many people would think impossible—to drop far behind enemy lines to do a mission, knowing that if you don't succeed, you will lose 133 men and your own life along with theirs.

"But we had a unit that was willing to carry out the mission assigned to it without any question or saying, 'This can't be done,' or 'That can't be done.'

"Everyone had the attitude, 'It not only can be done, it will be done.' "

A thorough officer, Lieutenant Ringler sent two of his men behind enemy lines to study the landing hazards for the paratroopers.

Having just received word of Pete's safe arrival at the Eleventh Airborne's Headquarters, Ben Edwards was relishing a time of relaxation when Lt. Roger Miller and Sgt. Robert Turner arrived under orders from Lieutenant Ringler to study the landing sites for the paratroopers. Ben describes their journey:

"We left Banhaya in two sailing *bancas* that evening and began the trip back to the area of the internment camp.

"One of these men was interested in the location of the power lines that angled through a portion of the lower camp area as well as the railroad tracks.

"I pointed out a road the paratroopers would take to get from the drop site to the main guardhouse and camp where the internees were imprisoned, and also showed them the two southern guard posts. We were so close to the camp fence that we could hear sounds from one of the barracks, probably the one where the Catholic sisters were housed—number twenty."

Only a short distance away in my barracks, number eighteen, I was weak, starving, diseased with beriberi, and praying desperately that if necessary God would send His angels and the hosts of heaven to rescue us from the threatening shadow of General Fujishige and his thousands. I did not know that He had two earthborn "angels" near my barracks planning that very rescue.

When Miller and Turner secured the needed information, Miller made haste in returning to headquarters, while Ben and Freddy went back to Nanhaya in the darkness of the night to await further developments.

Since Sgt. Robert Turner had to send up a flare to mark the drop zone for the paratroopers when the planes came at dawn, he stayed nearby at the home of a guerrilla leader, Colonel Price. Before the dawning of the morning, Turner would be in place, watching, and listening for the roar of our approaching planes, his hand and arm ready to throw a white phosphorus grenade indicating the drop zone for the paratroopers. Timing and accuracy in throwing were of vital importance.

CHAPTER 37
Picayune Me
Los Banos Internment Camp
February 20, 1945

"TIME FOR ROLL CALL!" our barracks monitor called out.

Everyone able to walk had to line up four deep in front of the barracks each morning. We were growing weaker, our shoulders slumping, hands hanging limp at our sides. It became increasingly difficult to stand erect while the guards counted all of us.

During roll call one day in Santo Tomas Internment Camp, a guard had rammed the sharp end of a bamboo pole into the ribs of a fifteen-year-old boy named Henry Johnson, further damaging an already injured rib that had prevented the lad's standing erect enough to please the guard.

Transferred to Los Banos, Henry now stood in our line at roll call, where all of us were too weak for standing up straight any length of time.

Just one thing made roll call tolerable. As we waited for a Japanese officer to come and count us, information and rumors were whispered along the line from one to another. It became our news network.

On the morning of February 20, 1945, word came down the line, "Mr. Blair died this morning of starvation."

Everything within me cried out *No! Not Mr. Blair!* Stunned

by the news, I was hardly aware of the soldier who methodically numbered me along with the others.

When we were dismissed, I went to our cubicle, picked up my Bible and walked slowly to the chapel, my mind in a turmoil.

A man of sterling character, Herb Blair had been one of the finest men in our camp. His degree from Princeton University bore the signature of Woodrow Wilson, who before his presidency had been head of Princeton.

Having served in Korea for thirty-four years, Blair was one of the builders of the fine Korean churches that became famous for their prayer meetings held daily in the early dawn. Just before the war, on his way home to America, he had stayed in Manila to help the church there. Although in his sixties, Herb had been a vigorous man when he arrived at Los Banos, always encouraging us younger ones.

Did a clergyman's dying of starvation nullify some of God's promises?

As one devastating circumstance after another assailed my faith in that concentration camp, I felt the meaning, purpose, and roots of my life were being torn from me.

I had to find an answer to Mr. Blair's death, or my work as I envisioned it was finished, along with some of the values on which I built my life. All of us were far down the road called beriberi, and the end of that road meant death.

Having learned the vital importance of listening to what the Lord would say to one's heart in a time of crisis, I sat in the chapel with bowed head and tears brimming, flowing, rolling down my cheeks. It seemed as though I was at the bottom of a dark abyss, with everything crashing down on top of me as I tried to reach upward, grasping for some glimmer of light and hope where all seemed dark.

After an immeasurable time, I felt the Lord saying to the waves of my storm, "Peace, be still."

This question began growing in my mind: Did I have faith to

accept Mr. Blair's death without having to know why, to believe
God permitted it for reasons unknown to me?

As I became quieter, thoughts turned to the apostles when
the Lord was dying on the cross. They did not understand the
reason, and it seemed to destroy all they had believed and
hoped for in the future.

Taking a deep breath, I prayed, "Lord, somehow give me
faith to believe it's all in Your plan and I don't have to understand why."

The internees made a coffin for Herb from one of the few
remaining outdoor dining tables that resembled the long picnic tables one sees in a public park.

That afternoon I stood at the graveside. The internees had
only enough strength to dig a shallow grave.

As Rev. John Crothers spoke at the service, I studied his
face. John and his wife had been like a father and mother to
me in that internment camp. Mr. Crothers had been a col-
league of Herb Blair's, giving a lifetime of service in Korea.
Now elderly and weak from starvation, John knew that if our
American army did not come for us soon, he probably would
be the next one to be laid in a shallow grave. Instead of a
shadow or tear on his face, there seemed to be a quiet, peaceful joy.

He did not feel God had failed Herb, who had died praising
Him and thanking Him he was soon to be in His presence. It
did not matter to Herb whether the Lord took him home to
glory from a prison camp or a hospital in America. He never
questioned God's purpose.

For Herbert Blair, death was not an ignominious end but a
triumphal entry into the Kingdom of Heaven, after having
been a faithful ambassador to the planet Earth.

Standing there comprehending this, I prayed God would
make picayune me into a worthy emissary on this earth for the
King of kings. As I lifted my face heavenward, peace came to
my heart. I had found my answer in the sovereignty of God.

In memory I could hear the congregation of the Church of the Open Door at home singing to me the words of this old hymn:

When through the deep waters I call thee to go,
  The rivers of sorrow shall not overflow;
For I will be with thee thy trials to bless,
  And sanctify to thee thy deepest distress.

I later heard that, unknown to his sickly wife, Mr. Blair had been giving her his meager portion of food along with her own, while he tried to continue living by eating slugs. Mrs. Blair survived, and she never knew of her husband's sacrifice that she might live.

CHAPTER 38
"Scheduled for Massacre"
Guerrilla Camp
February 18–21, 1945

"YOU ARE TO DESTROY your radio, code, and encoder if captured or death seems imminent." These were the instructions given a young radio operator named John Fulton when he volunteered for a perilous journey into enemy-held territory.

After penetrating Japanese lines, John was to locate and join the loyal Filipino guerrillas who were hiding in the area and establish radio communications with the Eleventh Airborne Division Headquarters.

Here is the story in John's own words:

"I prepared myself and equipment, which consisted of a small but powerful radio, hand generator, code, and encoder, plenty of extra clips of ammunition, as many grenades as I could stuff into the pockets of my jacket, a knife, and some food. I would be my own message center.

"A Filipino scout soon joined me and an American soldier who had escaped capture after the bombing of Pearl Harbor. We made our way in the darkness to the shore of Laguna de Bay. For security reasons, my radio and I were hidden in the false bottom of a typical outrigger-style, Filipino fishing boat. In case we ran into a Japanese patrol boat, I had two grenades ready to blow up my equipment, not to mention half of our boat.

"I felt apprehensive, slightly claustrophobic, increasingly nauseated because of the stench of dead fish in very close quarters. I also felt excited, very much alive, and intensely aware of what I was doing. Extremely anxious to get ashore, I was enjoying it.

"In the blackness of that dark night, we crossed the lake without incident. On landing, we met some Filipino guerrillas and headed inland by foot, finally arriving at a sort of camp.

"I verified with the Eleventh Airborne Headquarters and with the guerrilla commander, General Umali, and then encoded and radioed a few messages that were waiting for transmission.

"During the next few weeks I received dispatches from couriers sent by a guerrilla commander, Col. W. C. Price, and other guerrilla groups, and was kept busy verifying, encoding, and radioing communications to Division Headquarters, and then receiving replies back.

"Then in the early evening of February 18 I received this message, with the original spelling and wording preserved:

GUERRILLA HEADQUARTERS
LOS BANOS PATROL CP
18 Feb. 45
12: noon

Sargent Fulton, I am sending for the transceiver. The situation is such that that radio is very far from my CP where it should be, delaying the action on my part of important messages. Couriers to the place where you are now and up to this place takes more than three hours hiking and another three boating.

I am sending you a party of five armed men with tommy and the rest M-1's. I will be expecting you and the rest of the party to be here tonight or at least before dawn. Major Vanderpool will be here by tonight and he might want to use that radio for important last minute communications with hq of the 11th Airborne Div. It will be just too bad if he asks for that set and it is not around on our part.

Gustavo Inglis
Lt-Col., GSC (Guer)
Inspector General

"So off we went, the five guerrillas and myself, heading north as darkness closed in on us. Once during the night our point man came running back to alert us of an approaching Japanese patrol. We quickly slipped into deep underbrush on either side of the trail and 'froze' until the clanking of equipment, the squishing of boots, and murmuring of voices faded away into the night.

"Somewhere between three and five o'clock in the morning we made it into Inglis's camp. He was happy and relieved to see us. Encoding, transmitting, receiving, and decoding messages kept me very busy during the next several days. Inglis's assessment of his need for the radio proved right.

"A few days later Colonel Price handed me this message to encode and send immediately: [Parenthetical portions added]"

USPIF
(United States Philippine Islands Forces)
HQ., Red Lion Division 25th Div PQOG
In the Field
21 February 1945

To: Sgt. J. Fulton—Please transmit this communication upon receipt:

URGENT
ESPINO TO VANDERPOOL
HAVE RECEIVED RELIABLE INFORMATION THAT JAPS

HAVE LOS BANOS [Internment Camp] SCHEDULED FOR
MASSACRE PD SUGGEST THAT ENEMY POSITIONS IN
LOS BANOS PROPER [the area] AS EXPLAINED MILLER
BE BOMBED AS SOON AS POSSIBLE PD

W. C. PRICE
COL. GSC GUER
CHIEF OF STAFF

CHAPTER 39
Special and Secret
Mindora
February 21, 1945

DONALD ANDERSON RECEIVED a phone call regarding a mission that was so "special and very secret" that it could not be mentioned over the telephone.

A major in the United States Air Force, Don was stationed at their base on the island of Mindora in the Philippines. The man calling him was Lt. Col. Marvin Calliham, wing operations officer, who told Don to fly to the Eleventh Airborne Headquarters on Luzon, which was located in the commandeered house outside Manila.

Maj. Don Anderson tells his own story:

"We left immediately, landed in a rice field a mile or so from the house, and were driven to the headquarters and introduced to Colonel Quandt, who was the operations officer of the 11th Airborne Division.

"Colonel Quandt described the mission, which involved the coordination of the waterborne amphibious tractors and the dropping of paratroopers on the Los Banos prison. The area had been thoroughly scouted the day before. The key to the mission was the changing of the guard by the Japanese garrison and the brief exercise period of the new guard, at which time most of their weapons were in the guardhouse. This guard change took place at 7:00 A.M., some ten to fifteen minutes before full daylight.

"For us, it entailed taking off from Nichols Field in the dark, assembling our nine airplanes in formation, and arriving at the drop zone at precisely 7:00 A.M.

"We were to spend the night of February 22 in our airplanes with the paratroopers on Nichols Field, which had many recently filled bomb craters on the runway. I asked Colonel Quandt if we could delay our departure until 7:15 so we would have adequate light for takeoff and assembly.

" 'Let's ask the "old man," General Swing,' " he replied.

"The general had been resting and we awakened him.

"Dressed in an undershirt and trousers, General Swing rolled sideways out of his bunk when Colonel Quandt stated the problem. The general looked me straight in the eye and said, 'It will be seven o'clock sharp on the drop and you'd —— well better be right!'

" 'Yes, sir!' I replied.

"We did learn that men from the Reconnaissance Platoon and guerrillas were assigned to every Japanese outpost, and there were no enemy troops on the hill at the south end of Laguna de Bay, which we had to pass over at an altitude of two hundred feet. The whole operation was timed by the opening of the first parachute, at which time the Japanese sentries would be neutralized and the amphibious vehicles hit the shore."

As squadron commander, Anderson, with his operations officer, Captain O'Grady, flew over Los Banos on a reconnaissance mission, flying at an altitude of five thousand feet, returning to Nichols Field to await the vital moment of takeoff for our rescue.

CHAPTER 40
Go Carefully—Danger Ahead!
February 21–22, 1945

WHILE ALL ASPECTS of the rescue had dangerous overtones, men in the Reconnaissance Platoon had to be both brave and bold. Loren Brown describes their perils on the way to rescue us:

"We were alerted to the raid on Los Banos Prison Camp, being briefed thoroughly in preparation for the mission. The information, statistics, and all other related matters given to us by Pete Miles and Lieutenant Skau were of vital importance.

"Not only were we given a detailed layout of the camp, but also the daily activities of the Japanese routine, which proved to be one of the most important aspects of the raid.

"Our mission was to infiltrate, surround, and eliminate all resistance before the prisoners could be harmed by their Japanese guards.

"The number in our platoon had been reduced by illness. Some had to be left in a hospital in Leyte, and others were sick from ingesting contaminated water. There were now about twenty of us, and we were briefed according to the four different patrols into which we were divided.

"Because of the difficulty and danger connected with infiltrating behind enemy lines, our platoon was sent two days prior to the planned day of attack, a stroke of wisdom.

"Our twenty men were placed in four different *bancas*, with five men squeezing into each boat. (A couple of approved newspaper reporters crowded in also.) We waited two hours after the sailing of each *banca* so we would not appear as a convoy. I was on the last to start across the lake.

"While some of the men reported that their boats ran into a stormy squall, we faced the problem of a sudden and absolute calm when we arrived at the middle of the lake. There was not a breath of air blowing, and the sail hung limp on the mast.

"The day faded into night, and still no wind rippled either water or sail. The only ripples we experienced that first night and most of the next day were those that came from a Japanese patrol boat that came out periodically and circled us.

"This was a time of great anxiety. Our boat was small; and in order not to be seen, we had to lie down low in the *banca*. The shortness of the boat required that we lie on top of one another in order to be low enough in the boat so we would not be visible to the Japanese.

"It was hot; and the heat, discomfort, and anxiety took their toll as the Japanese continued to circle around our *banca*. We were becalmed there all night of the 21st and all day of the 22nd."

Could they reach the camp on schedule? They had to be there in time to prevent the Japanese from shooting the descending paratroopers and the prisoners.

CHAPTER 41
"If Anything Can Go Wrong, It Will"

"SHORTY" SOULE CAME by his nickname because of his short physical stature, but in other ways he stood ten feet tall. He had received the Distinguished Service Cross and would become a major general, but for now he was commander of the Los Banos Task Force to rescue us.

While the amphibious tractors were making their long, slow trek across land and water to our Los Banos Internment Camp, Col. Robert Soule and the military units with him were riding along another route in trucks, feeling capable of coping with whatever they might encounter.

But one must always keep in mind Murphy's Law, "If anything can go wrong, it will." The Japanese had blown vital bridges and prepared for some future battle. Unknowingly, they had also blown the primary plan of transporting the rescued prisoners by these trucks to safety behind the American lines.

And more things would go wrong than broken bridges for the men riding in those trucks with Colonel Soule. The chief purpose of this Task Force was to draw away from the Los Banos Internment Camp the attention of the main units of General Fujishige's 8th Tiger Division, and to eliminate enemy positions endangering the rescue. The men in this Task Force undertaking that tough assignment were:

1st Battalion of the 188th Glider Infantry Regiment commanded by Lt. Col. Edward LaFlamme. (The 2nd Battalion was held in reserve.)

472nd and 675th Field Artillery Battalions

Company B of the 637th Tank Destroyer Battalion

Engineers with bridging equipment

While the engineers improvised ways for the trucks to cross where some of the bridges had been blown, it would be very difficult to get the trucks through now to the Internment Camp.

Although unaware of the pending rescue at Los Banos, the Japanese had fortified Lecheria Hills in anticipation of an attack there sooner or later by the American army.

After a bitter fight, Soule's forces seized Lecheria Hills, but the captain in command of the Tank Destroyer Company was killed by a bullet in the forehead.

Had this battle not taken place and the rescued prisoners been evacuated by the trucks as originally planned, they could have encountered gunfire by the Japanese in the Lecheria Hills area.

Now Soule and his military units proceeded toward the Rock Quarry, where more Japanese were located even closer to us. Fighting became intense.

Colonel Soule wondered whether they would be able to reach Los Banos. What would happen to those imprisoned there? He was overall commander of the whole rescue operation, but could not get to the prison camp with his troops, artillery, or trucks.

However, Soule felt Major Burgess, the troopers and artillery with him, the paratroopers jumping onto the camp, the Reconnaissance Platoon, and the helpful Filipino guerrillas could handle the actual rescue and take the prisoners out in those slow amphibious tractors if he could just keep the Japanese away from them long enough. And he put all his military skill and that of his Task Force into fighting the Japanese.

CHAPTER 42
Darkness before Dawn
Thursday, February 22, 1945

THE SERENE WATERS of a large lake called Laguna de Bay would soon be churning with the roaring motors and loud clanking of fifty-nine amphibious tractors that had covertly traveled from Manila. It was of vital importance that no one guess their purpose or destination.

These large, lumbering vehicles now sitting quietly in formation on the shores of this spacious lake were often called "Alligators" because their metal tracks supported them on land and drove them slowly on water. Some shortened their name to "amphtracs" and others to simply "amtracs." Whatever they were called, the 412 men and officers who would be crossing the lake in them before dawn were dedicated to turning those amphibious tractors into iron-clad chariots of freedom for the prisoners in the Los Banos Internment Camp.

Capt. Tom Mesereau stood looking out over that broad expanse of water they were to cross in the darkness before dawn. After a few moments of contemplation, he turned and surveyed all their vehicles of conveyance. How could they cross that big lake in those noisy amtracs in the dark, with no lights allowed, reach a pinpoint landing spot on the other side at the exact time designated, and do it without attracting the attention of Japanese in the area?

Although someone would be sending up a smoke signal to guide them as they neared the shoreline, it all seemed like "mission impossible."

An "All-American" football player from West Point, Mesereau by nature was brave and daring, and an unusual man whom men would choose to follow. He was twenty-two years old. In this assignment, Captain Tom commanded C Company of the First Battalion, 511th Parachute Infantry, a part of the Eleventh Airborne Division.

Gathering his men around him, Tom bent down and sketched on the ground the mission they were to accomplish in rescuing the prisoners at Los Banos.

Discussing the plan with Major Burgess was Lt. Col. Joseph Gibbs, the commander of the amphibious tractor battalion. Under his control would be the tractors and just the soldiers who operated them. Gibbs was astonished that he, a forty-year-old colonel, would be taking orders from Major Burgess, who was only twenty-six but a graduate of Harvard University and a sharp young officer.

Most of the soldiers were barely out of their teens. Thoughts of rescuing imprisoned Americans who were dying of starvation and under threat of massacre stirred the red blood flowing in their veins.

A surprise arrived in the form of Maj. Gen. Courtney Whitney with a civilian. They carried an order authorizing them to ride along to Los Banos in order to secure secret documents of military significance from the office of the Japanese in our camp. Whitney served as MacArthur's staff officer responsible for overseeing the guerrilla organization on the island of Luzon.

When everyone had more or less settled down, a Filipino walked up and asked what time they were going to hit Los Banos. Startled, Burgess wondered how he knew. If this Filipino told the Japanese, catastrophic tragedy would result. Burgess became suspicious and took him in his amtrac, where the

Filipino stayed, petrified with fear that the Americans might shoot him. He did not know that Burgess intended to let him go when they reached Los Banos.

The thrill and the danger of the impending rescue kept many of the soldiers awake that night, and some offered a quiet prayer. They did not know that alarming news had reached General Swing.

Pilots of the Black Widow night-reconnaissance planes reported seeing Japanese trucks, with lights shining, entering the Los Banos Internment Camp, halting, and then leaving the same way they came. Were they bringing in troop reinforcements, moving troops to more strategic positions, escaping entirely, or removing the prisoners?

When this report reached the Sixth Army on the same day as a report about the Los Banos rescue, the Chief of Staff, a major general, was sent to General Swing's headquarters to get more details of the rescue and with authority to cancel it, if he deemed it wise.

Consulting with Henry Muller in charge of Intelligence, and Doug Quandt of Operations, General Swing pondered what the results would be of a cancellation at this late and vital time.

The pilots, trucks, and amphibious tractors could still be called back, but men of the Reconnaissance Platoon were by then well behind Japanese lines. Groups of Filipino guerrillas were creeping through the rice paddies and bushes toward the internment camp to help in rescuing the prisoners. While the Filipinos might be able to disperse themselves, the men of the Recon Platoon would be trapped in their hiding places beyond recall and beyond help. They could all be massacred along with those interned at the Los Banos camp.

It was a time for even the bravest and wisest of soldiers to pray.

After considering all angles, General Swing firmly decided that the rescue must continue as planned and ordered the Second Battalion to be on the alert for call into action to help

Soule and LaFlamme if necessary. He had a command post set up near them at Calamba.

Then General Swing ordered his small observation plane readied so he could watch every aspect of the operation from the air.

CHAPTER 43
The Romance and Pathos of War
By courtesy of
Lt. Col. Henry Burgess
Lt. Col. Thomas Mesereau

IN THE DARKNESS before the break of dawn, the fifty-nine huge amtracs maneuvered into the lake at four o'clock in the morning of Friday, February 23, 1945.

Among those aboard and most excited of all was Peter Miles, the internee who had risked his life in escaping from our internment camp in order to give vital information to those planning our rescue. He was the "Prince Valiant" of Los Banos.

Of the 412 military officers and men being transported in those amtracs, I'll let Tom Mesereau describe his feelings while those noisy, bulky amphibious tractors were churning their way across the lake:

"Crossing this body of water in darkness was a new experience for all of us. There was excitement of the operation in a rather different way from the ordinary battles we fought. I can even use the word *romance*, because there was a lot of pathos attached to the thought of freeing hundreds and thousands of prisoners, most of whom were Americans.

"As very young people, we were able to envision how they would feel when they saw the first Americans.

"We were soon out of sight of land, and I have no idea how the amtrac commander navigated the trip of seven and one-half miles with such precision. The noise of all the vehicles was horrendous, and I could not understand why the Japanese were not on the beach to greet us with Samurai swords."

In another amtrac was Capt. Louis Burris, Commander of D Battery of the 457th Artillery Battalion. He was keeping an eye on his guns, ammunition, and other supplies, making sure they remained dry.

In order to avoid any hint to the Japanese about the movement of amtracs and troops out of Manila, very short notice had been given to those who would be riding in them. Captain Burris had to obtain and put aboard the necessary ammunition, supplies, and two 75mm Pack Howitzers, each of which had been transported in seven pieces. Burris would have to assemble them immediately on landing. They were short cannons that delivered shells with medium velocities, usually at a high trajectory.

Each of the amtracs had a mount and ring for a machine gun, and most of them carried 30-caliber machine guns, while a few had 50-caliber. Threatening as they looked, however, they could only turn off light firing.

To the credit of those who navigated those amtracs, let it be recorded that they crossed that lake in the dark, keeping in formation, making three required changes in direction, guided only by a compass, and arrived on time at 7:00 A.M. at their appointed spot, Mayondon Point. As they drew near, the Point was very faintly indicated for them by flares of colored phosphorous smoke sent up by men of the Reconnaissance Platoon.

Taking the three Recon men aboard, the amtracs headed for the internment camp, leaving two of Burris's howitzers and artillery men to take care of the Japanese who were firing sporadically at them. The amtracs were about two and a half miles from the prison camp.

Seasoned officer though he was, Burgess felt his whole physical and emotional being tightening up with suspense, hope, and anxiety mixed with a thread of dread of what they might find. Were the more than two thousand men, women, and children still alive, or did the Japanese carry out the rumored threat to massacre them? Had the Japanese received any advance word that the American troops were coming to rescue those helpless prisoners?

CHAPTER 44
Tomorrow—
Will It Be Heaven, Hell, or Still Here?

JAMES HOLZEM, A PARATROOPER, describes his impression of that crucial February day:

"Something big was brewing for our B Company. We could feel it in the air. What was it all about? The rumors! Something important was coming up.

"We were loaded into trucks and driven about twenty miles south of Manila to a large penitentiary called New Bilibid Prison. We were assigned cells and slept that night on cots with boards as mattresses. The reason we were spirited away to the prison was to maintain complete secrecy regarding our next mission.

"Our commanding officer, Lieutenant Ringler, told us about the upcoming operation.

"There were more than two thousand American and allied civilian prisoners in a Japanese internment camp about twenty-five miles beyond our front lines. Word had come from Filipino guerrillas that the Japanese were going to execute all those prisoners on the morning of February 23, shortly after 7:00 A.M., as soon as the guards finished their morning calisthenics.

"Our B Company was to jump on the camp, or very near it,

right at seven o'clock, while the Japanese were doing those exercises and had their guns stacked. The Filipino guerrillas and the Reconnaissance Platoon would be there, and the rest of our battalion would be arriving in amtracs.

"Proud that we had been selected for the most exciting part, we had mixed emotions. I believe that in all of World War II, we were the only parachute company to make a rescue jump like this. However, rumors were rampant and comments varied. 'This will be a suicide jump!' 'Few of us will return.'

"Our reactions were varied. 'This is what we have been trained so long and hard for.' 'This will be the ultimate battle.' 'This is the highlight of our combat career.'

"But for no amount of money could anyone have bought a seat on the plane from a Company B trooper.

"I suggested to Oscar that he return to Manila until this operation was over, but he wouldn't have any of that. He was a paratrooper now, and he had his boots to prove it! And whatever he left unsaid vocally, he more than made up for it with the pleading in his eyes.

"There were two other Filipinos with our Company, both a few years older than Oscar. They felt the same way about wanting to make the jump.

"So three of us 'big brothers' and the three courageous young Filipinos pleaded the case with the powers that be, arguing that they had already proven themselves under fire, had the courage to make the jump, and we needed them to interpret for us.

"The answer was Go, so the three Filipinos, named Carlos Pulverosa, Robert Fletcher, and Rosenda Castillo (Oscar) were given a three-hour, intensive parachute training course.

"Late in the afternoon we were again loaded into trucks and driven to Nichols Field. It was not known yet for sure whether all the Japanese had been cleared out of this area.

"But there on the runway were nine C-47 airplanes waiting for us. We were issued parachutes and served a hot meal. In an orientation session, each person was informed what he was to do and how to handle dangerous problems that might arise when we landed.

"Then came a minor problem with Oscar. He was willing to concede that the large pack on his back could contain a parachute; but there was no way, he argued, that the little reserve chutepack in the front could contain something as large as a parachute. He wouldn't let up on the subject.

"I insisted that there was and finally said, 'Enough! Take my word for it.'

"We slept that night on the runway under the wings of the planes. I doubt that many of us slept very much, as we were all high on excitement.

"What would it be like?

"How many of us would be alive twenty-four hours later?

"We all lay there, each with his own private thoughts about our loved ones back home, about whether there really was a heaven and a hell, and where would we be tomorrow night— heaven, hell, or still here on Luzon?"

CHAPTER 45
Prison Camp Ambrosia
Los Banos Internment Camp
February 21–22, 1945

"IF YOU COULD HAVE the most delicious meal in all the world, what would you choose?"

"Which mouth-watering, tempting dessert?"

"What would be your entrée?"

It became the camp fad, almost an obsession, to copy, compare, and discuss recipes for ambrosial delights. Any scraps of paper available were filled with directions for making the most exotic delectables our minds could imagine. Luscious pies, creamy cakes, and ice cream extravaganzas were popular.

In our thoughts during the daytime and our dreams through the night, we became gourmets feasting on the world's most exquisite cuisine.

While trying to remain sane, we were using a form of escapism.

But even our dreaming came to a shocking, abrupt halt when the Japanese announced there was no more food. As our last rations, they gave unhusked rice, known in the Philippines as *palay.*

Our doctors warned us that if we ate the rice unhusked, it would tear our intestines and cause death.

The camp had no way of removing the husks, so our com-

mittee asked the Japanese to send it out to a local mill, but
they refused.

We were each given a tiny portion of this rice which was sup-
posed to last for two days. Everything else had to be forgotten
in the struggle of husking that rice. We might have given up on
the difficult task had it not been for word circulating through
our camp that this was the absolute end of our food supply. No
more food at all.

We experimented with all kinds of unique methods to strip
off those stubborn, tough husks. The most productive way became rubbing the grain between two blocks of wood, blowing
away the chaff, and picking up the grains one by one, but this
required considerable energy, and wooden blocks were hard
to find. Some people pounded the grain in a jar.

Weak from starvation, we found the task of husking the rice
exhausting. For the children, the sick, and the elderly, it was
impossible. Some just gave up and boiled the unhusked rice,
drinking the liquid, and throwing away the residue, hoping for
some minuscule molecule of nourishment.

In our cubicle, Ruth Woodworth asked, "How are we going
to get the husks off this rice?"

"Do you think Chips could get us a couple blocks of wood
from the carpenter shop?" Evelyn wondered.

"We do have one thing God has given us," I suggested, trying to be cheerful.

"What's that?" asked skeptical Mona.

"Our fingernails," I replied, holding up my hands.

"Mine are so weak and fragile, I don't think they could cut
into those husks," said Elda, and she was right.

Each one had to find her own method. Since we had no
chairs, I sat on the bamboo floor for hours removing the husk
from every little individual grain of rice with my fingernails,
which were already in bad shape. It seemed as though each
husk was stuck to its individual grain with impenetrable glue,
and my beriberi-weakened fingers and flimsy fingernails were

no match for the battle. My back ached from its hunched position, while my eyes hurt from the concentrated strain.

During all the clatter and frustration of husking the rice that was going on throughout the camp, I took a break to give my eyes and back a rest.

Having heard that a young American couple, Ruth and Herbert Clingen, were expecting a baby, I walked over to their cubicle to see how they were getting along.

My family name was Terry; and in the course of the conversation, Herb said, "My mother was a Terry."

"Where did she live?" I asked, my interest perking up.

"On Long Island, New York."

"Long Island!" I exclaimed. "My father's people lived on Long Island. One of my ancestors, Jeremiah Terry, was an officer in George Washington's army, and Thomas Terry a colonel in the colonial wars. They all lived on Long Island."

We traced it down to the very towns, and discovered we must be shirttail cousins.

"When do you expect your baby?" I asked Ruth.

"Almost any time now."

"Do you have any clothes for it?"

"I've managed to make a few little things," she replied, pointing to a box she was trying to make into a bassinet of sorts.

"What about yourself?"

"I don't have so much as a nightgown, but just so the baby's healthy, that is all that matters."

As I left their tiny cubicle, I wondered whether there was anything in my suitcase Ruth could use. My thoughts centered on a beautiful nightgown and negligee set that had been presented to me at a farewell shower given by the women of Calvary Church of Hollywood, of which Dr. S. H. Sutherland was the pastor.

Most of the gifts were practical things, suitable for the plain life of a single girl working in an orphanage and rescue home in India; but one delightful person had brought as her gift such a beautiful negligee set that one of the women smilingly remarked, "That's a bit glamorous for someone isolated over there in a girls' orphanage. It's more suitable for a bride."

"I think Carol should have something dainty along with the practical things," remarked the dear woman who had brought the pretty gift.

The negligee set was so beautiful that I couldn't bear to leave it behind for looters when I packed my small suitcase for the prison camp. I delighted in the loveliness and enjoyed looking at the ensemble, but I had never worn either garment. Somehow a prison camp was not the place to wear such dainty attire.

Opening my suitcase, I held up that pink nightgown and negligee, shook out some of the wrinkles, and then went over and presented those treasured pretties to Ruth. Her ecstasy brought tears to my eyes. When I went back to husking my rice, the task did not seem so arduous as my poor fingernails struggled with those tough husks.

Cae Paget describes the scene:

"All day we labored. In our barracks we worked steadily from the moment that we were released from roll call until it was too dark to see at night.

"We were now very weak and had formed the habit of lying on our beds every moment we possibly could. Now we were forced to sit up over this grain all day long, working desperately against the fading light. Our backs ached; yet we kept on, only to realize at the end of the day we couldn't possibly prepare the short daily ration, even if we worked every available moment.

"Many were so weak already that they could not get about. Some were in the hospital. Many were aged, and utterly unable to husk grain at all. Who was to do the work for them, when each individual found it almost impossible to do even his own? Those who had very small children couldn't cope with the situation. Some of the children were already ill from undernourishment.

"On the second afternoon a few of us laid down our work to spend an hour together in prayer. Surely God would do something. Unless He did, and that quickly, there was no alternative but death from starvation.

"What an hour of prayer! We rose from our knees with wet eyes, but with hearts at peace. Whatever came, we had the assurance that God was with us, and His presence hovered near like the fragrance of a sweet perfume. Refreshed and strengthened in spirit, we went back to our arduous task of husking the rice."

Leaving that prayer meeting, I felt keenly aware that in life and in death I was a child of God, and I offered a faint little plea to Him as my heavenly Father: "Whatever happens, be it life or death, help me to trust You."

When the dark hours of the night closed in, they seemed endless. As I lay there sleepless in my upper bed, the words of this old hymn, that I had always thought was meant for men on skid row who had sought shelter in some rescue mission, became alive for me:

Abide with me, fast falls the eventide;
  The darkness deepens, Lord, with me abide;
When other helpers fail, and comforts flee,
  Help of the helpless, O abide with me!

One of the Catholic priests in camp evidently felt the same way as he said to a nun, "If we're going to get out of this alive, we better pray."

And the nun devoutly replied, "If we're going to get out of this alive, God will have to send the angels."

CHAPTER 46
Becalmed and Circled

STRANDED ON THE LAKE with no wind for their sail and a Japanese patrol boat circling them, Loren Brown and the reconnaissance men with him were deeply concerned that they might not be able to reach the Los Banos Internment Camp in time to carry out their vitally important assignments. Their responsibility was to eliminate the Japanese sentries in the pillboxes and those doing their exercises before they could shoot at the paratroopers descending from their planes.

Until the wind would blow and the Japanese patrol boat leave, there seemed nothing that Loren and the men with him could do. Loren appealed to the only source of help available —he prayed. After the war he would become a minister.

Seeing nothing suspicious, the patrol boat finally left. And on the day before the raid, the wind billowed out the limp sail.

Loren relates what happened then:

"We reached our appointed place near San Antonio. The other boats having already arrived, the men had left. Although they intended leaving someone to let us know that everything was fine with them, the shortness of time required that they continue toward their assigned posts.

"It was a wise decision not to wait. Among their several duties, three of those pathfinders had to send up columns of smoke into the air by using phosphorus to mark the landing zone for the amphibious tractors that would be crossing the lake in the darkness of the night, while others had to mark in a similar way the landing zone in which the paratroopers were to be dropped from the planes.

"We now headed for our assigned positions near the camp. The night was very bright, with the moon shining. This made it a little easier to navigate our way along the dikes between the rice paddies, but it also made us much easier to detect.

"The guerrillas had informed our group about one Japanese outpost. As we approached it, we thought the soldiers there had seen us, but that was not the case, and we 'neutralized' them.

"Because of the long delay on the lake, it was now absolutely essential that we speedily arrive at our assigned posts around the internment camp. In order to be in place on schedule, we had to run the last quarter of a mile. Some of the Filipino guerrillas could not keep up and had to be left behind, but a number of them remained with us.

"We approached the guard located on the hill behind the camp and arrived just as we heard the planes coming. The Japanese guard in the pillbox also heard the planes coming and was so busy watching them he posed no threat to us.

"Pete Miles had brought the daily schedule of the Japanese guards. Their strict adherence to this routine became the single most important key to the rescue. He said that the guards not in the pillboxes would be taking their exercises in the compound at 7:00 A.M., with their guns stacked and locked in an arms rack inside a barracks. (One guard would be getting ready to take the camp's roll call.)

"When we arrived, we saw the guards exercising and noted a few firearms at one side stacked in the shape of an Indian tepee."

Keeping out of sight, Loren tensed up as the planes roared

toward them, watching for the signal to start the attack and firefight—the opening of the first parachute.

They had to eliminate the guards before the Japanese could shoot the descending paratroopers and the prisoners. The tension while waiting for that first parachute to open was incredible.

CHAPTER 47
Angels with Great Wings of Silk
Nichols Field 6:45 A.M.
February 23, 1945

AS PILOT OF THE LEAD PLANE, Maj. Don Anderson describes the action:

"We took off from Nichols Field about 6:45 in the morning, assembled in formation, and learned that one of the planes had not pulled the landing gear pins, so they could not retract their gear. They asked what to do, as it would not be possible to maintain position at normal cruise power with the gear down.

"I replied, 'Full throttle even if you burn up the engines, but stay with us.'"

Los Banos Internment Camp 6:50 A.M.

"Time to start moving out for roll call," announced Ruth Woodworth in our cubicle. Having been an experienced teacher, she kept us on our toes in many different ways, and in such a gracious manner that we enjoyed it.

Straggling down the barracks aisle that I had swept many times as one of my off-and-on-again jobs, we looked like wilting, drooping, fading weeds that had finally lost all their chlorophyll. Starvation had robbed us of our strength and all that made our bodies vibrant with life.

But that was not the only reason our women were walking halfheartedly down that aisle. One of them near me expressed the fear lurking in all our minds, "Do you think they will massacre us at roll call, machine-gunning us?"

Overhearing this question, another women half whispered, "One of the men told me he saw the Japanese digging a big ditch."

"For us or for themselves when our army comes?" I chirped up, trying to put a spark of hope in their thinking.

"Oh, I know our American forces will come for us sooner or later, but later may be too late," commented a fearful woman.

We were unaware that outside our fences:

Amphibious tractors were roaring toward us.

Planes were flying.

Reconnaissance men were scrutinizing.

Guerrillas were creeping.

All were waiting for the planes.

Our conversation continued:

"Can we hold out until they arrive?"

"Will the fighting in Manila ever end?"

"Do you think they won't rescue us until all the territory between here and Manila is in American hands?"

"There's the gong for roll call. Pray they won't shoot us."

Time for roll call—7:00 A.M.

"Listen! Quiet everyone! Is that thunder in the distance or airplanes?"

"Look over there! Airplanes!"

"American or Japanese?"

"Oh, pray God they're American!"

"How low they're flying!"

"If they are Japanese, they could mow us down while we stand here in line! Maybe that's the way they'll do it."

"They're flying right toward us!"

"God help us if they are Japanese!"

"Something's falling from them!"

"Could it be bundles of food?"

In the flash of those few moments, thoughts whirled in our minds.

As the planes flew by, I yelled, "Stars! I see stars! *They're American!*"

The very air seemed electric with excitement. Then one of the men called out, *"They're paratroopers!"*

Everyone started pointing and screaming with joy, "They've come! They've come!" It became the vibrant song of heart and soul.

The little nun who had said, "If we're going to get out of this alive, God will have to send the angels," stood looking up at the white silk parachutes floating down in the blue sky. With an almost worshipful expression on her face she said, "He sent the angels!"

Grace Nash commented that they looked "like Greek gods coming down from heaven."

Hysterically happy, we were not in a position to see the paratroopers land, but we heard gunfire that seemed to come from several different directions. Most of us ran inside our barracks and dived for some kind of cover. Having survived almost three and a half years as prisoners, we did not want to be killed in the final moments of rescue.

Our barracks of thin, woven matting and thatched roofs provided little protection against flying bullets.

There was no firm shelter, no place to hide.

Almost mesmerized by the sight of American planes flying right toward them and paratroopers descending, some of the Japanese guards just stood there in stupefied surprise, while others ran for the deep ravine.

Loren Brown describes the action: "When the planes were flying low over their heads, those Japanese doing exercises were distracted. We then eliminated them and confiscated their stacked guns.

"For a moment we thought there were Japanese behind us

on the hill shooting in our direction. Both the M-1 and the carbine shots from our rifles were flying, as well as 25-caliber shots from Japanese weapons, which turned out to be captured Japanese rifles in the hands of our friendly Filipino guerrillas."

Other men of the Reconnaissance Platoon were eliminating Japanese in pillboxes and wherever they spotted them. While one of these recon men was hiding behind a pillbox in the dark hours before dawn, waiting for the planes to come and the paratroopers to drop, the Japanese sentry in that pillbox unknowingly relieved himself right on the head of that American soldier who dared not move.

Loren Brown continues his experience: "All but one of those threatening pillboxes were eliminated within ten or fifteen minutes. When we were going down the hill, Japanese in that one pillbox sighted us and began firing. We took refuge behind a palm tree that had fallen diagonally on the hill. Jumping over it one by one from different spots behind the log, we then ran on down the hill.

"When my turn came, I jumped over the log, intending to keep very low, but my foot caught the log, and I sprawled head first on the ground. As I fell with my rifle in front of me, my face struck the rifle, and it bloodied my nose.

"Reaching for my helmet, which had fallen off my head, I discovered a bullet hole in the front and in the back, and thanked the Lord my head was not in it at the time!"

Ben Edwards could not see the inside of the camp from where he was hiding outside the fences, but he did see the C-47 transport planes carrying the paratroopers and the fighter planes accompanying them. Not knowing much about grenades, Ben threw a phosphorus instead of a fragmentation grenade. However, it did land in a guardpost.

Climbing over one fence and under another, Ben saw a Japanese running into a culvert. A Recon Platoon man flipped a grenade into the culvert, and a Filipino guerrilla administered the *coup de grace*.

Ben describes those fiery, battling moments: "There was considerable fighting for a few minutes. The tracer ammunition someone was firing looked like tennis balls floating through the air. Sometime during the attack, a bullet hit the ground in front of me. I was wearing the same khaki shorts I had worn during my escape, and either fragments of the bullet or rock splinters hit my legs, causing small wounds on both shins."

When Ralph and Grace Nash and their two little sons heard the gunfire, they ran to their cubicle. Ralph pulled the two boys into the soggy, spidery foxhole they had dug underneath their cubicle for just such an emergency. Grace carried baby Roy into their dugout; and then Ralph quickly grabbed slats from the boys' frame beds for a covering over their heads and was stashing a mattress on top just as bullets whizzed right over them. Their forethought and labor in digging that foxhole probably saved their lives.

Flying bullets are described by Jesse Tribble, who lived in Barracks Five:

"I realized what was taking place as soon as the first parachute opened and the shooting started.

"In one end of Barracks Eight lived the Kramer family. Harry was a veteran of the Spanish-American war and was voicing loud and clear his opinion of the Japanese. Being diagonally across from the Japanese Commandant's barracks, which was number three, Harry attracted gunfire from the Japanese compound.

"I grabbed my mattress as a shield against the flying bullets and rushed over to try and calm Harry down. I told Mrs. Kramer, her daughters Georgette and Effie, and son Donald to lie on the floor behind my mattress, which stopped many, but not all, of the bullets.

"Mrs. Kramer was hit in the arm below the elbow.

"Georgette received a bullet wound through the stomach wall—in one side and out the other.

"I was hit in my right hand with a bullet that remained there until it could be removed later at the field hospital in Muntinlupa.

"Harry Kramer, who drew the gunfire toward us, remained untouched!"

The walls of our barracks were made of *sawali* matting—thin, unable to stop bullets, and like kindling wood for any fire.

I had neither foxhole nor mattress, but needed some kind of armor to shield me from flying bullets.

Grabbing a nearby suitcase, navy blue in color and medium in size, I crouched behind it. Of light weight, it would not provide much protection, but it might slow up or deflect some bullet coming my way. I tried to keep my head down, but the compelling desire to watch what was happening often overcame my caution. However, each time I peeked, I saw nothing, just heard shooting.

Our barracks had some long, wide openings in the sides, four or five feet high and several yards long, with flaps to put down in case of heavy rain. In all the bedlam, no one thought to put those flaps down.

Suddenly four little brown men carrying guns jumped through the opening near me, waving their guns and shouting something we could not understand. I do not know who was the more concerned, those impassioned men or us, as they kept yelling unintelligible sounds.

Then Ruth Woodworth, who had lived in Manila for years and understood their accent, grasped what they were shouting: "Any Japs in here? Any Japs in here?" They were Filipino guerrillas searching out Japanese who might be hiding in our camp.

"*No!*" called out Ruth.

As they ran by, I had a vague impression that each one had a feather on some kind of headgear. I heard later that each one wore a feather from the tail of a rooster as an identifying mark, the logo, so to speak, of a guerrilla band known as "Terry's Hunters." Their idea of the feather came from Robin Hood. A respected ROTC group, it was led by Terry Adevozo, who later became Secretary of Labor for the Philippine government. It seemed an odd coincidence that of all the guerrilla groups, Terry's Hunters came to our barracks. My name at that time was Carol Terry.

In the meantime, the paratroopers had landed safely in the designated place on the other side of our camp's fences, where James Holzem was having trouble getting Oscar to move after landing. Oscar was more interested in opening his little reserve parachute pack to see whether there really was another parachute in it. He stood there astounded to find it true, while Jim tried to get him moving, and fast!

Colonel Ringler and most of the paratroopers quickly crossed the terrain and came into our camp, while the remaining paratroopers began eliminating specific targets on the perimeter and Japanese hiding in that area.

Inside the camp things were going a bit wild. One of the Japanese officers leaped through a window, heading for some foliage, but recon men soon ended his flight. Some Japanese tried hiding around the barracks area of the prisoners and had to be ferreted out, while others tried fleeing into a nearby culvert. Among those who safely escaped were Okamoto and the camp villain, Konishi.

While the intensive firing lasted no more than twenty minutes, it seemed like forever to us. As it tapered down into sporadic firing, some of our starving men raided the Japanese food supplies, gorging on their sugar and cooked rice, a few carting it off to their cubicles to share with others, while eyes of dead Japanese stared up at them.

Excitement, gunfire, danger, killings, men running here and there, mothers comforting frightened children, Filipino guerrillas dashing about—all causing tension and confusion. The capable Lieutenant (later Colonel) Ringler took control.

Feeling a little braver myself, though trembling a bit inside, I joined the other women in our barracks, slowly creeping out from our hiding places. Then seeing some of the paratroopers, we ran, overcome with unrestrained joy and unaware that we were still in danger, and hugged those wonderful men. They didn't object!

Colonel Ringler describes the scene: "There was much jubilation, with everybody wanting to hug the men and congratulate them. My effort was to eliminate all of that and immediately get the people organized."

Just then we heard a roaring sound, and many of us women prisoners panicked. Postponing until later the hugging of our heroes, we shouted, "Jap tanks! Jap tanks!"

Terror filled the hearts of some prisoners who realized that the dreaded General Fujishige and his ten thousand soldiers could massacre all the prisoners as well as the relatively small force of valiant soldiers who had come to rescue us.

Colonel Ringler explains the action he took: "We had to react to this, because in our position we did not know whether they were Japanese tanks or our own amphibious tractors. We relocated a couple of our bazookas to counteract them."

The very air now became laden with tension and suspense. I fled back to my barracks and the little hiding place behind my suitcase. Located at the far end of the camp, our barracks would probably be out of the direct line of fire. We were also some distance from the center of any news and had no way of knowing what was happening.

I chose safety over news, but who would be safe if those tanks roaring toward our camp carried Fujishige's ten thousand troops? In a women's barracks, perhaps I was in the most dangerous place of all.

CHAPTER 48
Escape at Dawn

AS MAJOR BURGESS and his amphibious tractors roared toward Los Banos Internment Camp, a Japanese officer rushed out of a house, carrying his sword and trying to pull up his pants at the same time. A shot from the leading amtrac finished him.

Guns pointing at them from a stone pillbox looked threatening, but the occupants had been grenaded by the Reconnaissance Platoon.

Riding in the lead amtrac, Burgess felt his heartbeat quicken and his whole body tense up as they crashed through the prison's gate and barbed wire fences. What would they find on the other side?

Before he had time to look around, the soldiers poured out of those amtracs like water from a fountain. Since the Reconnaissance Platoon had reported locations of Japanese soldiers in the peripheral area, squads from Mesereau's C Company had already fanned out to designated positions, with the immediate mission of preventing Japanese reinforcements from reaching the camp, especially Fujishige's.

"We could hear firing from the direction of the camp," commented Mesereau, "but could only wonder what was transpiring. I was kept partially informed by battalion radio." Captain Mesereau and his C Company troopers waited and watched, alert to every snap of a twig and movement of a leaf.

Lieutenant Fraker, with about fifty men from A Company, protected the loading area.

"For some time after we secured the camp," commented Burgess, "our troops continued to find Japanese hiding in the area several hundred yards around the camp, which resulted in isolated, sharp clashes and bullets flying over everyone.

"I was appalled at the condition of the internees. None of us was prepared for what we found, most of the men weighing no more than 110 pounds and the women resembling sticks. A few children had survived and were very weak. The prisoners were now in a condition of hysteria and euphoria and they didn't know where to go nor what was expected of them. Time was running against us in such confusion. The two hours we had figured before elements of the Japanese 8th Division could arrive had started ticking away."

The 1st Battalion of the 188th Glider Infantry Regiment had not arrived with trucks for evacuating the freed prisoners and no one could establish radio communications with Colonel Soule, although firing could be heard from their direction.

Time was of the essence and immediate action had to be taken. The men, women, and children were scrambling here and there, many hiding in the barracks because of hearing gunfire. There was no loud-speaking equipment to use for communicating with them. Paratroopers were sent running through each barracks ordering the people out to the assembly area.

The internment camp covered sixty acres, with twenty-eight long barracks in rows, housing more than two thousand people.

I received no news and could not interpret the sounds. On hearing the roar of tanks, none of us knew whether they were Japanese or American. As the paratroopers tried to get the people out, some were slow to comprehend the need to leave at once.

Like most everyone, I thought the American army had come in to seize the whole area. Our dullness and inertia must have been frustrating to the paratroopers, who knew that their lives and ours depended on fleeing immediately before Fujishige's thousands could entrap us.

Hiding behind my little fortress of a suitcase, I felt a false sense of security.

Then suddenly appearing from somewhere, a towering giant loomed over me. Clad in olive-drab green, with a large helmet on his head, boots on his feet, and a gun in his hand, he looked like someone from another world. As this "super human" spoke, his voice was not gentle and soft, but strong, pressured, urgent, and compelling in its intensity, "Lady, you've got five minutes to get into an amtrac."

I didn't have the faintest idea what he was talking about. Still crouching behind my suitcase and looking up at him I asked timidly and politely, "What's an amtrac?" It sounded like the name of a prehistoric monster.

The paratroopers still had hundreds to notify and time was running out. He looked at me with desperation and a command not to be ignored, "Now you've got *two* minutes to get in that amtrac," and moved on to tell others.

"What is an amtrac?" I still wondered. *"How will I recognize it? Where will I find it? How do I get there?"*

Giving little thought to what my suitcase contained, I threw some clothes into it and ran toward the front of our barracks. Suddenly I remembered my hidden tin can. Without a thought of being shot or left behind, I wheeled around and ran back toward my cubicle, passing the paratrooper who had ordered me out.

With a look of desperation, that wonderful paratrooper shouted, "Wrong way!" and chased after me.

Reaching the little garden of weeds outside our cubicle, I

started digging frantically with my bare hands, shouting, "My tin can! My tin can!"

The paratrooper dug it up and thrust it into my eager hands, probably thinking he had rescued my family's jewels. Its buried treasure was far more valuable—my diary, written partly in tiny shorthand.

In no uncertain terms he indicated I was to run "on the double" and get into an amtrac. Having been a track star in my school days, I made it, scrambling up the rear ramp of an already crowded amphibious tractor.

Some firing could still be heard in the direction of the "piggery," when a woman grabbed Ben Edward's arm and pointed to our arch black marketeer, the "king of the weasels." "Shoot him!" she screamed. "He's a traitor."

Ben did give her request some thought as he remembered how that man had fed canned salmon to his pet cat while little children starved.

In that excited, moving mass of humanity, Ben then spotted two soldiers carrying our camp hero, Pete (Prentice) Miles, on a stretcher. Afraid Pete had been wounded, Ben rushed to his side. Exhausted but conscious, Pete was clutching his prized rifle, which he asked Ben to keep for him. Miles had not been wounded, but his daring and arduous journeys in his efforts to save us had drained all his strength. We were to lose our hero to a heart attack in 1962.

Time was running out, and Colonel Gibbs was becoming nervous. He wanted to get his amphibious tractors out of there because they were slow moving, and let the trucks coming with the 188th Glider Infantry Regiment evacuate us as planned. But the 188th had not arrived yet, and Burgess could not establish any radio contact with them. Very faintly he could hear firing still coming from their direction. Although the colonel outranked the major, Burgess convinced him he must stay. The 188th never did arrive with the trucks. Had the amtracs gone off and left us there, we would have been massacred by the Japanese.

In all the confusion and excitement, people were dillydally-ing in their barracks, trying to decide what to take and what to leave behind. When some did not respond to the paratroopers' orders to get out immediately, Ringler noted that the Japanese barracks were burning from the firefight, causing people to run away from the flames toward the amtracs. Burgess then gave an order, "Fire the barracks!" Soldiers began running through each barracks, shouting, "EVERYBODY OUT IN FIVE MINUTES!"

Trying to avoid flying bullets, Mrs. Silen and her three young daughters were keeping low and huddled together when a bullet whizzed through the thin *sawali* walls and struck her twelve-year-old daughter. She had no medical supplies and dared not try to reach the hospital in all the confusion and bul-lets flying.

When an American soldier came running through her bar-racks shouting, "Everybody out of this barracks in five min-utes," she called out to him, "My daughter has been shot. She's wounded."

The soldier, whom Mrs. Silen thought to be a sergeant, ran into her cubicle, quickly examined the child, and then or-dered, "Leave her. We'll take care of her."

Almost gasping in unbelief that she had to leave her wounded, bleeding daughter, she gave the child a clean cloth for wiping away the blood and found a little something to give her to eat, and then, blinking back tears, took the hands of her other two children and walked away, trusting God and the army to take care of the little girl she had to leave behind. What faith in God and in our soldiers!

The three of them were guided toward an amtrac and climbed up its rear ramp. People from all over the camp were now surging towards the amtracs. Mrs. Silen's eyes searched and searched in vain for a glimpse of her wounded daughter.

Ben Edwards describes his efforts to help get people out and into the amtracs. "We encountered almost complete non-cooperation from some older men who refused to leave with-

out their trunks, boxes, and other belongings, most of which
was probably just junk, but considered treasure because it was
all they had. Some were so confused they did not know what to
do. I made one last appeal to them, and when they didn't
leave, I set fire to the far corner of the barracks with a carefully
placed incendiary grenade. They moved out then!"

"Get packed to leave!" was the order yelled at Peter and
Cae Paget.

"I fled down to the front of the barracks and looked out,"
Cae remembers. "The barracks just two doors down was in
flames, so I rushed back.

"'Let's take what we can carry and get out,' I said to Peter.
We seized what we could manage to drag and rushed outside,
Joy clinging to her battered doll, Ruth.

"'Who wants sugar?' someone across the way asked. We
paused, even in this moment, to grab a cupful and take turns
eating by spoonfuls.

"Then we were staggering along the road. The barracks on
either side of us were by this time ablaze, and the air was thick
with flames and smoke, the heat licking at us as we passed
along. Everywhere was confusion. Ashes fell in showers. Heat
of the fires reached out from all sides, as people were struggling along, dragging luggage.

"Soldiers appeared everywhere carrying rifles, their young
faces curiously tense. 'Hurry! Hurry! Hurry!'

"The soldiers cheerfully packed us into great, monstrous
amphibious tanks. The men who manned the tanks were like
beings from another world, so young and sturdy and ruddy
and altogether beautiful were they—only youths, but to us, de-
liverers.

"Several women had put on their entire wardrobe, in order
to save what they could of their belongings, and were gasping
in the heat and dust."

When Isla Corfield, a sophisticated Englishwoman accustomed to the finer things in life, heard the planes and saw the
paratroopers dropping, she realized rescue was near but con-

tinued preparing some breakfast for herself and teenaged daughter, "Gill."

Whatever happened, food was important, and she had no thoughts at that moment of having to flee.

Then a paratrooper appeared at her cubicle. He said politely but with authority, "You've got five minutes to pack and get out," and offered her a welcome cigarette.

Picking up the two suitcases she had kept packed for such an emergency, Isla and her daughter joined the cavalcade of men, women, and children heading for the amtracs, some half carrying, half dragging old suitcases, mothers shepherding their children, everyone holding an out-of-shape old box stuffed to overflowing or a bulging bag containing all they had left of material things in this world. In the rush and crush, little ones were stumbling and crying, frightened by things they did not understand. Priority on the amtracs was given children, the sick, and the elderly.

This surging mass of humanity resembled the "children of Israel" fleeing from the Pharaoh and his armies in Egypt.

As Isla was nearing the amtracs, she remembered that she had forgotten her daughter's favorite suitcase and ran back to their cubicle.

Not only were the Japanese barracks burning, but some of the prisoners' barracks were now on fire. It took a brave and determined woman to run near those flames. Grabbing the suitcase, she ran back to the main gate as the roaring sound of the amtracs mixed with smoke from the fires.

Isla made it to the last amtrac just in time to see it moving away from the camp. Stunned, she stood there with her daughter in unbelief. They had "missed the boat."

A soldier came over to the dismayed group of unfortunate people who had delayed too long in spite of warnings and said, "I'm sorry. You'll have to walk with us. We can't risk staying here any longer." General Fujishige's horde might come pouring over the hill any moment.

Among the internees having to make that long and difficult

walk to the lake, as they carried bundles and suitcases, was a stranger. Fifty-six years of age, Frank Smith was a parachuting newspaper reporter from the Chicago *Sun Times*. As an experienced war correspondent, he was accredited to General MacArthur's command and had taken part in several landings, including New Guinea and the Philippines.

Smith came in with our rescuing forces. He had wandered around the camp, looking in various barracks, and then came to the one used as a Catholic chapel. Walking through it, he saw a large pulpit Bible that would soon be burned by the approaching flames. Everyone had left the area. Taking it reverently in his hands, he carried it with him on that long walk to the lake.

As the prisoners trudged along, scattered firing from the Japanese sent them running for ditches beside the road, some tumbling into them. But Lou Burris and his artillery soon silenced this firing from enemy soldiers who seemed to be hiding in caves and in deep foliage.

Fighter planes from our air force were providing air cover, keeping the Japanese away from us. General Swing and Major Anderson continued flying overhead, watching everything; Filipinos were carrying suitcases and bundles for the weak but happy rescued prisoners.

Many prisoners had no shoes, just blocks of wood held on their feet by straps. This greatly complicated their walking.

Colonel Burgess describes the scene as the freed prisoners rode and walked more than two miles to the lake:

"The walk was an ordeal for the internees. We gave them all our rations, which were rich, high protein, and concentrated, causing many of them to become ill. Some internees were traveling so slowly that it was going to take many hours to reach the beach. Two malfunctioning amphibious tractors left behind had now been repaired and were used to shuttle many people unable to continue walking to the beach.

"Among such groups were several priests and a large number of nuns. They were loaded into a tractor, and as it ambled through the troops, it brought forth gales of hearty laughter. Following the custom of all GI pilots and truck and tractor drivers of painting the name of a girl friend on their vehicles, the amtrac driver evacuating the nuns had named his the "Impatient Virgin." (The driver's fiancée in America had signed one of her letters to him, "The Impatient Virgin," and he used that for the name of his amtrac.)

"One of our strongest, toughest, and smartest men was Sergeant Muntz, a great football player and the Battalion Operations Sergeant. We came upon a woman near the end of the column with a baby in her arms, so exhausted she could no longer carry her child. I insisted that Muntz carry the baby, which brought forth some catcalls until Muntz told the hecklers he would wait for them on the beach. By the time he reached the beach, he was devoted to the bundle. It was such a transformation of the man, but not permanent."

Unaware that some had missed getting aboard the amtracs, we were riding to freedom with the greatest of joy. As we clanked along the roads, Filipinos came out of their homes and waved at us, while we waved a small American flag.

Pockets of Japanese still remained in the area, and while we were rambling along, reveling in fun and fellowship with our rescuers, the sound of gunfire startled us.

"*Get down!*" our heroes shouted, swinging their guns into action. A piece of hot metal, maybe one of our own spent gun shells, fell on my bare foot. I was wearing those wooden clogs held on my feet by a strap over the toes.

When the gunfire ceased, the soldiers could not stand our pitifully starved faces and gave us treats from their supplies.

Riding in another amtrac, our camp songwriter, James Reuter, composed this farewell song to our Los Banos Internment Camp, written to the tune of "Good Night, Sweetheart."

'Bye, Los Banos, I am going home;
'Bye, Los Banos, you stay here alone!
I like your sunset and beautiful dawn,
But in the morn
I want more than corn!

So I say—

'Bye, Los Banos, with your blue lake beside you,
'Bye, Los Banos, 'mid hills that almost hide you;
I can't abide you!
I've been too long inside you!
'Bye, Los Banos, good-bye!

Feeling secure in our armored chariots and guarded by our own soldiers, we rode merrily along. It truly was one of the happiest times in our lives. No one knows what it is like to be free until he has been a prisoner. And the young men who rescued us entered into our happiness as almost no one else on earth could have done. I'm sure their chests were swelling with pride as we praised and thanked them.

Unaware that these amtracs were amphibious, I was dumbfounded when we reached the lake and saw no boats to take us across. We were still in Japanese territory. Could we be ambushed here?

The following stanzas are from a long poem entitled "The Soul of a Soldier," written by Robert A. Edwards, D Battery, 457th Parachute Field Artillery Battalion, one of the soldiers who crossed the lake in amphibious tractors coming to rescue us. Edwards, strongly influenced by the Los Banos experience, later became a Doctor of Divinity.

A sound of rapid gunfire not far ahead
Foretold the prison camp's rescue now begun.

Short minutes later we rounded a bend
And found a bamboo wall, looming high.
Thus, we knew we had arrived at last
And Los Banos prison would be no more!

A shifting of gears, a sudden lunge
Of a vehicle, the barrier crashed down.
Exposed to our curious eyes, a large stockade
And a group of ragged souls
Standing, staring, too stunned to move,
Not able to comprehend that they were free!

Then silently, slowly at first, then faster yet
They walked toward us, toward the gap in the wall,
Toward the light of the sky, toward the
Arms of Liberty, the freedom of soul!
Ragged and torn, pale and wan, they walked,
Not daring to breathe, too frightened to speak.

Can I ever forget their faces? The look in their eyes?
Can I ever forget the trembling hand which grasped mine?
Can I ever forget the faltering steps they took
Upon crossing the line where once stood a wall?
Or the uncontrolled pride as they softly said,
"Somehow we just knew you would come!"

A thousand nights of fighting, of bitterness, of hell,
A thousand nights of banzai attacks, hand grenades,
    and shells,
A thousand nights of watchfulness, of sudden screams
    of death,
All, all compensated by the rescued one's tears.
A thousand island beachheads, jungles, caves, and hills,
A thousand jungle fevers, accidents, and ills.
A thousand soldiers' bodies passed by on the roads,
All, all for the gratitude in the rescued one's tears.

It was then I knew I was seeing God!
I saw Him in the eyes of toughened soldiers,
I saw Him in the eyes of sick and suffering souls!
And suddenly I wanted to fall upon my knees in prayer...
I opened the doors to the church of my being.
The music was sung by the choir of my soul.
The sermon of Love was delivered by God
And found its place in my heart, my heart.

CHAPTER 49
Fleeing to Freedom

AS WE SURVEYED the large expanse of murky water, we were surprised and happy to see a line of our big amphibious tractors curving across Laguna de Bay, leaving a trail of churning foam and little waves in their wake. The amtrac did not resemble a sleek and smooth sailing yacht racing in the wind, but looked more like a big walrus lumbering through the water. The horrendous noise of them shouted to the wind and to the Japanese that we were there, but they were chariots of iron for our salvation.

Our amphibious tractors continued entering the lake one after another, stirring up its waters. But the artillery had to be called when the Japanese began firing at the last few amtracs as their final "good-bye."

Ed Allman describes the action: "We received a radio message that the departing amtracs were being fired upon from a point of land east of the beach area. After establishing communications with the guns, Captain Burris began adjusting fire upon the bunker. No more than a few rounds had been fired by our guns when we ourselves came under fire, evidently from a sniper in the wooded area of the hill in front of us.

"We quickly disassembled the radio and hightailed it down

the road toward the Bay, coming upon a trail that looked as though it led right up to the point and the Japanese machine-gun emplacement.

"Again the radio was set up, communications to the guns established and adjusting fire resumed, using two of our howitzers."

While this was going on, Graham Nelson, a British geologist, was riding in the thirteenth amtrac. The driver decided to cut parallel to the shore at less distance than the other craft in order to avoid their backwash. Nelson describes the comedy of serious mishaps:

"So that I could get a better view of the action, I climbed onto the ledge and lay down to watch the planes flying overhead and the numerous amphibious tractors pouring into the lake—over fifty in all. Machine-gun fire suddenly erupted from the nearby shore and raked some of the amtracs, including the one in which I was riding. Before I could duck down into the hull, a bullet entered my left leg, shattering the large bone. Everyone was huddled in the craft when I came tumbling down. I fell in such a way that the lower portion of my injured leg lay on the lap of another internee.

"When firing had first started from the well-hidden Japanese machine-gun nest ashore, the two soldiers manning the guns on top of our cab began returning the fire. Things became a bit hot, however, and one of the gunners jumped into the hold and landed on top of my already broken leg, breaking the smaller bone. I was pretty unhappy at that time.

"The driver of the amtrac began pulling away from the shore at top speed.

"My leg was bleeding profusely, and one of the soldiers on our amtrac applied a tourniquet and tried to make me as comfortable as possible."

As the amtrac in which I was riding lumbered into the lake, it reminded me of when the Red Sea parted before the Israelites, with the promised land on the other side, as we fled across the water with the enemy pursuing us.

One of the rescued internees, Leo Cullum, describes his experience: "When we left the camp, space inside the amtracs was reserved for women. I noticed there was room on the 'forward deck' of an amtrac and climbed on, joining a paratrooper there, possibly Albert Jones, who had injured his leg in the jump onto the camp. While we rode along, other pedestrians tossed their bags to me.

"As we entered the lake, Albert Jones and I were seated on cushions there on the forward deck. The lake was shallow and uneven, and our amtrac hit a shallow spot, climbing up and diving down the other side, causing a wave across the forward deck that washed Jones and me overboard. The buoyant cushions and valises floated us off.

"I was in no danger because a valise popped up alongside of me and served as a life buoy. However, Jones, with his injured leg, was in trouble. He yelled for help, and paratrooper Paul Schramm dived in and rescued him."

(Cullum's students later joked that his teaching notes had fallen overboard and he had dived into the lake to rescue them!)

"There was some irregular shooting by the Japanese from the shore. One spent bullet landed in the amtrac."

When out of reach of the Japanese guns, we started enjoying our trip across the lake. A few brought out small American flags they had kept hidden through the years and joyfully waved them. No Fourth of July parade could equal in patriotism and joy our parade of rescued prisoners across that lake as we fled from the Japanese just in the nick of time. No one ever loved America more than we did that day.

As I stepped out of the amtrac into American territory, there flowed through my whole being an intense feeling of love and appreciation for my country and for every person helping us win the war. Standing by the lake, I offered thanks to God and a prayer for America that it would remain forever free.

Some of the rejoicing ex-internees raised both arms heavenward in exaltation, some thanking the soldiers, others running to greet fellow ex-prisoners, sharing experiences, hugging, enjoying. *We were free!* Who can describe it? It was like breathing fresh air after having been smothered.

Milling around in that rejoicing crowd of people still lugging their awkward bundles or dragging suitcases and wiping away perspiration in that humid, muggy weather, I searched for the Pagets but could not find them.

In our excitement, most of us did not realize that only fifteen hundred internees had been transported in those amtracs, with a few soldiers to guard us. More than seven hundred of our fellow ex-prisoners were still on the Japanese side of the lake, waiting for the amtracs to return and pick them up. Each amtrac could carry only about thirty-five internees with their luggage. Protecting the waiting group were some of our officers and troopers as Japanese started firing at them.

As more and more of the amtracs returned and the waiting crowd grew smaller, the Japanese became braver and drew closer. In the midst of all this, Major Burgess received a radio call from General Swing, who was flying overhead in a Cub plane.

Burgess reported the situation to him. Pleased at the successful rescue, Swing asked whether Burgess and his troopers, after they had safely evacuated all the ex-prisoners, could capture the town of Los Banos and then move on to link up with the 188th Infantry without serious casualties.

Major Burgess was so startled by this suggestion that he turned off the radio to give himself time to think through the suggestion, risking reprimand for breaking communication with the commanding general. It was a tough decision to make with more than two thousand rescued men, women, and children still in his care. He considered the following factors:

1. Some of the troops had marched all night, and the others had had little or no sleep.

2. They had no food, as the troopers had given all of theirs to the starving prisoners.

3. He could not establish radio communication with the 188th Infantry and did not know whether they were still at Lecheria Hills or the Rock Quarry or on their way to Los Banos.

4. Up until now every soldier knew exactly what he was to do. Changing plans at this time could result in confusion. They would be marching for six or seven hours in enemy territory in unfamiliar terrain with no maps.

5. If his 460 men were attacked by General Fujishige's well-equipped thousands, the result could be catastrophic. He would not have the help of the amtracs and their operators because the XIV Corps general had ordered their withdrawal after evacuating the prisoners.

After considering all aspects of the situation, and since General Swing had put it as a question, not an order, Burgess decided the negatives were too many and continued with the established plan, probably saving his troops from being decimated.

Colonel Lahti had selected Burgess to be in command of our rescue because he knew him to be an excellent combat leader and trusted his judgment in a crisis. No reprimand followed because Burgess' decision was the right one.

Ben Edwards rode in one of the last amtracs to start across the lake under Japanese fire. Among the amtracs hit was the one in front of Ben, which he says for a short time "looked like it was riding a wave. The stern rode high and the bow low, as if surfing."

Major Burgess was in one of the last six amphibious tractors to enter the lake. Bracketed by Japanese firing, the amtracs zigzagged and escaped.

Among those riding in the last amphibious tractor were Lt. John Ringler, James Holzem, "Oscar," and a Filipino guerrilla.

Ringler describes what happened: "After crossing the lake, we were unloaded from the amtracs. We then reloaded on an amphibious duck. This is a four-wheel amphibious vehicle and not a track vehicle. The road was several feet above the rice paddies. As the vehicle slid off the side of the road and tipped on its side, we were thrown into the rice paddy. This was one of the rare times that I lost my cool and told the driver that I was going to court-martial him, for he had alcohol on his breath. After I had regained my composure, I did not take any punishment against the driver of the vehicle." No injuries occurred in the accident.

Captain Mesereau later described his feeling while crossing the lake in one of the amtracs carrying rescued prisoners: "There was just enormous excitement and joy in transporting those people to the other side of the lake. They were very happy and most eager for news concerning the progress of the war and events in the United States. We heard a lot of talk about eating a good meal again. They had been served some army rations, which had become somewhat tiresome to us but tasted like ambrosia to them."

I stood watching that joyous crowd on the beach at Mamatid —military men caring for us so efficiently and yet tenderly, trucks, ambulances, medics carrying stretcher cases, everyone so concerned and wanting to help us in every way. Our chariots, the amphibious tractors, continued arriving with jubilant people pouring out of them. Just a few hours earlier we had been prisoners, expecting to be executed. Now we were free!

Viewing the whole scene, I became overwhelmed by the magnificent greatness and wonderful heart of America. I wanted to stand there and sing out:

My country, 'tis of thee,
Sweet land of liberty,
Of thee I sing. . . .

The rescued prisoners were now being seated in trucks, with stretcher cases and those who were very weak being placed in ambulances.

Graham Nelson continues the saga of his twice-broken leg: "I was loaded onto a stretcher, but the toes of my broken leg became caught in the belt of the southern black medic carrying the front of the stretcher. Lots of noise was going on, and he did not understand the reason for my yelling and screaming. He just kept calling back to me in his rich southern accent, 'Nevah mind! The medics will soon have you fixed up.' Someone alerted him to the situation, and my foot was disengaged from his belt."

Suddenly I felt a soldier firmly take hold of my arm and guide me to an ambulance, helping me climb into it. Just before we drove off, I saw the Pagets watching me, perspiration streaming down their faces. Joy appeared very weak. On the spur of the moment, I called out, "Give me Joy!"

I do not know what might have flashed through their minds in that moment of time. We had been fellow passengers on the *President Grant,* had dodged bombs at the Oriente Hotel, hid from Japanese in San Juan, shared worries, prayers, and heartaches together, as well as starvation and illness in the Los Banos camp, becoming almost like a family. But to be separated from their little daughter in war?

Without a moment's hesitation, they thrust her into my outstretched arms, and the ambulance moved off toward a sanctuary prepared for us.

As I held the nine-year-old girl close to me, questions went through my mind. I did not know where the army was taking us. Would Joy and I arrive in a different place from her mother and father? They were British and I was American. Some time back Cae had given me the names and addresses of their relatives in Canada in case anything happened to them and I could save Joy.

The little lassie and I clung to each other. I stroked her fine blonde hair, wiped the perspiration from her face, and assured her everything would be all right now because we were safe in American hands. Her blue eyes looked up into mine with such trust, I would have given my life to protect that frail and frightened child.

Riding along in the ambulance, we could catch a glimpse now and then through the windshield of Filipinos standing guard for us along the roadsides, and I wanted to call out "Thank you!" I did give them the "V for victory" sign.

Then we approached a huge fortress with high walls and towers, which somehow reminded me of tales of the Foreign Legion and a book I had read years before, entitled *Beau Geste*. But flying from the top of a tower on this fortress was a large American flag. What a sight! Pride filled my heart and tears streamed down my face.

We were driving through the entrance of New Bilibid Prison at Muntinlupa, which had just been wrested back from the Japanese. The military selected this prison as our refuge because it could be defended and would accommodate our thousands. Colonel Lahti was there, with his wounded arm in a sling, waiting to welcome us. We were safe, secure, and happy in the care of our American army.

When our ambulance stopped inside the gates, its back doors were opened and a young and handsome soldier helped us out. On his uniform I noticed the letters "MP." Having come from a military family, I knew that stood for "Military Police," and I felt doubly secure. As I thanked him, it was the first time I had ever seen an "MP" smile. He looked so young, I wanted to give him a hug, but refrained, feeling that was not exactly the thing to do to a military policeman.

"Milk and soup are now being served," he informed us, indicating the direction.

Joy and I lost no time in getting there. Hand in hand, we almost ran.

The people serving the milk and soup seemed to be as happy to give it to us as we were to receive it. Watching Joy drink that milk brought tears of gratitude to my eyes and a prayer of thanksgiving, mixed with a request for God's blessing on the wonderful men in our American army. Much as I enjoyed my soup, it was seeing Joy drink the milk that stirred my heart.

We watched the ambulances and trucks arriving loaded with rescued prisoners.

"Who do you think will see your mother and father first, you or I?"

"I will!" she confidently exclaimed.

When I first spotted Cae coming in on a truck, I remained silent, so Joy could have the pleasure of calling out first.

Soon her thin little face lit up with excitement. "Mummy! Mummy!" she called out, waving her hand.

When Cae climbed down, Joy ran to her with arms outstretched, calling out, "Mummy, they gave me some milk."

We watched for Peter, and he soon came along in another truck.

"Come on," I said, after they greeted one another. "They're giving out milk for the children and soup for the adults."

Cae describes it: "We filled up the bowls they gave us and went into a long room that had been transformed into a large dining hall for us. I looked at Peter. He seemed to have lost ten pounds since I had left him on the beach at the lake, so drawn and skeleton-like did he appear to me. It frightened me. His eyes were fixed on Joy with the strangest expression in them.

" 'They have given her milk, Cae; she's drinking milk,' he said in a broken voice and laid his head down on the table. I blinked back my tears and swallowed hard, but we soon forgot everything in the luxury of dish after dish of that nourishing bean soup."

Those who were caring for us were kindness itself. Serving dinner that evening lasted until after midnight.

Along with everyone else, I had been in line four times for milk. Some men went through the dinner line several times, insatiable, not heeding warnings that eating too much in our condition would make us ill.

After getting milk for the two children with her, Mrs. Silen started searching for the daughter she had been told to leave behind in the midst of flying bullets and burning barracks. She did not see her until the next day in the medical unit of this monstrous prison that had been turned into a place of refuge and hospital for us, as well as for soldiers wounded on the front lines.

The medics had taken good care of the little girl, who had been transported in an ambulance from Mamatid, and she fully recovered.

Mrs. Silen's courage in leaving her wounded daughter when bullets were flying and barracks were burning, and her faith in the soldier's word that the little girl would be taken care of, is one of the finest examples of courage and trust to emerge from our rescue, and among the noblest of tributes to our American soldiers.

We now had the privilege to thank and honor them.

CHAPTER 50
Honoring Our Heroes
Muntinlupa Prison

"WHAT IS YOUR NAME?" asked the Red Cross worker sitting at a little table out in the open. In front of her were typed pages containing long lists of names.

"Carol Louise Terry," I replied, hoping she would find my name on the list.

As she flipped through the pages, I stared at them. They looked like the ones I had typed for our roster at the Los Banos camp. Our George Gray had brought my roster out with the camp's minutes and other vital documents he rescued before leaving the camp.

The worker found my name, checked it off, looked up and smiled, and then gave me needed information regarding our new abiding place.

Then I was handed a Hershey chocolate bar and several packages of cigarettes. Losing no time in tearing the paper wrapper off that chocolate bar and sampling its luscious taste, I then ate it voraciously. I could not stop until it was finished.

Some people felt that way about the cigarettes. They were so eager for them their hands almost trembled. But what should I do with mine? Then I saw Dr. Dana Nance strolling around. Knowing that he smoked, I went over and said, "Let me thank you, Dr. Nance, for the many times you helped me in the camp. I don't have any money to pay you in appreciation, but if you would like to have these cigarettes, I'd be very happy to give them to you."

"Oh! Thank you very much," he replied, and accepted the welcome gift.

Everyone was milling around, some hugging one another in uncontrollable happiness, others searching among the crowd for friends, hoping they had been rescued and were all right. Stretcher cases were being carried to the hospital wards.

Both Filipinos and Americans were imprisoned here during the war, and some had been executed. Since this big prison was located just a short distance behind the American lines, huge brown tents had been erected as hospital wards to accommodate wounded soldiers being carried in from the battlefront. I would visit and pray with some of them.

We were to occupy the prison wards and cells in the big cement buildings. I was given two khaki-colored army blankets and assigned a bed. Searching around, I found it in a long building with a room resembling a hospital ward, having two lines of decked beds made of flat boards with no springs or mattresses. I would have been glad to sleep on the floor or ground, so long as I was in American hands. How absolutely glorious!

Everyone in our cubicle at the internment camp had been assigned the same ward. I placed my two blankets on the bed above Ruth's.

Going outside, we heard excitement at the gate and rushed over there.

Our rescuers were marching in!

We cheered!

We applauded!

We threw kisses!

We reached out and touched!

Tears rolled down my cheeks and I made no attempt to wipe

them away. Nothing we could say or do could express how we felt.

Most of those paratroopers smiled back, others lowered their eyes modestly, with smiles trembling on their lips.

Our enthusiastic welcome reached through to each trooper. No words can ever describe the magic of that moment when our hearts reached out and touched theirs. For them, this moment made up for the hard times of war. These young men were only about nineteen years old, and the officers in their early to late twenties—the pride and joy of America.

And the military showed that it does have a heart. Our rescuers were allowed to stay there with us for a day or two before they marched away on another assignment.

Because the next day was my birthday, I was one of those selected to be interviewed on the radio. A breakfast was to be ready for us at 7:00 A.M., and that happened to be the time scheduled for the radio broadcast. Not wanting to miss the breakfast, I slept little and arose so early the stars were still shining. One of the first in line, I received my breakfast—a tablespoonful of cream of wheat and a half of a canned pear.

Sitting on the ground with a few others, I slowly savored every bite, wanting to hold it in my mouth for a while before swallowing it. Finally I realized there would be time before going on the radio to get in line for a second helping, and I promptly joined the line.

I was within about two people of getting my second serving when it was time for me to go on the radio. Thinking of what it would mean to my parents to hear I was alive, I had to choose between that and this second breakfast. I struggled in those few moments with making the decision and have been ashamed for the rest of my life that I chose the tablespoonful of cream of wheat and half of a canned pear! Starvation had warped our sense of values.

I sat down on the ground to eat with a small group of our rescuers, and as we chatted, I offered to write their parents when I arrived home and tell them of their part in our rescue since they could not do so for military reasons. They gave me the information, and on arrival home I kept that promise. Some of these letters were printed in their hometown newspapers.

In the evening we gave a program for our heroes. Among the songs was this favorite written by James Reuter:

In Honor of the Eleventh Airborne Division,
Which Rescued Us
To the tune: The Gay Caballero

There once was an airborne division
That jumped with machine-like precision,
They jumped out at dawn,
Right down on our lawn,
And we ate up all their provisions.

These soldiers who jump out of planes
Are handsome and very well trained.
They spread every Jap
All over the map,
And our losses were: One ankle sprained.

A great tank rolled out of the water.
Its driver took part in the slaughter.
He let down the back
Of his mammoth amtrac,
But he'd only take ladies aboard her.

That big tank rolled back in the water
With forty-five ladies aboard her,
Our gunner was grand
Until his gun jammed
Then he said things that he hadn't oughter.

But now all our dreams have come true
Because you jumped out of the blue.
The men have full plates;
The ladies have dates;
And we're all so grateful to you!

As I celebrated my birthday on that next day after our rescue, I thought what a present America had given to me—my
very life! I received birthday wishes from my "war pals" in
Los Banos and from Rev. E. J. Klippert, a fellow internee at
our camp, unknown to me but evidently a very alert and
thoughtful person. Each of us received an issue of candy and a
box of cookies. Word spread around that they were a gift from
General MacArthur. Whether this was fact or rumor I did not
know but saved the wrappers from the box of Nabisco Vanilla
Wafers and from a stick of Teaberry chewing gum for lifetime
souvenirs.

CHAPTER 51
We Thank Our God

Now thank we all our God
With hearts and hands and voices,
Who wondrous things has done,
In whom His world rejoices.

ON SUNDAY we gathered to give thanks to God for our thrilling escape at dawn, for those who planned it and the valiant men who risked their lives to give us freedom at sunrise.

Though not personally present, General MacArthur joined us in spirit with this message:

Nothing could be more satisfying to a soldier's heart than this rescue. I am deeply grateful. God was certainly with us today.
[Signed] Douglas MacArthur
General of the Army
Special Communique
24 February 1945

Since this large prison now served as a military hospital, soldiers who were recovering from other battles in the surrounding area came to the service in their maroon robes, some walking in on crutches.

Instead of giving the chaplain's sermon, I wish to record the words of Lt. Col. Thomas Mesereau given at one of our reunions.

While the paratroopers were descending to rescue us, the surprised nun who exclaimed, "He sent the angels," added a touch of reverence to this name for the paratroopers. It had been previously used as a sort of nickname for them in a slightly humorous sense.

Colonel Mesereau added more comparisons with these words from the Bible:

"Bring out the prisoners from the prison, and them that sit in darkness out of the prison house" (Isaiah 42:7, King James Version).

"The angel of the Lord by night opened the prison doors, and brought them forth" (Acts 5:19, KJV).

And the colonel commented, "That passage is not specific as to whether the angel was wearing an Eleventh Airborne 'patch' " (their insignia with wings).

"The chariots of God are twenty thousand, even thousands of angels" (Psalm 68:17, KJV). "This does not detail whether the chariots were C-47 planes or amphibious tractors."

Truly the tractors and planes were as chariots of God to us, and our rescuers as earthborn angels.

Mesereau continued:

"What is this magic, this nobility, this greatness of spirit that causes men and women to give of themselves and reach for the stars when pressures are so immense?

"Those of you who were soldiers in combat, and those who were prisoners of war, can relate countless stories of comrades who gave of themselves so unselfishly and sometimes died in the doing.

"Soldiering and imprisonment release qualities in human

beings that are often surprising, usually noble, and almost always unselfish.

"Among the holy deeds of a man of the clergy was substituting himself for another prisoner of war who was to be executed by the Germans during the second world war.

"Our Lord once said, 'Greater love has no one than this, that one lay down his life for his friends'" (John 15:13, New American Standard Bible).

> Lt. Col. Thomas Merereau
> One of Our Rescuing Officers
> Graduate U. S. Military Academy
> West Point

At the close of the chapel service, Communion was served. Beautiful Communion cups were used that had been fashioned from gun shells cut and molded into the shape of those used in churches, with the brass polished and shining like gold. They inspired and challenged me.

If God could cause a gun shell, which is an instrument of death and destruction, to be turned into a Communion cup representing communion with Himself and blessing as we remember Calvary, He can take our lives, no matter what has happened to us, and turn them into instruments of fellowship with the Lord and blessing to others.

The cups were collected at the close of the service, but after an appeal to the chaplain by a soldier who explained how I felt about them, he gave me permission to have one, a souvenir treasured the rest of my life.

Some time after our rescue, Thomas Mesereau went on to Japan as commander of Gen. Douglas MacArthur's Honor Guard. Over six feet tall, he stood near MacArthur during the signing of the peace treaty with Japan. This valuable document was then given to Major Mesereau to hand carry to Washington, D.C., and personally deliver to the president of the United States.

Anyone familiar with Tom Mesereau's integrity and battle record would know why he was selected to carry the peace treaty. An all-American football player for West Point, Mesereau had been equally aggressive in battle, noble and brave. He became known for picking up the enemy's unexploded, live hand grenades and tossing them back to explode on the enemy that had thrown them in the first place.

In his custody, the peace treaty would indeed have been secure. However, so much international publicity attended Mesereau's carrying the peace treaty that there was fear he might be attacked, perhaps killed, and the treaty stolen. Mesereau made the trip to Washington, D.C. with an official valise handcuffed to him as a cover-up, risking his life, and received the official reception in Washington. Meanwhile, the treaty was carried covertly by a secret courier to Washington, as a safeguard against any dissident who might want it destroyed.

Forty-one years later I received a call from his family to come at Colonel Mesereau's request to administer Holy Communion to him, as he had become seriously ill.

Considering it a sacred honor, I served him Communion from the gun shell communion cup that I had kept all those years.

Looking into my eyes at the close of the Communion ceremony, and knowing that he would soon be in the presence of his heavenly Commander in Chief, he said to me, "And now Tom Mesereau says good-bye to Carol."

A few days later Colonel Mesereau took his final "flight." I attended services for him in a cathedral and at March Air Force Base with tears in my eyes and a cross of white flowers graced with three red carnations—one each for his wife, daughter, and son.

We Thank General MacArthur
New Bilibid Prison
Muntinlupa, Philippines
February 28, 1945

Gen. Douglas MacArthur
Commander in Chief
U.S. Armed Forces in the Far East

Dear General MacArthur:

It is the unanimous desire of the former internees, who are now at this Camp, to express their sincere appreciation for release from the hands of the Japanese Army at Los Banos.

We request you to convey our deep feeling of gratitude to the officers and men of the military units which participated in the action last Friday.

Even the untrained observer was conscious that such an operation could only be achieved by the perfect coordination and timing of the Air Corps, paratroops, amphibious units and the guerrillas. Its success, which was effected without a serious injury to any of the 2,121 internees, speaks eloquently for the generalship and ability of the U.S. Armed Forces under your command. We are proud of them and we thank you.

Very respectfully,
Administration Committee
(Civilian Internees of Los Banos Internment Camp)
[Signed]
Murray B. Heichert, Chairman
L. T. Watty, Vice Chairman
George Gray, Secretary
A. D. Calhoun, Member
R. E. Cecil, Member
Clyde DeWitt, Member
W. F. G. Harris, Member

CHAPTER 52
Living with the American Army

EVERY DAY SOMETHING NEW made our lives exciting.

One day we suddenly heard the roar of planes overhead and were all startled and apprehensive to see parachutes drifting down right into our fortress. Deep in our thoughts lurked an ever-present fear that the Japanese might take reprisals against us, and some had become paranoid about it.

We stood staring almost hypnotized by those descending parachutes of various colors. As they drifted closer, we could see they were carrying packages, not people. Our soldiers around us did not seem excited, but secretly some of us wondered whether those packages contained Japanese explosives.

They contained food for us, the color of each parachute indicating the type of food being carried. I obtained a piece of a blue one for a souvenir. Why was our army dropping food by parachutes? Speculations abounded. "The Japanese have cut off our supply lines!" "We're starving, and they don't have enough food for us here." "We need food so badly they're flying it in, not waiting for trucks."

The truth may have been that it provided a faster and more convenient way for transporting our food supplies.

One morning I heard everyone shouting *"Mail! Mail!"* I

rushed out into the big open courtyard, and there posted on the side of one of the buildings were long lists of names from as high as we could read to the bottom of the wall. I stood watching as some people saw their names, jumped for joy, and ran to get their letters. Others stayed a long time scanning the lists and could not find their names. They turned away, their shoulders drooping, their hands wiping away tears. Seeing that, I wondered whether I had the courage to go up there and look. Not receiving a single letter would be hard to take.

After a while I took a deep breath and ran over there, found my section on the alphabetical pages, and searched down the list of names.

Then I saw it! Carol Terry—6. Six letters! One from Mother and Dad; one each from my brothers, George and Jack; and one each from Rev. Alfred C. Snead, representing the work I was going to in India, the Ramabai Mukti Mission, Mrs. Fay Eaton (one of my former professors at Woodbury College), and Zada Stevens of both Woodbury and Biola years. None of them could ever know what those letters meant to my heart.

All of us had worms. My friend Ruth had to be taken to the camp's hospital. While there she expelled a worm about six inches long. The army medics dished out pills every day to our crowd. We assumed that some of these pills were to get rid of our worms, but mine were enjoying themselves so much they refused to leave. They traveled with me to America, causing my mother great distress.

We were still in the fighting zone, and everything seemed to be bedlam—noise, guns, explosions, planes, parachutes, trucks, and wounded soldiers being brought in on stretchers. Though in the center of it all, we felt safe and secure behind those strong walls, with the Stars and Stripes flying high on a tower, and our American soldiers guarding us.

Rumors flew throughout the prison that General MacArthur visited us incognito, not with fanfare as at Santo Tomas for security reasons, but I questioned the truth of that rumor. It was

not his style. However, the treats we received this time were reported as gifts from him.

The Red Cross now gave pajamas to those who had none. I
had been sleeping in my dress. The prickly army blanket under and over me in that humid climate was uncomfortable, and
I was glad for the pajamas.

One day I wrote my mother, "I have no underclothes, but
the dress I am wearing is not transparent, so what does it matter?"

I also had no stockings or shoes, but those were mundane
matters compared to what they gave us now: Lipstick, red nail
polish, powder, and a hair brush. The men greatly appreciated
our having the cosmetics!

Then suddenly our fortress was attacked. We watched the
roaring about in tanks and firing by our soldiers as they returned the Japanese fire. While some of our women became
hysterical, I felt cold fear gripping my heart. If the Japanese
could get us back into their hands again, it would undoubtedly
mean torture and massacre. I thanked God our soldiers were
there.

We could not see what was happening outside our walls, but
the sounds were petrifying. I did not run about and scream as
some of the women did, but prayed to God not only for my
own protection but for our brave and alert defenders.

After a time the firing ceased. We never did hear just what
happened, but the Japanese kept sniping at us now and then.

The American soldiers were alert, brave, kind, and gallant—
as wonderful soldiers as ever were made anywhere in the
world. They took the children in their jeeps for joy rides
around the camp, played with them, and coddled us, putting
up good-naturedly with our internment-camp phobias. I heard
that one of the army doctors said none of us had yet returned
to normalcy. The following incident proves his point.

In the Los Banos Internment Camp, most of us did not have
any dishes and used coconut shells if we did not have a tin

can. We all preferred a tin can because it was easier to keep clean. We carried water, cooked, and washed ourselves in our treasured tin cans. They were our priceless possessions, but we could not take them with us when we fled from the Japanese.

One day at this fortress of refuge, some of our group spotted a garbage pit filled with empty tin cans dumped there by the army. We all stampeded for them. The soldiers argued in vain. They could not convince us that we could live without tin cans.

Finally the army gave in, and the soldiers brought out box after box of clean, shiny, empty tin cans and gave them to us. Many were to carry those cans clear to America and right into the reception and hospitality center of the beautiful Elks Club in Los Angeles.

The army continued to do everything they could for us, showing remarkable patience, caring for our aches and pains, feeding us with food that seemed ambrosial after the prison years. Because our stomachs had shrunk from starvation, we were fed according to doctor's orders and given only small portions at first. But some of our men were crazed for food. Seeing it stacked up in labeled boxes, they wanted more and more, and they wanted it *right now*. I marveled at the army's patience with all of us.

One day an announcement to this effect came over the loudspeaker: "When the internees at Santo Tomas Internment Camp were rescued, they were given all they wanted to eat, and some became ill and almost died from overeating. We rescued you, and we don't want to kill you now by giving you too much food. It will be increased gradually as you are able to assimilate it. There is plenty of food for everyone."

This quieted the men, and everyone began to relax a little.

Under General Griswold's command, the XIV Corps had the responsibility of taking care of us, under the immediate supervision of the corps surgeon, Col. Robert Allen. Everything needed was provided and more, including registration, food, medical examinations with appropriate care, and even music and movies. An important factor that meant a great deal was the kind and understanding manner in which they cared for the men, women, and children—all of us still troubled by our internment camp neuroses.

The officers and other personnel of our American army seemed to think of everything we needed and continued to be wonderfully kind to us, displaying no harshness or impatience with our dull stupidity and taking time to explain orders and situations we did not understand. In their dealings with us they were never harsh nor brash. I'm sure our crowd of more than two thousand must have tried their patience to the breaking point sometimes, but if that was so, they never showed it. Kindness, helpfulness, and at times even tenderness characterized their handling of us, while warfare continued outside our walls.

Watching all they were doing to help everyone, I decided to offer my services as one who could handle shorthand and typing.

After a few days I was called to the office of the Counter Intelligence Corps. They had set up a field office inside this fortress to gather information for various purposes. They needed an accurate typist who could be trusted to keep things confidential, and I was recommended by the officials from our internment camp at Los Banos, possibly because of my typing the internment camp roster.

The officer for whom I worked was Arthur A. Ellerd, a man of culture with a keen mind, an efficient officer, and a gentleman. I found it a joy to work with him for a few hours every day.

During those balmy evenings under the stars of a tropical sky, most of us socialized with the American soldiers, forgetting for a few enjoyable moments the war outside our massive walls and feeling secure inside our fortress, with its guards and military equipment protecting us. Since there was no shortage of soldiers, every girl could have a date with one or two or three or more!

Now that we were receiving good nourishment, our menstruation returned, and the Red Cross provided emergency supplies to take care of that problem.

And then suddenly a great surprise came my way.

Someone called me, "Carol, a soldier has just arrived in a jeep. He's asking for you."

Since I did not know anyone in all the Far East, who could it be?

CHAPTER 53
"Bill Has Found Carol!"

WALKING OUT toward the entrance, I saw a tall and slim soldier standing by an army jeep but did not recognize him.

"Carol!" he called out, walking eagerly toward me.

Puzzled, I asked, "Who are you?"

"I'm your cousin Bill."

"Bill?" I questioned, trying to tie in his present appearance with my sophisticated New York cousin.

Questions and answers flew back and forth. "I'm with the Counter Intelligence Corps," he explained, "and have just been stationed at the Santo Tomas Internment Camp in Manila. How about coming down there with me for a few days? You can bunk in with someone you know in the camp."

"Oh, Bill, I'd love to, but I'm also working for the Counter Intelligence Corps, and not sure I can get time off."

"Come on, we'll work it out."

Together we went to my boss, Mr. Ellerd. His first response was lukewarm, but when Bill showed his Counter Intelligence Corps credentials, that settled it.

Then I began having second thoughts. In New York Bill had been one of the best-dressed young men in the society circle. He now saw doubt creeping over my face.

"What's troubling you, Carol?"

Looking down at my old, worn dress, my legs without stockings, wooden clogs on my feet, and realizing, although he would not know, that I had no underclothes, I felt embarrassed. "Bill, I don't have any clothes to wear. You will feel ashamed to have people know I'm your cousin."

He drew closer, gently taking me in his arms. Putting one finger under my chin, he lifted up my downcast face until our eyes met. "Carol, we're in the midst of a war. Clothes do not matter here. I'm not exactly dressed for the opera, either. What's important is that America is winning the war, you and I are both alive, and some day we'll be back home again. That will be the time for nice clothes. Now we need good fellowship and kinship that warm the heart. Come along with me for a couple days. It will do us both good, and I'll see that you get back safely."

How could I resist? I realized anew why Bill had always been my favorite cousin, sensitive, gentlemanly, and with values that matched mine. As a child, he had been the leading choir boy in a large cathedral in New York City. Whenever we were together, he always played the grand piano and we sang. He had a beautiful tenor voice, and I could hardly carry a tune, but we enjoyed it. When he soared into opera, I remained silent and listened.

Soon we were riding merrily down the road toward Manila, my hair blowing freely in the wind. Jeeping along on war-torn roads was not like riding in Bill's car in New York, but somehow it was greater fun, and we laughed as we bumped along. I began to feel life flowing through me again.

My friends from the *President Grant*, Marion Childress, Anna Nixon, Dr. Evelyn Witthoff, and Geraldine Chappelle, gave me a great welcome and a place to stay at the Santo Tomas Internment Camp, which had been liberated before Los Banos. They also arranged for my food. How wonderful to have such friends! A few days after our rescue they had come by bus to the prison in Muntinlupa to see how I was and bring me little gifts.

Bill and I sauntered about and talked, sharing experiences. Toward evening, when darkness was falling, he said, "Let's go outside these walls. You've been behind prison walls far too long."

"It's dangerous out there, Bill, especially at night. Japanese snipers are hiding here and there."

"Yes, but I know a place where we'll be safe. The fellows congregate there. You'll be surrounded by soldiers."

I realized Bill spoke the truth. I had been behind prison walls and fences so long I was almost afraid to be outside them. Still feeling a bit timid about venturing out at night with Japanese around, I agreed.

When we came to the Santo Tomas gate, Bill showed his Counter Intelligence Corps pass and the guard let him through. "You can go," he said, "but the lady cannot."

"She is also working for the Counter Intelligence Corps," Bill answered. "Show him your pass, Carol."

After looking at my pass, the guard said to Bill, "She's come down here on business and you're taking her out socially. Is that the idea?"

"Well, not exactly," replied Bill. "You see, Carol is my cousin."

"Oh, yeah?" answered the guard. "I've heard that kind of story before."

Bill and I both laughed, and I assured the guard that we really were cousins.

Whether he believed us or not, he said to Bill, "Well, all right, but have her back inside this gate by ten o'clock, and I mean ten o'clock *tonight!*"

"Thank you," Bill courteously replied, and away we went, happy as two carefree high school kids out on a lark.

"There is only one place near here safe to be at night, Carol, and it's not like any place I would take you in New York

City. Soldiers will be there, some smoking, a few drinking any-thing they can scare up, but it's fairly safe from Japanese snip-ers because of the wall enclosing it and the number of soldiers who gather there."

We enjoyed the jokes and chitchat of the soldiers, but I pre-ferred a quiet time of talk and fellowship with Bill. "Is it safe to sit in the courtyard?" I asked him.

He nodded, replying, "Fairly," which was not too reassur-ing, in spite of the rather high wall around it.

However, the balmy tropic air felt refreshing, the sky spar-kled with stars, and Bill and I relaxed, enjoying the evening and sharing mutual memories. He gave me news of home and relatives. When ten o'clock drew near, I became a bit nervous. I still had a prison-camp mentality. "Bill, it's almost time to go back."

"Don't worry, Carol. I'll take care of it. Just relax. By the time we get there, another guard will be on duty. I'll handle it. Let's just forget the camp and enjoy the evening. We may not see each other again for a long time."

I experienced that warm, womanly feeling of how wonderful it is to have a man who cares looking after you.

"Won't the folks at home be surprised that in all this world at war, we met out here?" I asked him. "How did you find me?"

"Working with the Counter Intelligence Corps, I had access to records, and I traced you down."

"Isn't it an unusual coincidence that we should both be out here on the other side of the world at the same time and work-ing for the Counter Intelligence Corps?"

"I wonder where we'll meet again, Carol."

"Maybe the next time I'm in New York. When that will be, I don't know, probably years from now. You never come to Cali-fornia. But it will be the same whenever, wherever we meet again."

We wandered rather reluctantly back to Santo Tomas, holding hands as we walked along, enjoying the sky and balmy air.

As Bill had predicted, another guard was on duty. After looking at our passes, he waved us through without questions. I felt safer inside the big walls of Santo Tomas, but would remember all my life long that evening with Bill under the starlit skies of war-torn Manila.

When he drove me back to Muntinlupa, I stepped back inside my world of high walls.

Bill sent his mother in New York a message that he had found me, and she phoned my mother in California, "Bill has found Carol!" What joy beyond expression!

CHAPTER 54
American Intrigue

I WAS STARTLED to see the name Earl Hornbostel scrawled on the wall of a cell in this large prison where the Japanese had imprisoned and executed serious offenders. Could this mean Earl had been scheduled for execution?

Not only had I stayed in Earl's home with the Pagets when we were under house arrest, but I had risked my very life for him by smuggling those radio parts into Santo Tomas Internment Camp.

I later heard Earl's incredible story of how American ingenuity and intrigue survived under Japanese scrutiny.

Everyone wanted to know what was happening in the war, but the Japanese were determined that people hear only their interpretation of the news. They made it a death penalty for anyone to possess or listen to short-wave radios or to distribute news from them. However, a few brave and possibly unwise people, such as Earl, Johnny Harris, and I, ignored their threats.

Johnny Harris was not interned, because he had a Filipino mother, but the Japanese put his American father in Santo Tomas Internment Camp. An expert in short-wave radios, Johnny secretly installed one into the wall of his home. After listening to the news, he would write it in very fine writing on thin sheets of colored onion skin paper, roll each one tightly, and slip the tiny rolls into the cavities of the old Parker fountain pens that were much larger than ours of today.

While distributing these pens to his friends, Johnny also gave them to three men who were allowed to go outside Santo Tomas regularly to purchase medicine and other important items for the camp. They exchanged pens when they met, doing it carefully so as not to be seen.

When Johnny was caught, he admitted sending one of these pens into the camp to his father. The police then arrested the elderly man, and this opened up a Pandora's box of serious troubles.

The military police, known as the dreaded Kempetai, arrested Earl in Santo Tomas without giving any reason and put him in the chamber of horrors called Fort Santiago. When its cells became overcrowded, the Japanese moved him to a prison-like dungeon beneath an ancient Spanish mansion known as the Burke residence. Earl found himself in the cell next to Johnny's elderly father, who was about seventy-seven years old.

Earl could overhear the Japanese questioning Harris. The confused and weak old man told them Earl had given him one of those short-wave transcripts, but it actually was just a copy of the approved Japanese newspaper called *The Tribune*.

Earl knew then why he had been arrested. While the military police continued to question the old man, Earl listened through a small opening in the wall between the cells.

When cornered on something the elderly Harris told his captors, Earl gave Chungking as a legitimate source of news, because listening to medium-wave radio was permitted.

Then the interrogators zeroed in on Earl, fishing for information about subversive groups in Santo Tomas. When he said there were none, the police became furious. "We know there are groups called 'Clubs.' "

"Oh, yes," responded Earl, "I know about them. There's the Stamp Club, and the Catholic women get together." He named other obviously innocent groups, which infuriated his questioners.

Becoming tough, the military police began hitting Earl with bamboo. One officer took off his belt and whanged it around Earl's head, the metal buckle causing lumps and cysts, but he never gave them any information.

The Japanese moved Earl to Old Bilibid Prison, where he shared a cell with Johnny Harris and a number of other people. Not allowed to talk with each other, they had to sit in a squatting position sometimes sixteen hours a day. The Japanese wore soft shoes so the prisoners could not hear them when they approached or walked by their cells.

Using the Morse Code by touching a person's back with his finger, Earl taught his fellow prisoners how to communicate. He also showed them how to articulate by speaking from the side of the mouth so the Japanese could neither hear them nor see their lips moving.

Underestimating American ingenuity, they never discovered all the secret radio work Earl had been doing in Santo Tomas for which he most certainly would have been executed

Japanese officers had sent inoperative radios into Santo To-mas for a General Electric man and two Australian electrical experts to fix. Not trained in repairing radios, they secretly gave them to Earl for repair, sometimes telling the Japanese certain parts were needed, which they promptly provided. By adding parts, Earl quickly turned the radios into short-wave, listened to the war news from overseas, and then removed the extra parts before the radios were returned to the Japanese.

When the internees were allowed to put up an outdoor stage of bamboo and *sawali* matting, Earl hid a short-wave radio at the top of that stage, where facilities to light it provided electricity, and the long string of lights that could be disconnected would make a good antenna. Though it was in full view of the

Japanese Commandant's office, that official never noticed the radio, nor did other Japanese officers going in and out of his office.

Earl's turn for trial now came up, but it served as a trial in name only. The Japanese on their own decided the charge, the guilt, and the penalty ahead of time. Then they called the criminal, read the charges, and let him answer.

Standing before his accusers, Earl heard his sentence read in Japanese and then interpreted by a Japanese soldier who had nothing to do with the trial itself but simply served as an interpreter. His name was Richard Sakakida.

As Richard stood there translating Earl's sentence into English, the face of this interpreter seemed inscrutable. While hearing his sentence read by the translator, Earl did not know that this Japanese was a secret, undercover agent for the United States, America's counterpart of "Tokyo Rose."

Although now sentenced to three years of imprisonment, Earl was later scheduled for execution.

Had I been caught smuggling those radio parts into Santo Tomas the day Japanese officers questioned me, I might also have been standing before Sakakida with him as the interpreter at my trial.

None of the Japanese officers were aware of the history and true identity of this translator. Unknown to any of them was the incredible undercover work Sakakida was accomplishing for America in the offices of the Japanese military headquarters. After court-martialing Earl, the military police sent him to the prison at Muntinlupa, sometimes called "New Bilibid."

They placed Earl with a group of men scheduled for execution, each prisoner hoping his own execution would be delayed somehow until the American army arrived. Their physical condition became pitiful. Of the twelve hundred prisoners there, only four hundred survived. Many died from beriberi, the same disease with which I had become afflicted, caused by lack of vitamin B-1 accompanied by starvation.

One night when Filipino guerrillas raided the prison, they urged Earl to escape. Fearing the Japanese would take reprisals on his family, Earl refused. His father was in a military prison, his mother and sister in Santo Tomas, and another sister, Johanna, was in our camp at Los Banos.

On February 2, 1945, the Japanese lieutenant in charge of the guard detail in Muntinlupa prison received an order to execute Filipino guerrillas who had been sentenced to fifteen years or more, and all of the five Americans regardless of length of sentence, including Earl. Johnny Harris had been executed, and I could have been had they caught me.

Reluctant to carry out this order for mass executions, this Japanese officer went to the chief of the dreaded Kempetai with an appeal to cancel the order, but his request was denied. All day Saturday, against his will, he had to march out Filipino guerrillas in groups of twelve to be shot.

General MacArthur and his forces had now landed at Lingayan Gulf, and the 1st Cavalry reached Santo Tomas Internment Camp to liberate it on Saturday night, February 3. Expecting the Americans to arrive, the Japanese officer tried to delay executions.

They were continued on Sunday, February 4, when forty-eight Filipino guerrillas were executed. Earl and the other four Americans were called out at 3:00 P.M. to be shot. However, the execution squad did not return until five o'clock in the afternoon. With darkness soon to come, the executions were postponed until the next day.

Earl commented, "Providence provided me with a little help."

It was at this time Earl scrawled his name with charcoal on the wall of his cell, where I saw it at Muntinlupa.

A girl nicknamed Boots decided to try and save him. Before the war, this prison had been used for civilian criminals and was managed by a Filipino constabulary man. The Japanese kept him on to run the prison under their supervision. His daughter, Boots, was of mixed blood, half American. During the time Earl was imprisoned there, she had become attracted to him and within certain limits provided extra food for Earl. He became interested in her while fixing their radio.

Boots suggested to her father that on this Sunday evening they invite for dinner the Japanese officer in charge of this prison and executions. After warming up the officer with some pre-war Scotch whiskey, Boots and her father pleaded with him to save the five Americans scheduled for execution. He finally agreed to be derelict in his duty, which he didn't want to carry out anyway, though it was a very serious crime for a Japanese officer to commit.

After making this promise, he brought out a crucifix on a gold chain that he was wearing and gave it to Boots, asking her to get it to his mother in Japan after the war. One assumes he was a Catholic.

Earl later heard that this Japanese officer was then assigned to reinforce the garrison guarding the Los Banos Internment Camp. While he was on the way to our camp, he was killed by Filipino guerrillas.

Although this Japanese officer had arranged for the execution of many Filipino guerrillas because it was his military assignment, he did it reluctantly. The guerrillas did not know that, and they may not even have recognized him.

Earl received more help as the Japanese guards just walked out and left the prison at Muntinlupa when American troops drew near.

Instead of being executed, Earl received an invitation to have breakfast with General Eichelberger as soon as he could get there. The Filipino guerrillas were among those who helped Earl reach the general's headquarters in Paranaque.

The next time he saw Boots, Earl asked, "What can I do to thank you for all you have done for me?"

Her reply was quick in coming, "Marry me so I can go to the United States."

Since a mutual affection had grown up between them, Earl happily granted her request and they sailed together for America.

But not all wounds and scars of the war would heal as beautifully as those of Boots and Earl, and for me there still remains an unhealed wound.

CHAPTER 55
The Unhealed Wound

FLEEING FOR HIS LIFE during our rescue, the "camp villain," Konishi, had hidden in the ravine that Ben, Freddy, and Pete used in their getaway.

Along with other guards who had been hiding, Konishi made his way to the safety of Mount Maquiling. There he joined the Japanese Commandant of our internment camp, Major Iwanaka, who also had fled to the hill.

Ordered by Iwanaka to join the Saito Battalion, Lieutenant Konishi came under the overall command of the brazenly cruel General Fujishige, who had given the command: Kill all American soldiers brutally. Do not kill with one stroke.

And now Fujishige gave another order: Kill all guerrillas, men, women, and children in [the village of] Los Banos.

Fearing something like this might happen, Mrs. Espino, wife of the guerrilla leader, "Colonel Price," went to homes near our camp and warned people to flee into the nearby hills. Those who fled saved their lives, as the Japanese went first to this college area.

When the Japanese raided the chapel, Filipinos who had sought refuge there were killed as they tried to flee, while about seventy who locked themselves inside were burned alive when the Japanese set fire to the chapel.

Joined by a pro-Japanese group of Filipinos, the Japanese made raids during several nights, ravaging and killing Filipinos and Chinese in the area. The Chinese were very loyal to America, and it was reported that among Saito's orders were the words, "Kill all Chinese and Filipinos."

A few days later when they were near the area, Major Burgess and his battalion returned to the village of Los Banos. He and his troops viewed with horror the carnage there. Since villagers knew this might happen, it is a mystery and a tragedy that the people did not flee to the nearby security of the hills.

"I do not believe the atrocities in and around the college (at Los Banos) were the direct result of the liberation," commented Ben Edwards. "The Japanese were poor losers."

Whenever they were losing, they went on a rampage of killing. In Manila the Japanese not only destroyed the city, but killed more than a hundred thousand people. As the tide of war continued to turn against them, they went on more and more of these killing sprees against pro-American Filipinos living in the villages.

While the vast majority of Filipinos were on our side, some nationalist zealots called the *Makapili* considered the Japanese as liberators to free their land from America, not realizing what it would mean to have the Nipponese rule their country. These *Makapili* raided villages where Filipinos were pro-American, ravaging and killing. Ben Edwards feels that what they did in Los Banos was not unique but was in accord with their pattern of operation, as in the unrelated village of Calamba where they killed two thousand.

And it was, perhaps, not so much because we were rescued that the Japanese ordered this raid on the people in the area of Los Banos, but because Filipino guerrillas were seen assisting in the rescue. These atrocities could have been thought of as reprisals against them and their families. But who can fathom what was in the minds of men so vicious? Both the Japanese and their cohorts from a group of fanatic pro-Japanese Filipinos called the YOIN share equal blame.

And more than all, the soul of our camp villain, Konishi, was stained with the blood of his victims.

This raid on innocent people, whatever the reason, created in my heart a hurt that never goes away, like an unhealed wound, while Konishi himself came to an unexpected end.

CHAPTER 56
The Amazing End of Our Camp Villain

HE STOOD FACING HIS JUDGES at last, this camp villain responsible for the starvation, suffering, and deaths of so many Americans, Chinese, and Filipinos. Like his life, the military trial turned rather raucous, and the punishment fit the crime.

Konishi had been found guilty of willfully and unlawfully ordering or permitting soldiers under his command to kill the following unarmed, noncombatant civilians in violation of the laws of war and of committing other atrocities:

1. David Gardner, his wife Florence, and their infant son, James, who were American citizens
2. Silverio Seguerra, a Filipino citizen
3. Fifty other Filipino civilians
4. Ang Kai, a Chinese civilian
5. Sixty other Chinese and Filipino civilians
6. Attempt to kill two Chinese infants
7. Devised, aided, and abetted a policy of gradual starvation at the civilian internment camp near Los Banos, causing sickness, disease, and death to numerous American civilian internees.

8. Ordered Japanese soldiers to kill George Louis, an American civilian internee, and participated in said killing at Los Banos on 28 January, 1945.

Sentenced to death by hanging, Konishi sought a better life.

While incarcerated in a prisoner-of-war camp a few miles from the village of Los Banos, Konishi must have wondered about his eternal destiny as he talked with the Catholic chaplain, Col. John P. Wallace, who explains in a letter to Sister Louise of the Maryknolls what happened:

"I baptized him on June 17, 1947, and he was executed on the same day. It was my custom to baptize shortly before executions to eliminate the need of confession as I could not understand Japanese. I visited this person repeatedly and instructed him in the Catholic faith through an interpreter. His embracing the Catholic faith was genuine and sincere. He told me that he had been impressed by the example of Catholic sisters and priests whom he had encountered during the Japanese occupation of the Philippines. . . ."

It was my privilege to talk with this chaplain, Colonel Wallace, and he told me, "Shortly after baptizing him, I walked with Konishi to the place of execution, witnessed it, and saw him buried. The Filipinos who dug the graves removed shoes and uniforms from the Japanese before burying them, and I permitted it, as the clothing would be of no further use to the buried men."

Just before baptism, Konishi took the Christian name of "Peter." I felt "Paul" might have been more appropriate since he also had persecuted the Christians.

Whether Konishi's conversion to Christianity was a fire-escape conversion or sincere, only God, who knows the hearts of all men, can be the judge.

CHAPTER 57
Homeward Bound!

"PLANES ARE FLYING. Ships are sailing. Where do you want to go?" The army was sending us home!

For several days the loud speaker kept blaring out instructions that went something like this:

"Everyone line up for medical clearance."

"Men line up for 'GI' outfits."

"Women line up for WAC uniforms."

"Line up for overcoats."

"Line up for shoes."

In order to be sent home on a military ship or plane, everyone had to have clearance from the medical as well as from the Counter Intelligence Corps.

It was a busy time for our office, and Mr. Ellerd could not give me hours off to stand in line day after day. "Give me your size," he said, "and I'll have your outfit put aside for you."

After I had obtained my medical clearance, his plan seemed to solve our problem of getting the work completed in our office.

On the day our women were given "WAC" uniforms, I went over at five o'clock to get mine but they were all gone, and I had to settle for a man's "GI" outfit in khaki, too long and too big, but it did cover me and no doubt would be warm on the ship going home. The trousers would be good while sitting on deck if there were no steamer chairs. And who ever heard of steamer chairs on a military transport?

The next day after work I went over and received a navy blue overcoat, a bit large but warm and comfortable.

On the day shoes were being given out, I said to my boss, "Will you please tell them I am a woman and give my correct shoe size?"

He took down the information and assured me this time there would be no mistake.

When I went for my shoes, they were the correct size, but both for the left foot!

There were apologies, but I just laughed. Nothing could down my spirits now, except an attack by the Japanese, and we would soon be sailing away from them, I thought.

One day my boss, Mr. Ellerd, handed me this letter:

493rd Counter Intelligence Corps Detachment (Regional)
United States Army Forces of the Far East
APO 358
27 March, 1945
Subject: Letter of Commendation
To: Miss Carol Louise Terry

1. This is to express to you my very sincere appreciation and gratitude for the great help that you have been to me in my work as representative of War Department Military Intelligence in the New Bilibid Prisons, Muntinlupa, Rizal, P.I.

2. The time that you have spent in the compilation of data relative to our prisoners of war, the skill with which you have, of your own free will, without assistance from this office, organized the work for us, and the patience that you have shown in undertaking to do a most difficult clerical type of work for us are commendable in the highest degree.

3. If at any time this letter of commendation may be of use to you as a personal recommendation from me, it is hoped that I may thus in turn be in some small way the assistance to you that you have been to this office in your diligent, excellent work for us.

[Signed] Arthur A. Ellerd, Jr.

Arthur A. Ellerd, Jr.
Counter Intelligence Corps

But that was not the end of my work for Mr. Ellerd and the Counter Intelligence Corps. With that particular job finished, they now gave me another of a different kind, which resulted in my receiving the following letter:

493rd Counter Intelligence Corps Detachment (Regional)
United States Army Forces of the Far East
APO 358
6 April, 1945
Subject: Letter of Commendation
To: Miss Carol Louise Terry

1. This is to express to you the deep appreciation of our office for the work program that you have earnestly and sincerely carried out for us during our mission and operation at New Bilibid Prisons, Muntinlupa, Rizal, re the clearance and evacuation of liberated United Nations nationals, formerly of Los Banos Internment Camp.

2. Subsequent to our having drawn a series of excellent recommendations concerning yourself, and to our having selected you for highly confidential secretarial work, to the best of our knowledge the trust reposed in you has been honored and executed to the fullest extent.

3. If in any way my personal commendation of your admirable work for me may be of possible assistance to you in the future, it will be most gratifying to me to be able to be of this service to you. My office is very grateful to you for your services to us.

[Signed] Arthur A. Ellerd, Jr.

Arthur A. Ellerd, Jr.
Counter Intelligence Corps

When giving me this letter, Mr. Ellerd offered me a handful of Hershey chocolate bars, which I gladly accepted. Remuneration for my work was not financial but the joy of serving my country.

Then came an announcement, "Will all those wanting to leave for Australia please report immediately." Wondering whether the Pagets had heard the announcement, I had them paged. They were British and might go on from there to India or Canada.

Peter hurried over to find out what it was all about. "That's an idea to be considered," he replied in his conservative English manner of understatement. He talked it over with Cae. They were confused, not knowing what they should do. No word had come from their home office giving them instructions either to come home or continue to India. They were in no physical condition to go on to India at this time, but a rest and nourishing food in Australia might put them in first class shape.

Peter, Cae, and Joy walked over to the chapel and spent time in prayer. They came out different people. Their faces were shining, their decision made. After recuperating in Australia, they could continue their journey to India and the work to which they had dedicated their lives. Purpose and resolve had replaced confusion and indecision.

Time was short, and they hurried to get packed. A plane was waiting for all who were Australia bound. It would fly them to Leyte, where they would board a ship soon to sail for the land down under.

It was not without tears that I said good-bye to these wonderful people who had been family and friends through starvation, illness, danger, and the joy of our rescue. We were to meet in India two years later, when I would bring them needed things from America and a beautiful doll for Joy.

At last the day of our departure came. Each person was given a card designating the truck in which he or she would ride. Mine was "Section 3C, Truck #12B." In order to qualify for a place on one of these trucks, you had to have a note of clearance like this:

Headquarters
United States Army Services of Supply
APO 707
23 March 1945

Pursuant to instructions contained in letter. Headquarters USAFFE, dated 4 March, 1945, file FEGARP 704, subject: "Civilians Recovered from Enemy Occupied Territory," the bearer, Terry, Carol L., has obtained CIC and medical clearance and has been placed on orders for evacuation to the United States.

As we moved in a long convoy of trucks out of Muntinlupa, we saw a man standing alone, looking longingly at us when our jovial crowd rode away toward the ship and home. All indications were that the lone man required to remain behind was the king of the weasels. If so, he had received his comeuppance at last.

My heart was with the homesick soldiers we were leaving there. Every morning we had seen these fine American young men going out to fight the enemy. Each evening we watched some of them return, wounded, bleeding, and dying, carried in on stretchers. I wished it were possible to give one of them my place on the truck, and I prayed that America, and all who had the honor of living in our great country, would be worthy of the blood these valiant young men were shedding for us.

As we rode along, smiling Filipinos waved us good-bye. We were all very happy until we drove through the streets of Manila and saw the utter devastation wrought by the Japanese as they fought from building to building rather than declare it an "open city." It appeared that almost the whole city had been leveled, a shocking and sobering sight. I could not recognize or locate anything because all landmarks were gone.

A Filipino band played "Farewell to You" as we loaded into landing craft that took us past many sunken ships to a huge military transport in the outer harbor, the SS *Admiral Eberle*. I remembered having to climb up a rope ladder hanging over the side of one of my father's ships in order to get aboard. Surveying that tremendous *Admiral Eberle*, I knew a rope ladder would be too much for many of us to climb.

But as we drew nearer, I saw a kind of gangplank with steps not straight up the side of the ship but angled up its side, and possibly even with a rail to hang onto. When my turn came, I felt as though I were climbing up a skyscraper.

Watching the others, I noticed those shiny tin cans dangling from their bundles and luggage.

We were assigned accommodation on the ship according to our physical condition. The hardier ones were put in the lower regions in large compartments, with four-decker beds. These were the regular accommodations for troops. Since I was comparatively young, I took the uppermost bed, so older and weaker women would not have to climb up there. Each time I had to shinny up the pole, I felt like "Jack and the Beanstalk."

That evening a young sailor came along and started fastening shut the doorway into the next compartment. "Why are you doing that?" I asked.

"If a torpedo hits your compartment," he answered, "you folks will drown, but the next compartment and the rest of the ship will be saved."

For a while, I thought the women were going to mob him. They would not let him lock that door shut. Better psychology on his part would have been to say, "If a torpedo hits that other compartment, the people there will drown, but you will be saved."

However, maybe he did it purposely to have a little fun watching our reaction. If so, I think it was much stronger than expected, and he had a tale to tell his buddies.

But the Japanese were not ready to give up on us yet. The next day our ship's siren warned of danger. Word spread that a Japanese submarine had been spotted coming after us— rumor or truth, we did not know.

We had two destroyer escorts that were submarine chasers, and we heard they took off after that Japanese sub, but had no confirmation of it. To our knowledge, we were not bothered again. The incident did make us realize we were not out of danger yet, but we had the protection of a mighty America. When we reached safer waters, the destroyer escorts left us and did not return. We were now on our own!

After we arrived at the island of Leyte, soldiers came aboard going home on leave. They were as excited and pleased to see us as we were to have their company.

Some of these men stood behind the food counters serving us all through the journey home. How wonderfully everyone treated us! The food was abundant and delicious, with all restrictions now lifted. We had fun with the soldiers and sailors, and they found pleasure in it, delighting in seeing some of our good-looking girls who were now losing their starved appearance.

It was a long trip. There were no steamer chairs, so we sat on boxes or just on the deck, relaxing, enjoying, dreaming, catching up on the news of the war.

While we were en route, President Roosevelt died, and we had a memorial service for him. Then a little girl became ill and passed away. We had a service and watched her burial at sea. It seemed a lonely place to leave a tiny child, out in the middle of the Pacific Ocean.

When we stopped at Honolulu, we were not allowed ashore, but United States officials came aboard and continued the trip with us, interviewing each rescued prisoner and picking up our passports.

As we drew closer to California's shores, we were strictly warned that on arrival home we were not to reveal any war information that might be helpful to the enemy. Since I knew speaking engagements would be scheduled for me, I sought further clarification of what could and could not be told. Referred to a certain officer aboard ship, I walked in and found three young men in uniforms sitting at desks. They all looked up when I entered, waiting for me to speak.

"Is there anyone here who can answer my questions?" I innocently asked.

The soldiers stared at me for a few seconds, and then one fellow stood up, expanded his chest and answered, "I think I'm old enough!"

Startled by such an unexpected answer with its implied meaning, we all burst out laughing.

We sailed into the Port of Los Angeles on May 2, 1945, with 2,499 former prisoners of war on board. A military band on the dock welcomed us home. Tears rolled down my cheeks, tears filled with love for my country and thankfulness to my God.

As soon as the gangplank had been put in place, a handsome naval officer in a white uniform with gold braid strode aboard. After a short time, an announcement came over the loud speaker, "Will Carol Terry report to the troop office."

Startled, I thought, *My sea captain father must be behind this.* When I arrived at the troop office, there stood that handsome officer in white and gold.

"Are you the daughter of Captain Terry?" he inquired.

"Yes, I am."

"Get your things and come with me."

I didn't have much to gather up; but by the time I was ready, most everyone was more or less lined up halfway around the ship waiting to get off. Some still hung about the rails, watching all that was going on at the dock and the tying up of the ship. A few parents in line were trying to keep their children from running around. It was a happy, informal scene as we all waited for that longed-for moment when we would at last step on the shores of our homeland.

The handsome officer now offered me his arm. With my head held high and arm linked with that of my knight in white and gold, I walked with him past more than two thousand ex-prisoners. A buzz of comments erupted from those standing in that informal line. Not turning my head to left or right, I walked on with my ears picking up the remarks that went something like this:

"Who's that being escorted?" someone asked in a surprised voice.

"Isn't she the one who typed the roll call in Los Banos?"

"Why! That's Carol Terry!"

"How come she rates such royal treatment?"

"Is there something about her we don't know?"

"I saw her working for the Counter Intelligence Corps."

"Could she be a secret agent like Earl Stanley was in Santo Tomas?"

"Naw! That's too far out."

I could hardly keep a straight face as I walked on with the officer. When we reached the government official seated at his desk near the gangplank, I did not have to say a word. My "knight" handled it.

At the foot of the gangplank, in that highly restricted area, stood my father. As my escort turned me over to him, he said, "Captain Terry, this is my way of thanking you for saving my life on your yacht in that storm. Here is your daughter."

Outside the restricted area, our car was waiting, with my

mother, brother George, his wife, Amy, and their children, Orlie and Bill. Happy beyond words to express, we drove to our home on Balboa Island. But that was not the end of the saga.

Large buses were waiting at the dock area to take all the rescued prisoners to the Elks Temple in Los Angeles, where the Red Cross provided nourishment, toys for the children, coupons for clothes and rationed meat, railroad tickets to their home towns, local hotel accommodations, and first aid. Everything possible was done to help these ex-prisoners still holding on to their shiny tin cans!

Since it had been publicized that all rescued people would be taken from the ship to the Elks Temple in Los Angeles, Dr. Sutherland, for whom I had worked in my student days at Biola, went over there. Seeing a Red Cross worker at a desk checking names, he waited his turn and then asked, "Is Carol Terry on the list?"

After glancing down the long, alphabetized list, she replied, "Yes."

"I cannot find her. Carol's father is a sea captain. Could he have taken her off that ship and on home without her coming here?"

And the Red Cross lady replied, "I don't care if her father is the president of the United States, he could not have taken her from that ship and away without her coming here first."

So Dr. Sutherland started scanning closely all the people standing in lines for this and that. He recognized Mr. LaPorte, who had been in Princeton Seminary with him. Going over and greeting Mr. LaPorte, he asked, "Do you know whether Carol Terry was on your ship? I don't see her here."

And Mr. LaPorte replied, "The last time we saw Carol she was walking off the ship on the arm of some high officer from the navy."

"Thank you," said Dr. Sutherland, "that's all I need to know."

Later, when Dr. Sutherland told my father what the Red

Cross lady had said, Dad chortled. It became his favorite story for the rest of his lifetime.

The next day I reported at the Elks Temple in Los Angeles, where some of our people were still being processed. I did not need housing or tickets and clothing for travel, but I gladly accepted the coupons for rationed meat and thanked the people for all they were doing for us.

After being at our home on Balboa Island for a few days, I started expelling a few worms about five or six inches long. Mother almost fainted at the sight of them. I realized it was time for me to see my physician, Dr. E. Forrest Boyd, at one time chief of staff at Hollywood Presbyterian Hospital. His sister, Mary Stagg, had been unmercifully tortured and beheaded by the Japanese in Manila. How could I tell him?

During this time of recovering my health, lost through starvation and disease, God lifted my eyes to far horizons where I was to realize His reasons for my prison-camp years, and the purpose for which I was on this earth.

CHAPTER 58
Relaxation and Fun

RELAXING AT MY PARENTS' HOME on Balboa Island seemed like paradise. Sailing with Dad in a small yacht over the blue waters of the bay, the wind billowing out the sails, a breeze blowing a gentle spray of mist into our faces, I felt the horrors of war dropping from my shoulders, cleansing my heart of pain and hurt. A feeling of peace started slowly creeping into my mind, body, and soul.

Jokes about my worms spread among family and friends. One day I happened to meet Dr. Louis Talbot, president of Biola. As pastor of the Church of the Open Door, he had baptized me when I was a teenaged student at Woodbury College. Walking along with him was Dr. Samuel Sutherland, then dean of Biola. "I say, Carol, did you get rid of all the worms?" asked Dr. Talbot.

Seeing a gleam of mischief in the eyes of the two men, I replied, "All but two."

Laughing heartily, they shared the story with others until it seemed as though almost everyone I met had heard about my "two worms."

During the time required to recover my health, I studied for a degree at Biola's seminary, later called the "Talbot School of

Theology." While preparing the program for graduation, Dr. Talbot decided to brighten up the commencement exercises by having me give a five-minute speech about my war experiences. His secretary confidentially told me that he said, "I'll not tell Carol ahead of time. If she's called on without warning, the shock might make her testimony more exciting."

"Then I'll give him a shock," I replied, and had the tassel of my mortarboard electrified. While conferring my degree and changing my tassel from one side to the other, he received a shock that slightly shook his hand. The four thousand people present laughed, thinking he was humorously shaking his fist at me, as though I were a problem student they were all glad to see graduate. When the prank was explained to him later, he accepted it with his great humor.

Sailing again for India in 1946, I wrote down in phonetics a short speech in the Marathi language to give at the welcome service for me on arrival there. My traveling companion, Elda Amstutz, helped me with the strange sounds of that language.

While I was sitting on deck struggling with those Marathi words, a passenger named Don Hillis walked by. "What are you doing, Carol?"

When I explained, he said, "Let me see how you've written it."

I handed him my speech meticulously written in phonetics.

Glancing over it, Don remarked, "I'm doing this for Dr. Talbot." Then he held the paper out over the ship's railing and said, "Carol, you'll know it better for having to do it twice." He let it go and it drifted into the ocean below.

I gasped in unbelief. I had spent many hours struggling to put that message into phonetics and memorize the sounds, and I had no copy.

I had first met Don during my student days in Woodbury College. At that time he was a student at Biola and sometimes spoke at our Philologus Club meetings. Aboard ship, Don taught a Bible class every day. Because this had been an old troop ship, he was quartered with the men, while his wife and baby son were in a compartment now used for women. I spoke to a young Presbyterian missionary by the name of Nelson, who was on his way to India for the first time. Telling him the story, I asked, "Do you know where Don keeps his Bible when he is at breakfast?"

"Yes, right by his bunk."

I explained what I wanted him to do. "Tomorrow morning when Don is at breakfast, look in his Bible, take out the notes for his morning Bible study, and put this note in their place. He will probably check over his notes some time before the Bible study class and will have time to prepare again or ask for his notes back."

Mr. Nelson cooperated, but Don did not look in his Bible after breakfast!

He stood up before the group to teach, opened his Bible, and flipped the pages looking for his prepared notes, but could not find them. In their place he saw a little note with the same words he had given to me, "You'll know it better for having to do it twice."

Surprised, but realizing he had it coming, Don hesitated for a moment and then went on with the Bible study from memory. He had told his wife that he knew I would get back at him some way, and he accepted it in good humor.

Startled to realize that the captain of our ship was the same one who had put us off the ship in Manila when war broke out, and then had gone off and left all the passengers stranded there, I sent him a gift-wrapped sour pickle with a note and a little humor. As one sea captain to another, he had promised my father he would look after me on that first voyage, a promise he never kept. I had tried to ask his counsel when we were put off the ship but could not see him. The sour pickle was to be considered a gift from my father. When Dad later heard about that gift of a pickle, he chortled again. He would have enjoyed giving it to that captain himself.

As we entered the harbor of Bombay, my whole being thrilled at reaching the land of God's calling for me. I could hardly wait now to arrive at the orphanage, located about a hundred and fifty miles inland from Bombay.

For this I had trained, been imprisoned, and twice crossed half the world.

CHAPTER 59
The Challenge of India

AS THE TRAIN CHUGGED up the hills and whistled through the plains on its way from Bombay to Poona, and then on to the small and dusty village of Kedgaon, I felt my emotions, my nerves, muscles and every part of my body and soul surging with excitement. For years I had studied and prepared for this moment. Some monkeys, running about and screeching on the rooftop of our railway station as the train slowed to a stop, seemed as excited as I.

Waiting to carry me in style from this railroad station to the gate of the Ramabai Mukti Mission was a highly festooned bullock *tonga* pulled by two large white animals with horns. As we bumped along the dirt road, I could see lines of people, each woman draped in a colorful sari, and men wearing turbans of red and white, all waiting and watching for my arrival.

Stepping down awkwardly as someone helped me from the bullock *tonga*, I found myself surrounded by people carrying flowers. Garlands of pink, white, and red flowers mixed with greenery were draped around my neck, and a tiara of small fragrant white flowers placed on my head.

Soon each finger of both my hands was being held by some smiling child whose brown eyes were shining with welcome.

The bows of blue and pink ribbons tied on the ends of their braids seemed to dance with glee as the children began jumping up and down with joy. They all looked so happy and healthy compared to some of the starving children I had seen living on the sidewalks of Bombay.

Then as I happened to turn, I saw a thin old grandmother sitting near the gateway. Draped in a worn and faded sari, she had brought a baby in an open basket. As I stared at her, she looked up and held out the baby. Tears welled up in my eyes. She did not have to speak. Many of the happy little girls now dancing about me came like this, unwanted by the father because the mother died in childbirth.

For this I had come to India; for this I had starved and lived in rags in the prisoner-of-war camp; for this I was rescued; for this I was born.

A row of paper flags led to my room as I was escorted there by an entourage of children. Soon thirty of them would be my own special little girls to cherish.

Inside the room, I was glancing at the mail awaiting me, when a few teenagers dressed in brightly colored saris gathered at my doorway and wanted to enter. I invited them in, and they chatted away in the Marathi language. I could not understand a word they were saying. In an effort to converse with them, I called Miss Craddock, who lived in the room next to me. She was a stately Englishwoman and superintendent of that great work. One day I would take her place as superintendent, but for now I was a raw recruit. I thought she might interpret for us.

But before she arrived in my room, so close to hers, all those teenagers had disappeared in a flash. I wondered why.

The next day I heard that a rumor had circulated throughout the whole orphanage, school, and rescue home that I was "very strict."

Stunned, I asked someone, "How did I get myself called that?"

"When you called Miss Craddock, the girls thought you were reporting them to her for being in your room without permission."

"But I indicated to them they were to enter."

"Learn a lesson from this, Carol," one of the seasoned workers counseled me. "In an orphanage, you don't report the girls to the superintendent unless it is serious."

"But I wasn't reporting them. I just wanted to know what they were saying to me in the Marathi language."

"But they thought you were reporting them."

"A fine kettle of fish I've got myself into the very first hour!" I remarked. And in all the years I lived and taught and raised children there, I never lived down the impression that I was "strict." However, the time came when it changed to "strict, but nice." In the Marathi language it sounded like "kurduck pun chan."

The teenagers watched closely any new worker that arrived and gave her a name they felt described that person. The name given me was "Anandee Moushie," meaning "Joyful Auntie." I rejoiced that they did not call me "Strict Auntie."

Since none of the children and very few of the adults understood English, I had to learn Marathi. Until you passed your final exams given by the official Marathi language school after two years of intensive study, you were considered "on probation," with no voting rights or say in mission affairs.

While studying Marathi, I was given oversight of the "Blossoms," thirty adorable little girls aged six to eight. We could not understand each other's language, but it became fun communicating with our hands and eyes. I made certain their matron kept them clean, fed, and well. On Sundays we went out for a frolicking walk. However, in my adjustment to this orphanage, school, hospital, and rescue home, in all about eight hundred people, I found myself in another predicament.

One day Beth Albert roared up to our gateway in her jeep. A graduate of Biola, she worked with lepers. She was bringing to us a leprosy-free baby born to leprous parents. We invited her to dinner and to spend the night with us.

While we were chatting together in the dining room, Beth said to me, "Carol, my sister has sent me some phonograph records of hymns sung by George Beverly Shea. I brought them along. Would you like to hear a few?"

"Oh, we all would!" I exclaimed.

Turning to Miss Craddock, I asked, "Could we have an evening of sacred music in the drawing room tonight? Beth has brought some hymns sung by George Beverly Shea."

"Yes, but I cannot be present because of other things I have to do."

For an hour most of our staff were inspired by listening to wonderful hymns sung by that dedicated, master artist of song.

When the records were finished and Beth started to put her phonograph away, she said, "Oh, I have one more, just the opposite of what you've been hearing. In order to let me hear the awful music that is popular with the young people in America now, my sister sent me one of the records. The music is called 'rock and roll.' Would you care to hear it?"

Feeling a bit curious, we agreed.

Beth put on that record blaring out rock and roll music just as our stately, dignified, English Miss Craddock walked into the drawing room.

Stunned by what she heard, Miss Craddock looked at me and her face froze. "So this is what *you* call an evening of sacred music!"

She turned and walked out of the room. I followed her, trying to explain, but she would not listen. All the way to her room I was naming the hymns we had heard on the phonograph, and I kept saying, "Miss Craddock, we did have an evening of sacred music."

Going into her room, she shut the door. Wonderful woman that Miss Craddock was, she did not really hear what I was trying so hard to tell her. Many young people say to their parents, "Mom and Dad, you're not hearing what I'm saying."

When I returned to the drawing room, I found my friends collapsing in laughter at my plight! I had received a lesson in listening.

As the years passed, Miss Craddock and I were to become good friends, appreciating each other. But now the Lord was trying to tell me what to do about the old, falling-to-pieces Bibles in the Marathi language. However, I did not understand what He was saying to me as I was given an additional assignment. The founder of this institution was Pandita Ramabai, one of the most brilliant and famous women India has known. She was at one time listed among the ten greatest women in the world, giving refuge to almost two thousand women.

Among her fabulous accomplishments were translating the Bible from Hebrew and Greek into the Marathi language, buying huge presses, and teaching illiterate women how to set type in those languages as well as in English. When she completed the translation, the Bible was printed in Marathi on those presses, the trays of type still in place in the same room.

But that was many years ago. Ramabai was in heaven, the big presses had been sold, and the Bibles were now so old they were falling to pieces, the pages crumbling.

All that remained was an old treadle press on which stationery and receipts were printed in English for the institution. A few of those who had set type for Ramabai in their youth still worked there, old, feeble, and crotchety.

Day after day for a year I had to go to work in that dismal room of faded memories, pushing the large treadle with one foot, balancing myself on the other, while one of the elderly women pulled the big iron arm that turned the wheel, and another placed and withdrew each piece of paper as it was printed. Nearby a third woman, the rather cantankerous Pushibai, stood all day long at the big trays, setting type and complaining that things were not as they used to be when Ramabai was there and they were printing the Bible. In hot, humid weather, the perspiration streamed down my face and neck as I worked that old treadle press.

One day the white-haired, elderly woman we called "Aji-bai," an affectionate name used for a grandmother or an old woman, was sitting on the floor, a thread wound around her bare big toe to hold the thread firm as she rebound one of Ramabai's old Bibles. The paper was falling to pieces in her hand, and the spine side of the pages had been trimmed so many times in rebinding, part of the printed text had been cut off.

Sitting there struggling with it, dear old Ajibai said, *"Arey, Deva!"* meaning, "Oh, God!"

"Ajibai!" I called out in Marathi, "you mustn't take the name of the Lord in vain like that."

"I wasn't taking His name in vain. I was praying. I'll need His help if I'm going to rebind this Bible."

The depressing, meaningless work and hours spent supervising and helping operate that old treadle press, just printing stationery and receipts for the Mission, began creating a rebellious spirit in the depths of my being.

Going to my room, I knelt in His presence and told Him my complaints. "Lord, I didn't get all that education and go through those prisoner-of-war years to print receipts and bind worn-out, almost useless Bibles. If this is Your plan, then show me its purpose so I can do it with joy."

One big lesson I had learned in the prison camp was to get alone with God when things were too much for me. Now I sought Him again. For an unmeasured time, I knelt at my bedside, waiting quietly on the Lord, letting my spirit become meek, so He could speak and work out in me and through me His reasons, His plan.

How long I knelt there, I know not, but after a time, a certain quietness calmed my frustrated spirit. And then the Lord seemed to say to my heart, "But that is why I put you in that old printing room, to see those worn-out Bibles, the treadle press, and the many trays of Marathi type sitting there unused. Like most languages through a long period of time, there are some changes in it.

"Why don't you get together a group of scholars in the Marathi language? Do not have them change Ramabai's translation, but bring the language up to date. You can have the women set the type there in that little printing room, run the proofs off on the treadle press, and give them to the revision committee for checking. When the proofs are all perfect, take them to Bombay and have the Bible reprinted there that the people may have it in the Marathi language of today."

Kneeling there, I felt stunned. I had been so blind about what the Lord was trying to show me. Instead of listening, I had been rebelling. Now, kneeling before Him in wonder, adoration, worship, and thanksgiving, I marveled at His patience with me and His plan.

"And now, Lord," I prayed, "will You tell the Executive Committee the same thing?"

When this prestigious, ultra-conservative committee met, I received permission to present this tremendous project of having the Marathi language in Ramabai's translation brought up to date and the Bible reprinted.

Wonder of wonders, the committee approved!

A group of excellent Marathi scholars, all dedicated Christians, worked for years on this project as they were able to give time to it, with Rev. Fred Schelander as the capable chairman. An American born and brought up in India, he knew the Marathi language well, and the other scholars counted it a privilege and joy to work with him. He was loaned to us for this project by the Christian and Missionary Alliance.

When I announced that we needed some copies of Ramabai's Bible for the Revision Board, elderly women brought out their hoarded, treasured copies, giving them to me so each member of the Revision Board could have one to use.

We set each page in type at our little printing press, making corrections as the revisers changed this and that word. The day came when the whole Bible was completed, with every page set perfectly by these elderly women who had done the original Bible for Ramabai. That antiquated, dismal printing room became alive with joy and enthusiasm, as perfect proofs of every page were printed on that old treadle press. It brought meaning and purpose into the lives of these women to whom life had become uninteresting and boring. Even Pushibai stopped her complaining and rejoiced in setting type once again for the printing of Ramabai's Bible, with the language brought up to present-day Marathi.

We were not able to secure in India the proper paper for printing the Bible. Due for furlough, I returned to America and prayed that somehow the paper could be purchased there, although I did not have the necessary money.

After my arrival I participated in a conference in Grand Rapids, Michigan. On Sunday evening about a dozen speakers were allowed one minute each to give on the radio a request for prayer. In my one minute I told about the Bible and our need for paper on which to print it.

In a rather distant city in America, a Christian organization that provided paper for printing tracts came to the end of its fiscal year with an unusually large balance. How best could it be used?

The chairman, Don Falkenberg, had been in India a few years back. I had asked him at that time about his providing paper for the printing of our Bible, but he responded that Bibles were not included in their field of service, which was limited to tracts.

Now unexpectedly faced with a large balance, he remembered that interview. Through our mission's office in America, he located me in Grand Rapids. On the phone he said, "We have come to the end of the fiscal year with a balance of $. Did you secure the paper for your Bible?"

"No. I've been praying for it."

"Will this amount meet the need?"

"It is just the amount required!" I excitedly replied.

A one-minute prayer request, backed with previous times in prayer, was answered by God in His time, which is always the right time. We accepted the gift as His seal of approval on all the dedicated work that went into preparing Ramabai's translation of the Bible for republishing.

Being in America at just the right time, I was able to purchase the very type of paper we needed from the Zellerbach Paper Company in Los Angeles, which shipped the paper to Bombay. There the Bibles were beautifully printed.

Because over in India I had taken time alone with God to seek His purposes regarding my assignment to that old treadle press, thousands of people in India today have the Bible translated by Ramabai into a language they can easily understand.

How I thanked God for the lesson learned in those prison years of spending time alone with Him and listening to what He would say to my heart.

After Miss Craddock and some of the other senior workers retired, I found myself appointed superintendent of the whole Ramabai Mukti Mission in India.

New challenges mountain high now faced me.

CHAPTER 60
When You Need a Miracle

SLIPPING HER SANDALS OFF outside the screen door of my office at the orphanage in India, Sonubai gave a slight cough.

I looked up from my desk. "Come in, Sonubai."

Seeing the seriousness of her face, I knew she must have come about something important. As she walked in barefooted, the gentle, graceful folds of her white cotton sari revealed a thin body.

"What's the problem, Sonubai?"

"We're running out of food. We only have enough to last for three more days."

"We're also running out of money," I replied. "How much do we need?"

"Three hundred dollars by Friday to get the rice and wheat."

"At the moment our Mission doesn't have it, and neither do I. We'll have to do what our founder, Ramabai, did—pray."

Sonubai smiled. Her gray hair was evidence that she was old enough to have known our founder. "Yes," she replied. "I remember when Ramabai called us all into the church to pray because we were out of wheat. While we were praying, she was called to the gate. There was a man with a bullock cart full of wheat, and one of the wheels had fallen off right in front of our gate. Some of the sacks of grain had fallen on the ground.

" 'Can you fix my bullock cart?' the man asked.

"Ramabai sent for some men from our maintenance department, and soon the bullock cart was ready for the road again. The man appreciated it so much he gave Ramabai some sacks of wheat.

"She sent a message back to us in the church that went something like this, 'Stop praying and start cooking.' "

"But that was many years ago, Sonubai," I said. "Do you think the Lord will do the same thing for us now?"

"Yes, He will," was her emphatic reply. As she left my office, her straight carriage was indicative of the integrity of her character. She was in charge of our food supplies for over five hundred of our children and infirm, unable to cook for themselves.

That afternoon when I saw our hundreds of children pouring out of school, their faces haunted me, and I went to my room to pray. "Lord, I don't mind being hungry. I learned to be hungry in the internment camp, but this time it's the children. Please send us some rice and wheat or lay it on the heart of someone somewhere in the world to send us three hundred dollars before Friday."

For a couple of days this prayer constantly ascended from my heart. When trying to answer a letter in the office, I found my head bowing in prayer about the needed food. When overseeing work in one of the compounds, I found my eyes turning heavenward in prayer for $300.

I knew that in the history of the Mission there had been lean times, and the Lord had always supplied from somewhere. But this was the first time such a need had arisen since I had become superintendent. Humanly speaking, it was my responsibility to see that those under our care were fed—the blind, the crippled, the sick, the destitute, the rescue cases, the orphans, the widows, and the aged. I bowed my head, "For these, O God, I pray."

Each day when the mail came, I almost tore it open in my eagerness to see if there was a check for $300, but there was nothing.

And Sonubai was praying. When our paths happened to cross, her eyes sought mine with a question in them, and I answered with a negative shake of the head. The next day was the deadline.

And then it happened. Three hundred dollars came by cable from someone I had never met, but who had heard of my work in India. The letter that followed was addressed to the Ramabai Mukti Mission, care of our office in America, which had cabled the $300 to us and forwarded the letter by air mail:

I have been quite ill in the hospital for almost a month.

About midnight, as I lay in my hospital bed the other night, the name "Carol Terry" suddenly began to go repeatedly through my mind—"Carol Terry, Carol Terry," perhaps 30 or more times,—almost as if by teletype. I wondered!! Just before daylight, the same thing started again, but that time it was "Carol Terry $300—Carol Terry $300"—etc.

You will find enclosed my check for $300 for Carol Terry, to be used by her as she desires, either for some personal need of her own or for the work of the mission in India, whatever she wants to do with it.

I felt that perhaps Carol Terry, or her work in India, might have some special need at this time!

Thanking you for sending this gift on to her for me, at this time, I am
Sincerely,
Katherine T. Weakley

As I read the letter, my eyes misted, and I bowed my head in thanksgiving to a great God, our heavenly Father, as the following verse came into my mind:

"Before they call, I will answer . . ." (Isaiah 65:24).

The letter had been written before Sonubai had told me our need of $300 for rice and wheat.

When I wrote Miss Weakley and told her how we had been praying for $300, she replied that she was not surprised, because the message to send it had been so clear.

The Lord had even taken into account the time required to get the $300 to us for the day it was needed.

I had graduated from another course in God's university in prayer and faith and trust. I prayed that my relationship and fellowship with the Lord would be so close and sensitive that my heart would respond when there was some person He wanted me to reach for Him or some need He wanted me to meet. "Give me ears to hear, a heart to feel, a will to act, and faith to trust always."

When Sonubai came into the office to see if any money had arrived, I repeated to her the words of Ramabai, "Stop praying and start cooking." She raised her eyes in thanksgiving to God and then skipped out of the office clapping her hands.

CHAPTER 61
A Little Child Shall Lead Them

HER SKIN WAS THE SOFT, silken tan of India, and in her wide brown eyes was the hurt of an innocent fawn that does not understand why it has been harmed. The turbaned man carried her gently as he walked through the gateway of our orphanage. His face was worried and unshaven; his soiled clothes marked him as a man who belonged to the fields and villages. His whole attitude indicated desperation, but with it was a manly tenderness toward the frail little girl in his arms. He did not have to speak; I knew he had come for help.

I led him out of the burning sun to our shaded verandah. With a shake of the head he rejected the chair offered him and sat cross-legged on the floor, carefully holding the child. He spoke no English, and I was grateful for my years of studying the Marathi language.

"What has happened to the little girl?" I asked.

His voice became agitated as he told me the story.

"She was a happy, healthy girl six months ago when her mother, my wife, died. I could not leave her at home alone while I worked in the fields, so I took her to my sister's in a distant village. My sister was not pleased, as she did not want to be bothered with the child, but she finally agreed to keep her for me.

"Six months later I returned to visit them. I found Shaku crouching in a dark corner like a frightened animal. She could not walk or stand. She could not even sit up without bracing herself against a wall, and she would not talk. My sister walked out of the house without speaking, and I carried Shaku home with me. She told me then how my sister had mistreated her."

The man stopped speaking for a few moments while he tried to control his emotions. Then he showed me a lump as big as his fist, high on the child's spine, between her shoulders. She was breathing heavily, and although she was about six years old, she looked as though she would break in pieces if not lifted carefully.

I bowed my head over our admittance book in an effort to hide my tears. The man was illiterate and signed the necessary papers with his thumbprint. He stayed until Shaku was no longer afraid of us and then he slowly walked down the dirt road toward his village, occasionally looking back at the building where his daughter was lying in a soft white bed, the first bed she had ever known.

Because we did not have the medical facilities necessary to find out all the ways Shaku had been hurt, we took her to a large city hospital. When the day came for her return to us, we learned that she had only six months to live. In addition to the indignities she had suffered, Shaku had also contracted tuberculosis.

This meant we could not put her with the other children in our orphanage. The only place we had for her was in our tuberculosis sanatorium on a nearby hill. It was not a good atmosphere for a little girl who had already been scarred by life, but we had no other place. Sixteen complaining women, filled with thoughts of themselves and their disease, lived there. Nothing ever seemed to please them. If we gave them a large portion of food, they complained that we were wasting it. If we cut the ration, they said we were not giving them enough. One day there would be too much salt in the food and the next day not enough.

When we visited these women often, they thought we were spying on them; if we cut down our visits, they complained that we were neglecting them. We breathed a prayer for Shaku as, one evening, we put her among the grumpy women.

Early the next morning when we stopped at the sanatorium, one of the women was holding the child on her lap, another was putting her pillow behind Shaku's back, while still another was offering her a glass of milk.

The women tried every way they knew to erase the look of fright on the girl's face. Shaku became theirs, and they spent all their time and strength endeavoring to bring happiness back into that crippled life. The women found something to live for besides themselves; their faces softened and their dull eyes lit up.

Shaku responded like the opening of a flower to the summer sun. She loved them with all the generosity of a little girl's heart. A gentle smile replaced the sadness in her eyes, and she became a princess surrounded by a loyal court. The old women knew a love they had never known.

But the doctor's words came true, and Shaku began to fade. The day came when we stood around her grave. Tears streamed down the faces of the women whose lives she had transformed. They bowed their heads over the grave and thanked God that He had given Shaku to them and that He had given them an opportunity to make up for wasted years. They had been transformed from selfish complainers to noble women, and God had used a little child to lead them.*

*Carol Terry Talbot, reprint courtesy of *Good Housekeeping* magazine, January 1967, regional editions.

CHAPTER 62
When God Gives His Best

AFTER TWENTY YEARS OVERSEAS, I had arrived back in my home country to stay. Walking down Sixth Street in front of the Church of the Open Door in Los Angeles, I was thin and weak. The staph germs that had covered my body with sores in the prison camp had continually attacked my eyelids while I was in India, and the lids were badly infected.

I had just come from the office of the best eye surgeon on the West Coast. Surgery had been performed in India on my eyelids a number of times to remove infected cysts, then again in England by recommendation of their greatest eye surgeon, Sir Henry Holland.

Now this surgeon told me, "I do not ask you to give up your work, but you must give it up in India. So long as you stay in that country, you will have this problem."

All my strength seemed to have gone out of me. My parents were no longer living; I had no home and very little money.

A prayer went up from my heart as I walked along. "Lord, every time I get myself into a mess, You always manage somehow to give me help. Can You do it again soon?"

As I continued walking down the sidewalk, my eyes downcast, I almost bumped into Dr. Louis Talbot, by then the chancellor of Biola College, which later became a university.

We both stopped for a brief moment and stared at each other. "Carol?" he asked, surprised. "You look awful! When did you get back from India?"

"A few weeks ago. I spoke at some meetings in the East."

"Are you getting enough to eat? Do you have enough money?"

The answer to these questions was no, but I remained silent.

Right there on the sidewalk he took my purse, opened it, counted the money inside, and then said, "Come on, I'm taking you to lunch."

I had been asked to write a book of stories for boys and girls about our children in India. As my eyes permitted, I worked on this book. Dr. Talbot wrote the Foreword and Zondervan Publishing House published it under the title *Let's Go to India."*

During this time he sometimes asked me to dinner. He missed his wife, Audrey, who had been so beloved by him for many years but was now in heaven. He did not enjoy eating alone. Then one evening he asked me to go with him to the Griffith Observatory to watch a program on the stars. This became our favorite trysting place as the stars started sparkling in our eyes.

We were married in the home of President and Mrs. Samuel H. Sutherland, which was located on the new Biola campus, with Dr. Sutherland performing the ceremony.

God had given me the most wonderful man I had ever known in my life, His very best. Life with him was unusual, exciting, and always interesting. Louie's remarkable sense of humor kept things alive.

Our first guests at our apartment in Leisure World at Seal Beach were my brother Jack and his wife Crysta. Jack had managed to keep his distance from most ministers and took a rather dim view of having one in the family. I knew he would come with his defenses up and arguments ready.

I gave Louie detailed instructions how to handle Jack, what to do, say, and not say. "Take it easy with my brother Jack, won't you? No religious discussions, please, for this first visit, and by all means pay for the expenses of the day."

"Oh, sure!" Louie was most agreeable.

Knowing Jack enjoyed the sea, we went for an excursion in a motor launch, and Louie picked up the tab. Since everyone liked fish, we went to a seafood restaurant, and the whole day sailed happily along.

When the waitress put our dinner check on the table, Louie and Jack were engaged in a lively conversation and neither noticed it. After a time, I nudged Louie, but he evidently did not grasp the meaning of my nudge.

A few minutes later I gave him a kick under the table. Looking at me, Louie said out loud, "What are you kicking me for?"

Then Jack asked him a question, and the matter of the kick was dropped. Finally the conversation tapered off, and there sat the check. Jack reached over rather slowly and picked it up.

I snatched it from his hand and gave it to Louie. "You're our guests today, Jack, just as though you were in our home."

But Louie spoke up, "If Jack wants to pay the bill, why don't you let him?"

I just gasped, and then he said to my brother, "Jack, do you want to pay this or don't you?"

Jack nodded, but not very enthusiastically, and replied, "I'll pay it."

Leaning toward Louie, I whispered, "What's come over you?"

In a low voice that I was afraid my brother would hear, he answered, "We can't start feeding all your relatives like this."

Stunned, I blinked back the tears I felt coming.

Then Crysta spoke up, "Carol, I wonder if they're pulling something on you."

Quickly looking at both men, I noticed their eyes were dancing with mischief. Then they burst out laughing.

What had happened was this: When Crysta and I had gone to the powder room to freshen up after the boat ride, Louie shared with Jack every single thing I had told him. Then he gave my brother a twenty dollar bill, "I'm going to ignore the check, Jack, no matter what Carol says. After a while you reluctantly start to pay it with this money, and we'll see what we can do to get Carol upset."

The rest of the time together was all fun. Louie and Jack became great friends. My brother chuckled all the way to his home near Sacramento, and eventually Jack grew to love the Lord.

Life with Louie was always filled with the unexpected—his humor, his magnificent sense of true values, his love for people, our sacred times of prayer, and his deep reverence for God.

One evening toward the close of his life on earth, we were reviewing my years in the prison camp, the rescuing and raising of orphans in India, and the printing of the Marathi Bible. He said, "Carol, our Lord was working in you through the prison years to give you a deeper, more meaningful service in India, and in the ministries He has given you in writing and speaking across America, in Canada, and in England to help others experiencing heartaches. It was the way you responded to God's molding of your life during the difficult times in the prison camp and in India that drew me to you.

"Never doubt God's providences."

Lt. Col. Henry A. Burgess is awarded the Legion of Merit medal for his military skill and leadership in our rescue.

APPENDIX A
Citation for Legion of Merit

Lieutenant Colonel HENRY A. BURGESS, 0411435, Infantry, United States Army. For exceptionally meritorious conduct in the performance of outstanding services in Los Banos, Luzon, Philippine Islands, on 22 and 23 February 1945. As commander of a combined amphibious and airborne task force, Colonel Burgess skillfully executed a hazardous mission against the enemy concentration camp in Los Banos, wiping out the enemy garrison, freeing 2,200 Allied nationals and successfully withdrawing his force and the liberated internees. Colonel Burgess moved his battalion, less one airborne company, but with an artillery battery attached, by amphibious tractors across 5 1/2 miles of water under cover of darkness and landed behind the enemy lines east of Los Banos shortly before daylight. Skillfully deploying his force, he silenced enemy machine guns opposing his beachhead. He then moved inland two miles to the prison camp, meeting his remaining company, which had parachuted into the prison enclosure. While his troops were annihilating the enemy garrison, Colonel Burgess personally organized the 2,200 internees. Exhibiting great tact, leadership and force, he speedily moved the liberated internees to the amphibious vehicles. Only after all internees were dispatched did he execute a skillful withdrawal of his force. This difficult undertaking was accomplished in 14 hours from the time of initial embarkation to the return of the last internee and soldier to the same shore. Colonel Burgess's coolness, sound judgment and forceful leadership were largely responsible for the success of this historic mission.

APPENDIX B
Letter from Lt. Col. Thomas Mesereau
October 25, 1985

Dear Carol:

Thank you for your warm and welcome letter. My telephone call was not intended to bring tears to your eyes, but rather to include you in my list of dear friends with whom I wished to share this portion of my life. You are part of a very special list.

Thank you for your prayers, dear Carol. I know that your prayers reach our Lord by a more direct route than mine. Carol, I am not terribly saddened by being visited by cancer. I have the courage to fight it all the way and I am confident that I will win this battle. If God chooses otherwise, so be it.

He has given me greater experiences than most human beings. I have been to the heights and to the depths. I have tasted moments of glory and found love and truth in so many people.

I close this letter with love to Carol.

[Signed] Tom Mesereau

Some time later I stood with bowed head and a cross of white flowers by his flag-draped coffin in March Air Force Base Cemetery.

APPENDIX C
Interview with Daikichi Okamoto
Kyoto, Japan

He was a little different from most of our Japanese guards, even helpful at times. He served as the official interpreter for the Japanese Army from 1943 to 1945. Okamoto is our only surviving guard. We conducted our interview by air mail, with letters flying back and forth across the seas. His wording and spelling are preserved:

Q. How did you try to help us prisoners in the Los Banos Internment Camp?

A. I went out with driver Mr. George and YWCA people to buy many vegetables far away almost all every other day. I always sujest our commandant for improve for your camp life.

Q. How did you suggest it be improved?

A. One day chairman Carlfoun (Alex Calhoun) ask me to help to make water system simple type toilet in the camp, therefore, I explained to commandant to allow their application, because the American and Japanese life quite different at last and commandant understand.

Q. How else did you try to help us?

A. I always to sujest to Mr. Carlfoun and other to your committee to tell to all people pleasse be quiete and do not to escape from the camp for avoide any trouble.

Q. When all the Japanese officers and guards left our camp suddenly in the middle of the night, January 7, 1945, and came back January 13, where did you go and why did you leave in such a hurry?

A. Regarding on the 7 thru 13 January 1945, by order of our HQS. Manila to assemble and retreat to Mariquino mountain near Manila, then we came back and transferred under Fujishige division.

Q. Mr. Masaki tried to get medicine and food for us. What happened to him? Was he executed by the Japanese? If so, why?

A. Mr. Masaki tried to get medicine for a British people from in camp Holms Bagio. He was killed by unnamed the Japanese officer at the Bilbid camp in Manila during the war.

Q. Did your trying to help us get you into any trouble with your superior officers?

A. I was gloomy my camp life with Los Banos and Santo Tomas because the Japanese officers and soldiers said to me very often you are pro-American, therefore, our office personnels did not office work longer only within 6 months then transfferd other office.

Q. Did you expect the American army to rescue us from the Los Banos Camp?

A. I expected the American Soldier to rescue YOUR people at that time.

Q. Did you want the American army to rescue us?

A. Of course I want them to rescue US by that time.

Q. Where were you when the paratroopers arrived?

A. I was in my room.

Q. How did you escape?

A. I was escaped into concrete pipe near college orchard. I was surprised and I thought it was last time in my life.

Q. Where did you go after we left the area?

A. I was transfferd to 2nd battalion Fujishige division (they said suicide battalion) and on the 19th Sept., 1945, then I was surrender with 2nd battalion and to the PW camp.

Q. What was life like in the American prisoner-of-war camp where you were placed?

A. During my PW camp life not so bad. I was detained about 2 years at the war criminal camp and then released and sent back Japan from the Philippine on the 1st July, 1947.

Q. What happened to the Japanese guard, Mr. Ito? He showed a bit of kindness now and then.

A. Mr. Ito was Christian or Buddist unknown and who was dead by starvation in the mountain of southern Luzon territory.

Q. What is your religion?

A. I am Buddist but I love and respect for Christian.

Q. What happened to the Japanese doctor in our camp?

A. Medical officer Yoshimura was suicided at the war criminal camp after end of war.

Q. Where did all the other Japanese guards go?

A. Our Japanese guards under general Fujishige division were retreated to mountain and dead by starvation (7 out of 10 Los Banos personnel). The Japanese soldier will not dishonorable surrender.

Then Okamoto writes: "I was surprised and I am very sad to learn from your letter about killing of Los Banos (village) people after liberation. I dont know anything about this case because I was mountain with medical officer Yoshimura and about 3 soldiers after escaped from liberation day on the 23 Feb., '45. 3 days after we joined to Fujishige Div. and assigned 2 battllion stationed at Batan Gas. Killing of Los Banos people may have been ordered by general Fujishige and also I dont know captain Saito himself.

"Our Japanese surrender was very lucky by American instead of Soviet Union. All Japanese people does not forget kindly of all American people forever.

"Many many thanks for remember me my name. Please excuse me my poor English and sorry I can not familiar tape recorder.

Yours faithfully,

[Signed] Daikichi Okamoto

Kyoto, Japan

(Note: Some spelling errors may be due to his typing or that of someone typing for him.)

APPENDIX D
The Camp Roster

Here we are—all the men, women, and children who starved under the threatening guns of our Japanese captors in the Los Banos Internment Camp.

With the exception of a few scoundrels, such as the "king of the weasels," this is in a way an honor roll of valiant men and women striving to survive behind barbed wire.

This roster represents the countless hours spent keeping an accurate and current record as I typed on a "clunker" of ancient vintage. Rescued by George Gray when we fled, this list has been recognized by the United States government as the official census for our camp. I have reason to believe that my work on this roster was the basis for my being recommended to the Counter Intelligence Corps, an honor I'll cherish all my life long.

My roster was published in 1946 by Frederic Stevens. It also appeared in an anniversary program of the R.O.T.C. Filipino guerrilla group known during the war as "Terry's Hunters," four of whom jumped into our barracks seeking Japanese during the rescue, and I wish to honor them.

Those listed in this census who died between the time I typed this in February and the 23rd of that month when we were rescued are marked with an asterisk, with their age at death. Not mentioned is baby Lois McCoy, born on February 20. I am listed under my maiden name of Carol Louise Terry.

LOS BANOS INTERNMENT CAMP

February 1945. The last roster I typed in camp. Those whose names are marked with an asterisk died in the Internment Camp due to beriberi caused by starvation, or due to other diseases, or were executed.

American
Adams, Elbridge M.
Adams, Gustav Adolph
Adams, Owen
Adams, Welba S.
Adrian, Kathleen Halloran
Adrian, Michael Joseph
Agnes, Sister Inelda
Agnes, Sister Regina
Ahern, Hilary
Aimee, Sister Marie
Aiton, Joe E.
Aiton, Felicimo L.
Aiton, Josepha D.
Albert, Daniel Louis
Ale, Francis Harvey
Allen, Robert Coleman
Alness, Mark Gerhard
Alphonsa, Sister Mary
Alsobrook, Anthony Leonidas
Amstutz, Elda
Ancilla, Sister Marie
Anderson, Charles Richard
Anderson, Charles Stewart
Anderson, Theodore Maxwell
Anderson, Oscar William
Ankney, William Edgar
Antoinette, Sister M.
Andrew, Sister Mary
Apelseth, Clement Anders
Appleby, Blanche
Aquinata, Sister M.

Arana, Bernardina
Arana, Esther
Arana, Cesar
Arick, Melvin Ray
Arida, Jodat Kamel
Armstrong, Robert Worthington
Ashton, Sidney
Assumpta, Sister M.
Augustus, Sister Mary
Avery, Charles William
Avery, Henry
Axtman, Boniface
Ayres, Glen Edwin
Babbitt, Winfred Howard
Backman, Herbert
Bagby, Calvin T.
Baker, Rowland John
Balano, Felix
Baldwin, Rena
Barnaby, Catherine
Barnes, Charles Irwin
Barnes, Evelyn Crew
Barnes, Richard Porter
Barter, Fred
Bartgis, Fred
Barth, Phyllis Ludwig
Bartlett, Mildred Glaze
Bartlett, Sydney Stockholm
Barton, Roy Franklin
Bateman, Jack
Bateman, John James
Bateman, Sallie

Bauman, William McComb
Baxter, Cecil Marie
Baxter, Sidney
Bayley, Harold Raymond
Bayouth, Khallel Assad
Beaber, H.
Beata, Sister M.
Beaty, Truman Carlson
Bebell, Clifford Felix Swift
Beck, Emsley William
Beck, Francis Harold
Becker, Frank Emil
Bee, Edwin Joseph
Beeman, Frank Robert
Beeman, Maude Rona
Beeman, Narvel Chester
Beeman, Raymond Richard
Beeman, Wallace Earl
Begley, Charlie
Beigbeder, Frank Michael
Bennett, Frank Cantillo
Benninghoven, Edward Robert
Berger, William Harris
Bergman, Gerda Ottelia
Besser, Leo
Bezotte, Fred
Billings, Bliss W.
Binsted, Norman S.
Binsted, Willie M. G.
Birsh, Charles
Bissinger, George Henry
Bissinger, Winifred Allen
Bittner, Joseph
Blackledge, David
Blackledge, Helen
Blackledge, Robert
*Blair, Herbert E., age 65
Blair, Susan
Blake, Lila
Blake, Mary
Blake, Owen A.

Blakeley, Mildred M.
Blalock, John
Blanchard, Harold Mason
Blanton, Charles Maxwell
Blanton, Dale Lincoln
Blechynden, Claire Louise
Blue, Harry Coleman
Bogacz, Francis
Bogle, Edwin Carmel
Bolderston, Constance
Bollman, Benjamin B.
Bollman, Elsie K.
Bollman, J. W.
Bollman, Lynn B.
Bond, Leo
Bonham, Rex
Boomer, Louise Charmian
Boomer, Joseph
Boston, William
Boswell, Eleanor Madaline
Bousman, H.
Bousman, James
Bousman, Martha
Bousman, Nona
Bousman, Tom
Bowker, Bayard Jordan
Bowie, Harold Dewell
Bowie, Leah Lourdes
Bowie, Paquita Rodriguez
Boyce, Leila Susan
Boyce, Viola Ceres
Boyd, Joseph
Boyens, Ernest
Boyers, James Simon
Boyle, Philip
Bradfield, Elizabeth Shortridge
Bradley, Brant
Bradney, Reuel
Bradanauer, Frederick W.
Bradanauer, Grace A.
Bratton, Charles Henley

Brazee, Albert John, Jr.
Brazee, Nancy Agnes Erwin
Brendel, Oswood Roland
Brigitine, Sister
Brink, John William
Brink, Maude E.
Brink, Myron
Brink, Pamela
Brink, Robert Arlington
Broad, Wilfred
Brock, Joe O.
Brockway, Alex Grove
Brockway, Merna Morris
Brook, Walter Leroy
Brooks, Horace
Brown, George
Brown, Harry John
Brown, Helen Margaret
Brown, Katherine Ellis
Brown, Mary Martha
Brown, Nell McAfee
Brown, Ray
Brown, Richard Sefton
Brown, Roy H.
Browne, Leslie
Browne, Pilar
Browne, Robert
Brush, John Burk
Brush, Lois Bogue
Brushfield, Elizabeth
Bryan, Arthur
Bryan, Edgar Robeson
Bryan, Winifred
Bucher, Anna L.
Bucher, George Scott
Bucher, Henry H.
Bucher, Henry H., Jr.
Bucher, Louise S.
Bucher, Priscilla J.
Buckalew, Donald Howland
Buckles, Frank Woodruff

Budlong, Vinton Alva
Burke, Harry Taylor
Burkman, Charles Harris
Burlingame, Walter Michael
Brunham, Edward Frank
Burns, Francis
Burns, James
Burns, James (2)
Burrell, Louie Grant
Burton, Edith Ganz
*Burton, Harry Royal, age 68
Burton, James Edward
Butler, John Nicholsen
Butler, Linnie Marie
Cadwallader, Helen
Caecilius, Sister M.
Cain, Claude Oliver
Cain, Thomas
Caldwell, William A.
Calhoun, Alexander Dewey
Calvert, John Ellis
Calve, Elisa Warbaugh
Cammack, Larue
*Campbell, Guilford E., age 77
Campbell, Leo Lee
Campp, Anthony L.
Canson, John
Capen, Morris Noel
Caritas, Sister M.
Carlisle, Mabel Burris
Carlson, Alvin
Carlson, Imogene Ina
Carlson, Lawrence
Carlson, Mark
Carlucci, John (Boniface)
Carpenter, Henry
Carson, Hilton
Carter, Roland van
Carty, George B.
Carty, Eleanor May
Carty, Jean Pearl

Casanave, Andres
Casanave, Emilio
Casanave, Grete
Casanave, Pedro, Jr.
Casanave, Pedro Andres
Casanave, Peter A.
Casanave, Rachel Olive
Casanave, Teresa E.
Casanave, Theodore
Casey, Edward
Cashman, Michael
Cassel, Henry D.
Cassell, Marie
Cassell, Marion Reedy
Cassell, Maurice Arnold
Cassidy, John Patrick
Catherine, Sister M.
Cease, Forrest Lee
Cecil, Robert E.
Celeste, Sister M.
Chambers, Bunnie, Sr.
Chambers, Bunnie, Jr.
Chambers, Isidra
Chambers, Katherine
Chambers, Maria
Chantal, Sister M. de
Chapman, Corwin Clyde
Chapman, Mary Frances
Chapman, Virginia Dewey
Chase, Leland Preston
Chatman, Littleton
Cheek, Jesse Willard
Chester, Harold Dean
Chester, Pearl Eileen
Chestnut, James Edward
Chew, John Hamilton
Chichester, Robert Oxley
Chickese, Ernest
Childers, Ralph Leroy
Christensen, Edward
Christensen, Joseph

Christie, A.
Chisholm, Robert
Cillo, Thomas
Clare, Joseph-Mother M.
Clark, Andrew
Clark, Rush Spencer
Claude, Henry Louie
Clayton, Noel
Clifford, Carl Gaines
Clifford, William Dennis
Clingen, Herbert Signer
Clingen, Ida Ruth
Clingen, Robert Fraser
Cobb, Laura May
Coffey, Henry A.
Cochran, Donald Lewellyn
Cofer, Newton
Coggeshall, Roland Roberts
Cogswell, Gladys Jessie
Cole, Birnie
Cole, George Edward
Cole, Minnie
Coleman, Barbara M.
Coleman, Marjorie K.
Coleman, Marshall L.
Coleman, Patricia C.
Colin, Paul J.
Collier, Leonard Hooper
Collins, Joseph Davis
Collins, Thomas James
Colman, Sister
Conant, Ellsworth Thomas
Conant, Juanda June
Conant, Myra Belle
Cone, Hector Anthony
Congleton, Lucy E.
Conner, Herman Burt
Connors, John
Conway, Joseph Michael
Constance, Sister M.
Cook, James William

Cook, Maude Rose
Cook, William Sherman
Cook, W. Thomas
Cooper, Alfred D.
Cooper, Hugh Price
Copello, Thomas George
Copper, Robert Gamble
Corbett, Daniel
Cornelison, Bernice
Cort, Marcus Robert
Corwin, Alvah Oatis
Crabb, Josephine Rosalie
Craven, Louise Broad
Craven, Osgood Coit
Crawford, Joseph Claypole
Crawford, Robert Allan
Crawford, Virginia Hale
Crist, Ann Bennett
Crist, Lynn Levi
Croft, Selma Marion
Croft, Patty Gene
Croft, William Frederick
Croisant, Everett Albert
Cromwell, Robert Horace
Croney, Dorothy Fain
Crooks, William
Crosby, George Howard
Crothers, Ellen N.
Crothers, John Young
Cullens, James Wimberly
Cullum, Leo
Cumming, Clarence Warder
Cumming, Patrick
Cummings, Ernest
Cummings, Milton Weston
Cunningham, Frederick Noel
Curavo, Leonard Alexander
Curran, Elmer Hege
Curran, Howard H.
Curran, Hugh McCollum, Sr.
Curran, Hugh McCollum, Jr.

Custer, Theodore Hart
Dahlke, Gustav A.
Dahlke, Inga Hedwig
Dakin, Bess May
Dakin, Charles Austin
Dale, Billie Ann
Dale, Donna Lee
Dale, Edna Lee
Dale, Frank Emmit
Dale, Melvin Eugene
Dale, Roberta M.
Damrosch, Elizabeth H.
Damrosch, Leopold
Damrosch, Leopold, Jr.
Danie, Amelia Louise
Danie, Antony Joseph
Davey, Laura Emily
David, Sister M.
Davidson, Abraham
Davidson, Arthur Dewain
Davis, Marian Electra
Davis, Maureen Neal
Davis, Roger William
Davis, Rosella A.
Davis, Sun Ye
Dayton, Earl Tresiliam
Deam, Mary L.
Dean, Harry Wilson
Decker, Louis
De Coito, Louis
De Coito, Ann I.
Decoteau, Joseph
Dedegas, Basil
Deihl, Edith Jolles
Deihl, Renzie Watson
De la Costa, Frank A.
De la Costa, Jan
De la Fuente, Pelegrin
De Loffe, John
De Martini, Louise V.
Deppermann, Charles

Depue, Rodney Albert
Detrick, Herbert J.
Detrick, Lulu H.
Detzer, Linus William
DeVries, David Andrew
DeVries, Gene
DeVries, Gladys L.
DeVries, Henry William, Sr.
DeVries, Henry William, Jr.
Dewhirst, Harry Daniel
DeWitt, Clyde Alton
Dick, Thomas William
Dincher, Frederick
Dingle, Leila
Dingman, Arthur
Divine Child, Sister Mary
Doig, Leroy Dorry, Jr.
Doino, Francis
Dominica, Sister M.
Dorothy, Sister
Dow, William
Dowd, Austin
Dowling, Richard
Downing, Donald Clark
Doyle, Emily Norma
Doyle, Joseph Desmond
Downs, Darley
Dragset, Ingie
Dreyer, Karl Olaf
Drost, Leonard
Dudley, Earl C., Sr.
Dudley, Earl C., Jr.
Dudley, Susie Hall
Dugas, Alfred Frederick
Delaney, Frank Lorraine
Dustin, Herbert Warren
Dwyre, Allen Louis
Dyer, Althea C.
Dyer, Harlan L.
Dyer, June L.
Dyer, Mary

Eanswida, Mother M.
Earl, George Richard
Eaton, Gertrude Mary
Eaton, Leon Schultz
Ebbesen, Frank E.
Eddy, Arthur Louis
Edwards, Benjamin Franklin
Edwards, Herbert Kenneth
Edwards, John
Edwards, Mary Constance
Eison, George Simon
Ekstrand, Martin Eugene
Eldridge, Lawrence
Eldridge, Norma
Eldridge, Paul H.
Eldridge, Retha
Eleanor, Sister Frances
Elizabeth, Sister M.
Elliott, Francis Roy
Ellis, Adele Marie
Elstner, Josephine Elmer
Elwood, Joseph Donald
Emerson, Ause
Epes, Branch Jones, Sr.
Epes, Branch Jones, Jr.
Epes, William Fitzgerald
Erdman, Joseph James
Erickson, Eric Oscar
Erickson, Harry Eric
Evans, Bertha Rae
Evory, Harold William
Ewing, Margaret Greenfield
Ewing, Roy Emerson
Fairweather, Barbara Hayne
Fasy, Carroll
Fawcett, Alfred Edward, Sr.
Fawcett, Alfred Jr.
Feely, Gertrude
Felicidade, M. Mary
Felix, Harold (Raphael)
Fernandez, Carmen Mary

Fernandez, Gregoria
Fernandez, Joaquin Jose
Fernandez, Juanina Mary
Fernandez, Mary Louise
Ferrier, John William
Ferrier, Theresa Diana
Fidelis, Sister M.
Fielding, Ralph
Fisher, Arthur George
Fisher, Frederick Russell
Fisher, Ruth Lincoln
Fishman, Alvin William
Fittinghoff, Nicholas Alexander
Fleisher, Henry
Fleming, Joseph Lamar
Fletcher, Charles Falkner
Flint, Alvin Lovett
Flint, Sarah Viola
Florence, Paul Billington
Flores, Joe Tatani
Florez, Juanita R.
Florez, Julietta Lee
Florez, Ramona Samilpa
Fluemer, Arnold William
*Fonger, Burton, age 19
Fonger, Leith Cox
Fonger, William Henry
Ford, Charles Emery
Ford, Henry Tagros
Ford, William Munroe
Forney, William Thomas
Fowler, Ernest A.
Fox, Frank Christopher
Fox, Henry
Fox, James Joseph
Fox, James Roy
Fox, Mattea
Fox, Vincent Altizo
Francisco, Louis Joseph
Frantz, Daniel David
Fraser, Elvie

Frederica, Sister M.
Fredenert, M. M.
Freeman, Edward Francis
Freeman, Frances Mary
Freeman, Jo Fisher
Fricke, Herman Henry
Fricke, Dorothy
Friedl, Joseph
Fuller, Sumner Bacon
Gabrielson, Carl William
Gaffke, Albert A.
Gaillard, John Gourdin
Galassi, Dominico
Gallaher, Robert Franklin
Gallagher, Harry Joseph
Gallapaue, William Earl
Gallit, Henry Emil
Galway, Howard
Gardiner, Clifford A.
Gardiner, Elizabeth A.
Gardiner, William A.
Gardner, Claude Dennis
Garmezy, Samuel
Garrett, Elwood Llewellin
Garrigues, Dwight N.
Gavigan, Tripp G.
Genevieve, Sister Rose
Georgia, Sister M.
Gesemyer, Arthur K.
Gesemyer, Georgie C., Sr.
Gesemyer, Georgie C., Jr.
Gewald, Myrtle F.
Gibson, Alvin Harvey
Giles, Vinton Sela
Gilfoil, Katherine
Gilfoil, Katherine N.
Gilfoil, Lydia Alice
Gilfoil, Mary Louise
Gilfoil, Patricia Ann
Gilfoil, William Scott
Girard, Edward

Giucondiana, M. M.

Gisel, Eugene

Gladys, Sister M.

Glunz, Charles

Glunz, Henrietta H.

Godfrey, M. M.

Goebel, Otto John

Goldman, Edmund

Golucke, Louis Harold

Goodwin, Martin Luther

Gordenker, Alexander

Gordon, John J.

Gorzelanski, Helen Clara

Gotthold, Diana

Grady, Virginia H.

Gray, Bernice Louise

Gray, Edward James

Gray, George

Grau, Albert

Graves, Arthur

Greer, Henry

Griffin, Elizabeth G.

Griffin, Frank

Grishkevich, Vitaly Ippolit

Grode, Leo

Gross, Morton Robert

Guicheteau, Arnold J.

Gunder, Jack H.

Gunnels, Robert Lee

Guthrie, Mary J.

Guthrie, Richard S.

Guthrie, Romelda A.

Guthrie, William E.

Haberer, Emanuel Julius

Hacker, Leonard

Hackett, Alice

Hackett, John Alexander

Hageman, Marshall N.

Hale, J. Willis

Hale, Velma M.

Haley, Arthur Edward

Haley, James

Hall, Norman Shannon

Hallett, John Bartlett

Ham, Hugh Mack

Hammill, Dena M.

Hammill, Richard L.

Hammill, Rogers N.

Hammond, L. D. Lloyd

Hamra, Adeeb Joseph

Hancock, Lawrence Kelly

Hancock, Mary Edna

Hannings, Richard Edward

Hanson, Donie Taylor

Hanson, Rolf Hinnen

Hard, Herbert William

Hard, Marie Lucille

Hardy, Beverly Earl

Harms, Lloyd Frederick

Harper, Anita Mae

Harper, Arthur Edward

Harper, Betty Jane

Harper, James Albert

Harper, Steven Phillip

Harrah, Orville

Harrah, Rose Marie

Harrell, Richard Maxted

Harrington, Mary Rose

Harris, William S.

Harrison, Phillip Francis

Harshman, Albert N.

Harshman, Anita Wichman

Hart, Herbert Henry

Hart, Joseph Chittendon

Hartnett, Ernest

Hatcher, Benjamin Carlile

Hause, Charles David

Hausman, Louis Michael

Haven, Lewis Quincy, Jr.

Hayme, Carl

Haynes, Albert

Headley, Donald Grant

Healy, Gerald
Healy, John
Heath, George Eddy
Hebard, William Lawrence
Heery, Joseph Marion
Heesch, Henry John
Heichert, Murray Baker
Hell, Jan Howard
Hellis, Herbert Dean
Henderson, Barclay C.
Henderson, Dorothy Gardiner
Henderson, George William
Hendrix, Daisy
Hennel, Charles
Hennesen, Maria Alexandrina
Hennesen, Paul
Herndon, Alice Patterson
Herndon, Rees Frazer
Hertz, Harold Emerson
Hess, Arlene F.
Hess, Hudson S.
Hess, Lois Ellen
Hess, R. Bruce
Hess, Robert R.
Hess, Victor Glen
Hess, Viola Ruth
Hibbard, James F.
Hicks, John Thomas
Highsmith, Jerome
Hight, Allen H.
Hiland, George S.
Hildabrand, Carl
Hileman, Arthur Daniel
Hill, Alva J.
Hill, Jay Ward
Hill, John
Hill, Martha M.
Hill, Samuel W.
Hinck, Dorothy A.
Hinck, Edward M.
Hinck, John A., Jr.

Hinck, Mary L.
Hinck, Robert
Hindberg, Walter
Hinkley, Jay Augustus
Hinsche, Otto
Hobson, Henry
Hochreiter, Charles J.
Hodge, Julia M.
Hodges, Catherine Taylor
Hodges, Harry Mead
Hoffmann, Winifred
Hogenboom, David Lee
Hogenboom, Leonard Samuel
Hogenboom, Ruth Groters
Hogenboom, Stephen
Hokanson, Marie Corp
Hokanson, Mons
Holt, Jack Berger
Holt, Truman Slayton
Holy Name, Sister M.
Honor, Dorothy Y.
Honor, Herbert C.
Honor, Herbert, Jr.
Honor, Vera O.
Hood, Thomas Dewitt
Hook, Emil V.
Horgan, Gregory
Hornbostel, Johanna Mario
Horton, Frank
Hoskins, Colin Macrae
Hoyt, Jackson Leach
Hubbard, Charles R.
Hubbard, Christine
Hubbard, William Augustus
Hudson, Clay Menafee
Hudson, Lewis Clifton
Hudson, Primitiva Bertumen
Hughes, Harry Bloomfield
Hughes, Hugh John
Hughes, Russell
Hughes, Samuel Alexander

Hull, Edwin Miles
Hunt, Darcy Swain
Hunt, Phray O.
Hunter, John Jacobs
Hyland, Walter
Harpst, Earl Michael
Iddings, Paul Loren
Immaculate Concepcion,
   S. R. M.
Innis, Charles
Innis, David
Innis, David James
Innis, Donald
Innis, Frances
Innis, Joseph
Irvin, Tom B.
Irvine, Bessie
Irwin, Henry
Isabel, Sister M.
Jackson, Myrtle
Jacobs, Louis Welch
Jacobson, David
James, Elizabeth
Jamieson, William
Janda, Marie Wagner
Janda, Robert Lee
Jarlath, M. M. of S. T.
John, Rees Hopkin
Johnson, Cherokee Chickasaw
Johnson, Frederick Arnold
Johnson, Henry S.
Johnson, Ralph Murdoch
Johnson, Seneca O.
Johnson, Thomas W.
Johnson, Walter
Johnston, Doris
Johnston, William W.
Jones, Andy
Jones, Bernard Edwin
Jones, Charles Ernest
Jones, Elvis Everett

Jones, Ethel L.
Jones, Frank Dehaven
Jones, Muriel Gertrude
Jones, Robert Berian
Jones, William Henry
Jordan, Thomas Mark
Julian, Frederick
Juravel, Carl
Jurgenssen, August John
Jurgenssen, Jennie Grace
Justin, Sister M.
Kahler, Stannie Daniel
Kalkowsky, Adam Edward
Kapes, David
Katz, Anne
Katz, Frances Valerie
Katz, Isabella
Katz, William Allen
Kahn, Maurice
Kaminski, Nicodemus
Kavanagh, Joseph
Kay, Joseph Kerop
Kailen, Ernest
Keiley, Daniel James
Kelly, Harold Maxwell
Kemery, Mona Mae
Kemp, Oley C.
Kern, Helen
Kerr, Joseph
Ketchum, Gladys Esperanza
Keys, Harold Harte
Keys, John Dewitt
Kidder, Lucia Booth
Kidder, Stanley Rast
Kiene, Clarence Kirk
Kiene, Mildred Evelyn
Kienle, Alfred
Kilkenny, Edward Michael
King, Carl Philip
King, Josephine Cook
King, Mary Barbara

Kingsbury, Stanley Carlos
Kinn, Leo
Kinney, John Thomas
Kinsella, John Sylvester
Kitzmiller, Blaine John
Kitzmiller, Owen
Kleinpell, Robert Mensson
Klippert, Edward
Knaesche, Herman
Knowles, Sambuel Etnyre
Koestner, Alfred U. S.
Kolodziej, Antonio
Kramer, Amelia
Kramer, Donald
Kramer, Effie
Kramer, Georgette
Kramer, Harry
Knutson, Gilman Darrell
Koons, Harry Montford
Koons, Thelma Donnelly
Krause, William Owen
Kringle, Harry
Kuhlman, William Henry
Kundert, Paul Denton
Lacey, Betty
Lacey, Kristin
Lacey, Sharon
Lacey, William Edward
Lacy, Merrill Ghent
LaFouge, Edward Rudolph
Lam, Bo Ming
Lamb, William Lee
Lambert, Frederick Dankilla
Landis, Audrey Blanche
Landis, Frederic
Landis, Patricia A.
Landis, Richard
Landis, Roderic
LaPointe, William F.
LaPorte, Margaret
LaPorte, Otto

Lappin, Leslie Everett
Lauriat, Frederick
Lautzenheiser, Ora Ezra
LaVigne, Ernest Henri
Lawry, Gordon Langford
Lawton, Betty Estelle
Lawyer, Jerome
Leary, John (Jack) Thomas
Leary, Paul
Lederman, Daniel Bishop
Lee, Charlotte Kingsbury
Lee, C. W.
Lee, David
Lee, Elfred M.
Lee, Fred M.
Lee, James Milton
Lee, Margurite
LeForge, Roxy
Leighton, Ethel Packard
Leisring, Lawrence
Leitch, James Elmer
Leland, James Arthur
Leland, Rosamond Cooper
Leland, Shirley Mae
Leonarda, Sister M.
Lesage, Alphons Gerard
Lessner, Eva
Lessner, Hilda
Levy, Ruben
Lew, Wah Sun
Liggett, James Paul
Liles, Lawrence Poland
Limpert, John William
Lind, Niles John
Linn, Harold Adolphus
Lochboehler, Bernard
Logan, George Lafayette
Lombard, Harold Webster
Lombard, James Dino
Lord, Montague
Louis, George James

Lovell, Glenn Howard
Lovell, Ruth Patterson
Lowry, William Arthur
Lubarsky, Saul
Lucy, Sister Mary
Lundquist, Carl Axel
Luckman, Elsie Marion
Lyon, Herbert
McAfee, Clauda
McAfee, Robert
McAllister, Margaret
McAnlis, David
McAnlis, Jean
McAnlis, Josephine
McAnlis, Ruth
McAnlis, William
McBride, John Henry
McCaffray, Arthur
McCalister, Jacob
McCandlish, William Foster
McCann, James
McCarter, Edward Lee
McCarthy, Floyd Arthur
McCarthy, Marian Florence
McCarthy, William Ransom
McCarty, Leroy
McCarty, Edward Charles
McCloskey, Robert E.
McClure, Carl Hamlin
McClure, Ryanna
McCoy, May
McCoy, Oscar Gervius
McCune, Joseph Gerhardt
McDonough, Charles A.
McEntee, Samuel Sanders
McGaretty, Howard Carson
McGovern, Lee
McGrath, Peter William
McGrew, Kinsie
McGuiness, Joseph
McGuire, Grace Ann

McHugh, Patricia Willis
McIntosh, Melville Ethelbert
McKay, Jean
McKee, Robert
McKeown, Hugh Michael
McLey, Harold J. G.
McMann, Frank Patrick
McMann, James
McMann, John
McManus, Ambrose
McMullen, Joseph
McNamara, Francis Robert
McNicholas, John
McSorley, Richard
McStay, John
McStay, John Curry
McVey, Bunnie Cecilia
McVey, Charles David
McVey, Grace Alice Mary
McVey, Mary Cecilia
Mabry, Frank M.
Mabry, Opal Marie
MacDonald, Alyse Louise
MacDonald, Bob
MacDonald, George
MacDonald, Helen
MacDonald, John
MacDonald, Kenneth
MacDonald, Margaret
MacIntosh, James
MacKinnon, James Bowie
MacLaren, Donald Ross
Madigan, Francis
Madsen, Elmer
MaGee, George Lyman
MaGee, Mary Elizabeth, Sr.
MaGee, Mary Elizabeth, Jr.
MaGee, Philip Donald
*Magill, Charles Newton, age 68
Mahoney, John Joseph
Makepeace, Lloyd Brenecke

Malmstrom, Charles Clarence
Mangels, Franz
Mangels, Henry Ahrends
Mangels, John F.
Mangels, Margaretta Hermine
Mangels, Nieves
Mangels, Nieves Chofra
Mankin, James Percy
Manser, Daniel Leonard
Marcella, Sister M.
Margerita, Sister M.
Margulies, Ruben
Marion, Sister Cecilia
Marsden, Ralph Walter
Martin, Clarence
Martin, D. P.
Martin, Edgar
Massey, Charlotte
Masson, Philip
Matthew, Sister Rose
Matthews, William Jerome
Maura, Sister Bernadette
Maurashon, Sister
Maxcy, Joseph
Maxey, Wilburn
Maxwell, William Allen
Mayer, Harry O'Brien
Meagher, Bernard Joseph
Meagher, Zora Simmons
Mee, Louis
Meinhardt, Ruth
Melton, Jesse Edgar
Merrill, Robert Heath
Merritt, Isaac Erwin
Messinger, George Marion
Metz, Carmen Adoracion
Meukow, Coleman Arian
Meukow, George Osakina
Meukow, Nina Ruth
Meukow, Walter Trendel
Meyer, Gus Henry

Miles, Daniel Walter
Miles, Prentice Melvin
Miller, Charles Henry
Miller, Dorothy Veronica
Miller, Gilbert Charles
Miller, Helen
Miller, John Joseph
Miller, Maxine Margaret
Mills, John Andrew
Millward, Samuel James, Jr.
Miravalle, Andrew Nino
Miriam, Sister Agnes
Miriam, Sister Louise
Miriam, Sister Thomas
Missmer, George Washington
Missler, Carl Edward
Mitchell, John
Mitchell, Thomas
Mitchell, William Thomas
Moak, Conway Columbus
Mock, Charles Gordon
Mollart, Stanley Vincent
Monaghan, Forbes
Montesa, Anthony Joseph
Montesa, Edward William
Montesa, Henrietta F.
Montesa, John Phillip
Montgomery, Antonia Cantilo
Montgomery, Ethel Denise
Montgomery, Everett Verden
Montgomery, Fern Asunsano
Moore, Charles F.
Moore, Emma G.
Moore, George
Moore, Joseph Oliver
Moore, Joseph W.
Moore, Leonard C.
Moore, Mae Dancy
Moore, Patricia E.
Mora, Ernest Joseph
Mora, George Castro

Mora, Iberia Ortuno
Moran, Lawrence Richard
Morehouse, Francis B.
Morehouse, Phyllis Brenda
Morehouse, Winifred Louis
Morison, Walter Durrell
Morning, John
Morris, Leroy
Morrision, Carson C.
Morrision, Helena V.
Mortlock, Frank Oliver
Moss, George Herbert
Mudd, Maurice
Mueller, William Fred
Muldoon, Anthony Gregory
Mulry, Joseph
Mulryan, Alma Steiger
Mulryan, James Raymond
Munger, Henry Weston
Munger, Louralee Patrick
Murphin, William
Murphy, John Joseph
Murray, William Elmer
Myers, Kenneth Robert
Myers, William Tyner
McAfee, Leo Gay
Naftaly, Lillian Saidee
Naftaly, Nancy Nataly
Naido, Joseph
Naido, Ruth Louise
Nance, Dana Wilson
Nash, Gail Blackmarr
Nash, Grace Chapman
Nash, Ralph
Nash, Ralph Stanley
Nash, Roy Leslie
Nash, Margaret Alice
Nathanson, Nathaniel Arthur
Nau, Catherine Ludwina
Neal, James
Neal, Pauline

Neibert, Alice Julia
Neibert, Henry Edward
Neikam, William L.
Nelson, Thomas Page
Nelson, Valley
Newcomb, Water Cattell
Newgord, Julius Gerard
Nicholas, John Middleton
Nichols, John Randolph
Nichols, Leonard David
Nicholson, John
Nicholson, William
Nicol, Celeste Claire
Nicol, Charles Bertram
Nicol, Fedora Mary
Nicol, Jacqueline Winifred
Nicol, Normal Arthur
Nicoll, David
Nicholson, James Francis
Nokes, Wilbur Charles
Norton, Alfred
Nuger, Isaac
Nuttall, Edmond
O'Boirne, Vincent
O'Brien, John Robert
O'Brien, Michael Wilbur
Obst, Thomas James
O'Conner, Clarence
Ode, Carsten Linnevold
O'Hara, Kathleen F.
O'Hara, Lorraine Betty
O'Hara, Michael Joseph
O'Hara, Michael Joseph, Jr.
O'Haver, Goldie Aimee
Ogan, William Clarence
Olivette, Sister M.
Olsen, Lillian Agnes
O'Malloy, John Bryan
O'Neill, James
Oppenheimer, John
Osbon, Bert Paul

O'Shaughnessy, Martin
Oss, Norman Alfred, Jr.
O'Toole, John Patrick
Overton, Elbert Monroe
Owens, Hoyle Williams
Pacheco, Michael Angelo
Paget, Cyrus
Paige, Eldene Elinor
Palmatier, Ellery Leroy
Palmer, Clarence Hugh
Palmer, Mildred Ailene
Pangborn, Wallace
Parham, Archer Brandon
Parker, Bertha F.
Parker, Bertha Helena
Parker, Helen Dorothy
Parker, Roy Lester
Parker, Wilbur Clarke
Parquette, William Stewart
Parish, Edward John, Jr.
Passmore, Fred J.
Patricia, Sister M.
Patricia, Sister Marie
Patterson, Myron
Pauli, Ralph
Pawley, Charles Thomas
Pearson, Cecil Leroy
Peck, Lawrence Leroy
Peek, Elvin Roland
Penny, Harold Ray
Pepper, Charles John
Perfecta, Sister
Perkins, Willie Ray
Pearlman, Max O.
Perry, Walter Lee Gihon
Pflug, Emma
Phillips, Eleanor Marie
Phillips, Howard Lester, Sr.
Phillips, Howard Lester, Jr.
Philp, Dorothy Suzanne
Pickell, William H.

Pickens, Henri B.
Pickering, Camille Elaine
Pickering, John Kuykendall
Pierce, Margaret Helen
Pirassoli, Charles William
Pitcher, Susie Josephine
Plowman, Claire Elizabeth
Plowman, Elizabeth Oxford
Plowman, George Harden
Pohl, Gordon Robert
Pollard, Harriet Emma
Pond, Helen
Porter, Lloyd Thomas
Posner, Irving
Precino, Thomas
Preiser, Rosa Christian
Preston, Rose Marie
Price, Walter Scott
Priestner, Joseph
Purnell, John Ferguson
Purnell, Lillian Cottrell
Putney, Harry Bryan
Quillinan, Frank William
Quinn, Grant
Raleigh, Daniel Mead
Rand, Grace
Rast, Beni
Ratcliffe, Jesse Walker
Raymond, Mona
Reardon, Francis
Redard, Alexander James
Redempta, Sister M.
Reich, Bertha Harris
Reid, William Robert
Reilly, Matthew
Reinhart, James H.
Reith, Joseph
Repetti, William
Repikoff, John
Reuter, James
Rey, Sister Maria del

Reynolds, Ralph Leonard
Rhudie, Ada Woodsworth
Rhudie, Oscar Peter
Rice, Williard Lamont
Richards, Edwin Franklin
Richards, Mary Fielding
Riddle, Henry Hampton
Rider, Frank Jackson
Riffel, Dorothy Ann
Riffel, Esther N.
Riffel, Gordon William
Riffel, Retta Leona
Riffel, William E.
Riley, Charles
Rively, William
Rivers, William Richard
Rizzuti, Oarm
Robert Marie, Sister
Roberts, Elizabeth
Roberts, Galien Sofia
Roberts, Odin Gregory
Robertson, Joseph H.
Robie, Merle Steel
Robinson, Charles A.
Robinson, Graham Post
Robinson, Leslie D.
Robinson, Roberta May
Rodgers, Frances
Roebuck, Brooks Waldo
Roebuck, May Ephrom
Roehr, Oscar Carl
Roehr, Pauline Marie
Roeper, Ludwig Earl
Rohrbaugh, Olive
Rohrer, Helen Brian
Rohrer, Samuel Lewis
Rosabella, Sister
Roscom, Jerry Nicholas
Rose, Sister Catherine
Rose Jude, Sister
Rose Marie, Sister

Rosella, Sister
Rosenthal, Leon
Rosier, Warren
Ross, Ervin Clinton
Ross, George
Ross, Gladys Mary
Ross, Lillian
Routhier, George Silvio
Rowland, M. Elston
Ruane, John
Runyon, Richard Earl
Rurka, Steve
Russell, Aida B.
Russell, Diana Marie
Russell, Earl Edwin
Russell, Theresa White
Ryall, Theodore Lee, Jr.
Rydberg, Carl Gunnar
Safino, Esther A.
Sager, Frederick James
Salamy, Abraham George
Salet, Elizabeth Ann
Salter, Russell
Samara, Edward Thomas
Samara, Saleem George
Sams, Gerald R.
Sampson, James Stewart
Sanborn, Donald George
Sanders, Albert J.
Sanders, David J.
Sanders, Edna F.
Sanders, Florence Smith
Sanders, Phillip Herman
Sands, Martin Paul
Sands, Mildred Marie
Satterfield, Frederick Malone
Saunders, Emma
Saunders, Frank, Sr.
Saunders, Frank, Jr.
Saunders, Norma Louise
Sayre, Bruce

Scaff, Alvin Hewitt
Scaff, Lawrence A.
Scaff, Mary Lee
Scarlett, Jane Agnes
Scarlett, William John
Schechter, Seymour
Scheidl, Rudolph John
Scherer, Doris
Scherer, Morris C.
Scherer, Richard
Schermerhorn, William H.
Scheuermann, Dennis Friday
Scheuermann, Gustav John
Scheuermann, Gwendolyn Marta
Scheuermann, Helen Friday
Schier, Kathleen Grant
Schier, Samuel Saunders
Schmidt, Richard Joseph
Scholastica, Sister M.
Schoppe, Leonard Albert
Schoppe, Lillian A.
Schroeder, Louis
Schorth, Max Brune
Schubert, Edward C.
Schuster, Helene Rothmeister
Schuster, Helene Jeanete
Schuster, John Howard
Schworer, Donald Valentine
Scofield, Donald Eugene
Scott, Elizabeth Steele
Scott, Joe Edwin
Scott, Lyle Cecil
Seals, Margaret Mildred
Sechrist, David P.
Sechrist, Harold
Sechrist, John W.
Sechrist, Marguerite
Shaffer, William Robert
Shapiro, Herman
Shaw, Herbert Wesley
Shaw, Kate Sibley

Shaw, Walter Ray
Sherk, David Robert
Sherk, Gerry Ann
Sherk, Margaret Coulson
Shimmel, Edith
Shoemaker, Abbott Paul
Shropshire, Harry Wesley
Shurdut, Joseph Moses
Siena, Sister M.
Silen, Elizabeth Jean
Silen, Joan Bradford
Silen, Margaret Elizabeth
Silen, Shirley Ann
Silloway, Merle
Simatovich, Nicholas Joseph
Simmons, Ernest Edgeworth
Sklenar, Anthony Joseph
Small, Elizabeth Studavant
Small, Frank Sylvester
Small, Helen Elizabeth
Smallwood, Robert
Smith, Alfred Whitacre
Smith, B. Ward
Smith, Dewey Woods
Smith, Harry Josselyn
Smith, Harry Thurston
Smith, Joseph John
Smith, Paul L.
Smith, Stephen L.
Smith, Viola R.
Smith, Willard Horace
Smoyer, Egbert M.
Snead, Elizabeth B.
Snead, Mary Carol
Snead, Paul Kindig
Snead, Paul Laurence
Sniffen, Genevieve Marie
Sniffen, John Mark
Snyder, Gaines
Snyder, Mary Lucille
Snyder, William Raymond

Soares, John Stanislas
Sottile, Frank Joseph
Spatz, Oswald
Spear, Earl Franklin
Spencer, William Meek
Spencer, William Robert
Sperry, Henry M.
Stacy, Gertrude Rosie
Stahl, Alfred Joaquin
Stancliff, Leo
Stark, Clarence Theo
Starr, John Bernal
Stearns, Mary Jean Stephens
Steffens, Raymond Harold
Steven, Oswald Barnard
Stevens, Leslie Eugene
Steward, Basilia Torres
Stewart, John Norman
Still, Dorothy
Stiver, Edna Theresa
Stiver, Joseph Alfred
Stocking, Charles Samuel
Stokes, Henry Milton
Stoll, Eugene Leo
Stoneburner, Edna
Strong, James Walter
St. Thomas, Federico, Jr.
Stuart, David Lennox
Stubo, Knutty Christian
Stumbo, John David
Stump, Irene J.
Stump, Lawrence
Stumpf, William Jerome, Jr.
Sturm, Stanley Marcellus
Sudhoff, Raymond George
Sullivan, Edward
Sullivan, Russell
Suro, Reuben
Swanson, Ruth Pauline
Sykora, Frank
Tabor, John

Tapia, Edwin Joseph Jones
Taylor, William Leonard
Taylor, Willis L.
Tekippe, Owen
Terrill, Thomas Star
Terry, Albert Henry
Terry, Carol Louise (Talbot)
Terry, Joseph Edward
Teurnee, Maurice Conrad
Theophila, Sister M.
Theudere, M. Mary of S. P.
Thomas, Antonita B.
Thomas, Dollie Mae
Thomas, Florence A.
Thomas, Howard Wilton
Thomas, Robert Lee
Thompson, David Bill
Thompson, Floyd Addison
Thompson, Leslie Daniel
Tinling, Don
Titlow, Marian Phillips
Todd, Carrie Edwina
Todd, George, Jr.
Todd, Noel
Todebush, Ralph Bernard
Tootle, Mildred Caroline
Torkeson, Edward
Treubig, John F.
Tribble, Jesse Lee
Trogstad, Martha Bowler
Tuck, Ernest E.
Tuck, Helen G.
Tuite, Thomas
Tulloch, James Garfield, Jr.
Tulloch, William James
Tutten, Daniel Eugene
Ullman, Frank
Ullman, Tamara Alexis
Urquhardt, Edward J.
Urquhardt, Maud J.
Urquhardt, Stanley P.

Vandenplas, Pierre Gaston
Vandenburg, Charles Osborn
Vernick, Joseph Barry
Vicroy, Sigle Allen
Villar, Charles Herman
Vincent, Louis Lester
Vitalis, Sister Mary
Vogelgesang, John
Von Hess, Jack C.
Voss, William Frederick
Vinson, Olivert Castille
Vinson, Thomas Chalmers
Wagelie, Cunval Andreas
Wagner, John Robert
Wagner, Rudolph
Wahlgreen, Beulah King
Walker, Alfred Francis
Walker, Harold
Walker, Orian Love
Wallace, Frank Byron
Waples, James Francis
Ward, William Vines
Wareham, Johnson Matthew
Warner, Carl
Warner, Mary Delilah
Warren, Fred Prince
Warren, Harry Pre
Waterstradt, Albert Edward
Wathen, John David
Webster, Walter, Jr.
Weems, Alexander Murray
Weibel, Mary Eileen
Weil, Charles William
Welborn, George
Welch, Leo
Wells, James
Wells, Jessie
Wenetzki, Charles Eduard
West, Glenn Key
West, Hester D.
Wester, Arthur W.

Westmoreland, Graham Bradley
Westmoreland, Victoria Maria
Wheeler, Hiram Albert L.
Wheeler, Ida Ellen
Wheeler, Robert Antony
Wheeler, Robert J. M.
Whitaker, Evelyn Eddy
Whitaker, Helen Elizabeth
Whitaker, Jocelyn Alfred
Whitaker, Margaret Evelyn
Whitaker, Septimus Tom B.
White, George Henry, Jr.
White, Nathaniel Walker
Whitesides, John Garrett
*Whitmoyer, George Irwin,
   age 49
Wichman, Daniel Lee
Wichman, Douglas
Wichman, Ernest Hermsen
Wichman, Gladys Caroline
Widdoes, Alice S.
Widdoes, H. W.
Wienke, Carl Ludwig
Wienke, Carmen Aurora
Wienke, Edward Peter
Wienke, Elizabeth Carmen
Wienke, Frederick Johan
Wienke, Mercie Christina
Wienke, Theresa Victoria
Wienke, Violet Alma
Wilcox, Lyle
Wilcox, Wendel
Wilder, Charlie
Wiley, Samuel
Williams, Clyde Scott
Williams, Gordon L.
Williams, Greta R.
Williams, Jack
Williams, Leona H.
Williams, Roy Harold
Willmann, George J.

Barr, Fiona
Barr, Margaret
Barr, Ronald
Barrett, Cecil
Beck, Arthur Charlesworth
Beebee, Walter Willis
Beeman, Sarah
Behenna, Dorothy
Bennett, Lillian
Bentley, Edward
Birchall, James Richardson
Black, James
Blair, Leslie
Blechynden, Lindsey DeClarke
Boddington, Dorothy
Boddington, Richard John
Bonner, Norman Ellis
Bosch, Edward Henry Brett
Boswell, George James
Bradshaw, John William
Brambles, James Christopher
Brambles, Margaret Lillian
Brambles, Ralph Douglas
Brambles, Elizabeth
Brambles, Grace
Brambles, Patricia
Brambles, Ralph
Bramwell, Edward Kennedy
Bramwell, Helen L.
Breson, Lillian
Brewster, Charles
Brooks, Anna
Brooks, Cyril H.
Brooks, Kenneth S.
Brooks, Leonard C.
Brooks, Rose E.
Buckberrough, Rosa
Buhler, Charles
Burn, Robert
Burn, William Angus
Bush, Edward Stanley

Cameron, John Fraser
Corley, Thomas Ekstrom
Celestine, Sister M.
Chapman, Maurice Bonham
Chong, Charles
Christian, Frederick
Clark, Wallace Robert
Clarke, Esther Millicent
Clarke, Evelyn Victoria
Cohen, Florence Frances
Corfield, Isla
Corfield, Gillian I.
Coxon, Jane Margaret
Crabbe, Kenneth Murray
Creech, Henry
Crewe, James
Curtis, John Shearme
Dalgleish, Mabel Emily
Dalgleish, Mabel Margaret
Da Silva, Augustus
D'Authreau, John Harold
Dickson, Elsa Fanny
Dodd, Gloria Lydia
Dodd, Reginald Morris
Dodd, Zina Andreevna
Dolores, Sister Maria
Donald, William
Dos Remedios, Henry Joseph
Douglas, William
Doull, Agnes
Doull, William
Dow, James Frederick
Drysdale, Thomas Douglas
Duncan, Ian Murray
Dwyer, Thomas
Ethelburga, Sister M.
Gertrude, Sister Lane Fox
Fairweather, James Edwin
Falkner, Angeles Martin
Falkner, James Albert
Falkner, Ronald D.

Fitzgerald, Desmond S.
Fox, Catherine Mary
Fox, Christopher Charles
Fox, Charles James
Fox, Lawrence
Fox, Patrick James
Fox, Stephen George
Frampton, Amy Beatrice
Frampton, Muriel
Freckleton, Thomas
Geddes, Eric
Geddes, Jean Frances
Gillett, Bertram John
Gordon, Mary
Gordon, Matthew Dobie
Grant, Helen Gordon
Gray, Irene Betty
Green, Louisa
Green, Michael John
Greenland, Lucy Violet
Griffith, Owen Ambrose
Grimmant, David Henry
Haigh, Annie
Haigh, Jesse
Haigh, Renee Mary
Haigh, Victor Alfred
Hails, Henry Forster
Hallowes, Elsie Mary
Hamblett, James
Hanson, Frank Raymond
Hardcastle, Charles Otterson
Harris, William Francis Geo.
Hayes, Jean
Hayes, Kathleen Elizabeth
Hayes, Michael Aloysius
Haymes, Maxwell Freeland L.
Hearn, Martin Everard
Hill, Rowland George
Hodges, Arthur J.
Hodges, Eleanora
Hoey, Richard C.

Hoey, Ruth C.
Hollyer, William George
Horridge, George Redvers
Hughes, Donald Francis
Humphries, John Hugh
Hurley, Patrick
Hutchison, David Dick
Irvine, Jean
Ismail, Sheil Salim
Jackson, James Gregory
Jamieson, Stewart
Jaques, Stanley Heath
Jay, John Leslie
John, Dorothy A.
John, Helen M.
John, Kathleen Elizabeth
John, May
Jones, Henry Victor
Jordan, Kathleen Agnes
Kane, John William James
Kay, Aubony Taylor
Kennedy, Eileen
Kennedy, Erna V.
Kennedy, Kathleen M.
Kennedy, Robert C.
Kennedy, Robert C., Jr.
Kew, Cecil
King, Agnes Isabel
King, Charles Forrester
Kotliar, Betty
Lee, Ansie
Legg, John Alexander
Leith, Henry Earl
Leith, Mair
Leith, Rosemary
Leyshon, Frank Howard
Ligertwood, Charles Liddell
Lloyds, Edwin William
McClure, Lawrence Maxton
McGinness, Thomas John
McGregor, Robin

McKerchar, Ian
McLeod, Hugh
McMaster, John Wilson
McMaster, Norah Helen
McWhirter, Hugh Fergus
MacIntyre, Norah Peal
MacIntyre, Ronald
MacKay, Kathleen Mary M.
MacLaren, William Hart
MacLean, Hector James Hilder
MacLean, Margaret
MacWilliam, Jean Cowan Shanks
MacWilliam, Richard Niven
MacWilliam, Scott
Malcolm, Harry Redd
Malpas, William Richard J.
Mann, William Ronald
Mather, William Gladston
Maxima, Sister M.
Medina, Elfrida Elizabeth
Meadows, Gordon
Miller, Charles Walter
Miller, David Carlton
Miller, Patricia Ann
Miller, Robert Walker
Miller, Vera Alexandra
Moore, Calvert Hildabrand
Morley, Howard
Morris, Robert Owen
Morrison, Geoffrey Lionel
Morrison, Robert Alexander
Naismith, William Cunningham
Nathanson, Jean L.
Nathanson, Marie Emsley
Nelson, Archibald Graham
Newgord, Esther
Newsome, Peter Noel Vesey
Nicolson, John
Norton-Smith, Kenneth James
Oliver, Violet Lillian
Palmer, Bertha Lucy

Palmer, John Blything
Palmer, Ronald Singleton
Parker, Herman Vercomb
Parquette, Rosemarie Dorothy
Paterson, James
Paterson, Mary D.
Patey, Walter Bruce
Patricia, M. M.
Pedder, Gerald Herbert
Pedersen, Gwendolyn Florence
Perry, David Henry
Philomena, Sister Marie
Piatnitsky, Olga Pavlovna
Piercy, Arthur
Pollard, Arnold
Pollock, Yvonne Celia
Pope, Harvey Collie
Porter, Robert John
Price, Arthur
Price, Elizabeth Sible
Price, William Samuel
Prismail, Allen
Proudfoot, Alexander
Prout, James Ormand
Quinn, Bernard Alphonsus
Redfern, Foster
Reich, Joseph
Reid, George William
Richardson, William Bryan
Robertson, Howard Laird
Roche, Barbara Pavlovna
Roche, Mary Roberta
Rodda, Hababah
Rodgers, Albert G.
Rodgers, Marcus G.
Rodgers, Rosa N.
Royston, John
Rushton, Violet Edith
Rushton, George
Ryde, Sonia
Sawyer, Paula Adelatie

Schelkunoff, Vladimir Peter
Scott, David Alexander
Serephins, Sister Mary of the
Sinclair, Jeffrey Whitfeld
Small, William Valentine
Smith, George Albert
Smith, Joan Marie
Smith, John Alwynne George L.
Smith, Louis
Smith, William A.
Smith, Arthur Linton
Spackman, Harold C.
Spackman, Winifred D.
Steel, James Laurie
Stephens, Sydney
Stratton, Joseph Grant L.
Strong, Martin
Symonds, John
Templer, Angela Mary
Templer, Ann Hazel
Templer, James Robert
Templer, Jennifer S.
Thomson, Elizabeth Marie
Thomson, Robert Allison
Tomkin, Anna Georgvina
Tonkin, Marguerite Janet A.
Tonkin, Matthew McNair
Tonkin, William Charles Geo.
Turner, William
Tyre, Alexander James
Watson, William
Watt, Effie Margaret
Watt, Olive Charlotte
Watty, Lewis Thomas
Webb, Frank Hardy
Whittal, Henry Cecil
Wightman, Arthur John
Wightman, Eglington John
Wightman, Ethelgiva Frances
Wightman, Irene Nellie
Wightman, William Dana

Willder, Katie Agnes
Williams, Hugh Hosking
Williams, John Joseph
Williamson, Margaret
Wilson, Ian Thurburn
Wilson, Walter James
Windle, Wilfred Edwin
Wood, Charles John
Wooding, Wilfred
Wright, Arthur
Wulfildan, M. M.
Yewen, Nina Efgenievna
Zacharias, Hans

British Australian
Bargallo, Amelia
Bargallo, Salvadora
Best, Francis
Blanchard, Mary
Byrne, Joseph
Cruice, William
Deane, Patrick
Dougherty, John Hercules
English, Leo
Gygar, Andrew
Holt, Bridget Trist
Holt, Edna May
Hughes, Allen John
Jackson, Gordon
Kemp, Joy Elizabeth
Laycock, William Murray B.
Laycock, Kathleen
McCarthy, Charles
McGuire, Mary Kathleen
MacMaster, John Dunlop
Nield, Frederick Bodin
O'Donnell, Gerard
Pinkerton, Stanley Corey
Pinkerton, Velma
Richards, Thomas Robert
Ridley, John Edwin

Sagor, Amy Lida
Sexton, Francis
Smith, Flora Beryl
Taylor, Betsy Doris
Taylor, Charles
Thomas, George Frederick
Walsh, Francis

British Canadian
Abarista, Sister Mary
Alphonse, de Ligori
Angeline, Sister Mary
Ann Celine, Sister Saint
Ann Marie, Sister
Arcand, Ulric
Begin, Joseph
Benoit, Mother Mary of Saint
Bernard, Sister M.
Bleau, Albert
Brouillard, Rodrigue
Charter, Catherine
Charter, Luckey Kathleen
Charter, Thomas Henry
Christophe, Soeur Saint
Clotilde, Sister M.
Dalmis, Michael
Desmarais, Camille
Everista, Mother
Frician, Sister M.
Gabriel, Sister De-Anuncion
Gabriel, Sister S.
Geofferey, Joseph
Gustav, Sister Saint
Harper, Ella Mae
Hodgson, Francis Xavier
Holloway, Glen Irwin
Humphries, Robert Maxwell
Jarry, Andre
Jepson, Leon Baynes
Joseph de Bethlehem, Sister
Lawton, Herbert

Loptson, Adulsufinn Magnus
Loptson, Faith C.
McCullough, Henry
McKenzie, Catherine
McKenney, Warren Evans
Madeline Marie Barrat, Sister
Marie de Preciux Sang, Sister
Mathiew, Soeur Saint
Maurice, Sister Mary
Mooney, Luke Henry
Murphy, William J.
Nicol, Arthur Louis
Paget, Kathleen M.
Paget, Margaret E. J.
Paget, William H. W.
Palmer, Blanche Evelyn
Philp, George Ansel
Pierre Claver, Sr. S.
Rene, M. M.
Rosemonde, M. M.
Shaw, Alice Florence (Beyes)
Victorice, M. M. of Saint
Williams, William C.
Ymer, M. M. de Saint

Netherlands
Aalten, Hans van
Albana, Sister N.
Alarda, Sister M.
Aldenhuysen, Godfred
Alice, Sister M.
Alphonsa, Sister M.
Anastasia, Sister M.
Bathildis, Sister M.
Bieschop, Roosegaade J. Philip
Blans, Thomas
Blewanus, Gerard
Boggiam, Max
Borght, Francisco van der
Bos, Maria Theresa
Burer, John

Cajetani, Sister M.
Canisia, Sister M.
Coenders, John
Corsten, Andrew
Croonen, Joseph
Decorata, Sister
DeHaan, Isaac
Dekker, John
DeWit, E.
Donata, M.
Dyk, Francisco van
Egonia, Sister M.
Engelen, Felite van
Es, Roelof van
Evangelista, Sister M.
Fransen, Martinus
Gentila, Sister M.
Glansbeek, Reinier van
Groonen, Josef
Groot, Petrus
Hagen, Jan van
Hartog, William
Hendricks, Nicholas Wilhelmus
Houben, Arnold
Intven, Joseph
Janssens, Alberta
Janssens, Marius Cornelus
Jonkerguuw, Hubertus Josephus
Joseph, M.
Jurgens, Constans (Bishop)
Keet, Teodoro
Kemperman, Richard
Kilb, Antony
Loo, Cornelio van der
Lutgardis, M.
Magdala, Sister M.
Margretta, Sister M.
Mees, Gregory
Mees, William
Michels, Derk Aw.
Modesta, Sister M.

Notenboom, Jacobus Cornlis
Odyk, Anton van
Oomen, Antonius Paulus
Opstal, Van William
Polycarpa, Sister M.
Raben, Karel Hendrik
Reimers, Christian Hendrik
Reoinjen, Henricus van
Ruyter, Jan
Schaeffer, Johannes Henricus
Slangen, Peter
Sleegers, Henry
Smits, Andrianus
Steyger, Adrianus
Tangelder, Gerardo
Timp, Pedro John
Tonus, Cornelio
Trienekens, Gerardus F.
Van der List, Petrus J.
Van Overveld, Antonio
Van Vlierden, Constant Matthys
Verhoven, Joseph
Vincent, Jacobus
Vlasvelo, Pedro
Vrakking, Johan
Werff, Alice Catherine
Werff, Milagros Herrera
Werff, Pieter Hildebrand
Werff, Wanda Oliva
Werkhoven, Jacobux
Willemina, M.
Willemsen, Bernardus J.
Zegwaard, Francis Henry

Norwegian
Aanonsen, Nels Marion
Abrahamsen, Blarne William
Christensen, Yugvar Kjell
Eilertsen, Thomas
Einarsen, Ruben Helmer
Monsen, Olaf

Oyen, Nils
Pedersen, Erling Bjoern
Petersen, Knut Selmer
Petersen, Trygve

Polish
Adelski, Borys
Bieniarz, Edward
Gang, Samuel Sam
Hirschorn, Marcus
Keller, Harry
Krzewinski, Ludwig
Lerner, Helen
Lounsbury, Irene Olshenke
Mingelgruen, Wilhelm
Neuman, Rudolph Ham
Propper, Norbert
Rabinowicz, Icko
Rabinowicz, Mordchal
Sackiewicz, Alexander
Sackiewicz, Wladyslaw
Sielski, Wladyslaw
Sielski-Jones, Yadwiga Teresa
Soroka, Samuel Chaim
Strzalkowski, Henry
Szpigielman, Marek

Wahraaftig, Oswald
Werbner, Izydor

Italian
Bulli, Angelo
Coll-Mellini, Helen
Ghigliotti, Giuseppe
Ghigliotti, Lourdes
Gircognini, Lorenzo
Gircognini, Manuela
Gircognini, Maria Lisa
Gislon, Antonio
Givseppefranco, Altomonte
Mellini, Rudolph
Vigano, Angelo
Vigano, Camilla
Vigano, Tuillo
Vigano, Augusto
Vigano, Frederico
Vigano, Maria

Nicaraguan
Carcamo, Carmelo Noguera

French
Dreyfus, Jules

ACKNOWLEDGMENTS

One of the greatest joys in writing this book has been meeting and corresponding with officers of the Eleventh Airborne Division who participated in the planning and carrying out of our thrilling rescue from the Los Banos Internment Camp.

Brig. Gen. Henry Muller and his beautiful wife invited me into their home, where he explained how intelligence was gathered concerning conditions in the Los Banos Internment Camp and military information pertaining to our rescue.

Lt. Col. Henry Burgess shared his *Reminiscences*, which opened up the whole military story for me. He has been kind throughout my bombardment of him with questions, and his wife, Mary, is a jewel of rare quality who sought out important information that I needed.

Col. John Ringler provided vital facts regarding the spectacular jump of the paratroopers into our camp, while James Holzem personalized for me those "angels with great wings of silk" who descended as from heaven.

Lt. Col. Thomas Mesereau was the speaker at some of our reunions and the nobility of his thoughts inspired me.

Loren Brown revealed the dangerous work of the Reconnaissance Platoon.

John Fulton shared his story of radio communications behind enemy lines.

Earl Hornbostel, to whom I smuggled radio parts into Santo Tomas Internment Camp, sent tapes from Manila to explain his arrest, trial, incarceration, and sentence of execution interpreted by Richard Sakakida, a Japanese undercover agent for America whom I later interviewed.

Grace Nash shared episodes from her book, *That We Might Live*.

Mr. and Mrs. Gerald Sams gave me their daring adventures in creating and hiding secret radios in the internment camp.

My shipmates from the S. S. *President Grant*, Anna Nixon, and Dr. Evelyn Witthoff, related their experiences in the liberation and bombardment of Santo Tomas Internment Camp, while Jesse Tribble described his encounter in a fire fight with the Japanese at Los Banos.

Benjamin Edwards has been a good-natured, living encyclopedia about everything regarding Los Banos. He even traveled to Japan for an interview with our only surviving guard, Daikichi Okamoto. Anthony Arthur provided information regarding the end of our camp villain, Konishi.

In order that I might have the viewpoint of people not involved in the story, Dr. Foster W. Bens and Dr. S. H. Sutherland read portions of the manuscript.

Some of the photographs were furnished by Lt. Col. Glenn McGowan. It was a joy to visit with him and his wife in their home.

One of my most unique experiences in doing research was interviewing Lt. Col. Richard Sakakida, the nisei who added a bit of spice as America's undercover agent in Manila.

Other friends who have given special help along the way are Mr. George Doherty, Mrs. Evelyn Gibson, Mrs. Janice Grubb, Dr. James A. "Al" Sanders, Mr. William Skinner, Mr. James Vaughn, and Mrs. Cornelia Westlund.

I wish to thank McGraw-Hill Book Company for the privilege of quoting from *Reminiscences* (copyright 1964 Time Inc.) the statement by General Douglas MacArthur regarding our rescue.

Carol Terry Talbot

366